Social Movements

Social Movements

The Structure of Collective Mobilization

PAUL ALMEIDA

University of California Press

University of California Press, one of the most distinguished university presses in the United States, enriches lives around the world by advancing scholarship in the humanities, social sciences, and natural sciences. Its activities are supported by the UC Press Foundation and by philanthropic contributions from individuals and institutions. For more information, visit www.ucpress.edu.

University of California Press
Oakland, California

Library of Congress Cataloging-in-Publication Data

Names: Almeida, Paul, author.
Title: Social movements : the structure of collective mobilization / Paul Almeida.
Description: Oakland, California : University of California Press, [2019] | Includes bibliographical references and index. |
Identifiers: LCCN 2018033480 (print) | LCCN 2018035307 (ebook) | ISBN 9780520964846 | ISBN 9780520290914 (pbk. : alk. paper)
Subjects: LCSH: Social movements—Textbooks.
Classification: LCC HM881 (ebook) | LCC HM881 .A397 2019 (print) | DDC 303.48/4—dc23
LC record available at https://lccn.loc.gov/2018033480

Manufactured in the United States of America

26   25   24   23   22   21   20   19
10   9   8   7   6   5   4   3   2   1

Contents

Illustrations

Acknowledgments

This book derives from my fifteen years of teaching social movement courses at the undergraduate and graduate levels along with my research on collective action. I owe gratitude to dozens of individuals (and hundreds of students in the classroom). Rogelio Saenz, Harland Prechel, and Sam Cohn of Texas A&M University encouraged me to offer courses in social movements early in my career. Nella Van Dyke at the University of California, Merced, did the same. An army of student research assistants at UC Merced also made this manuscript possible, including Anna Schoendorfer, Joselyn Delgado, Maria Mora, Miriam Mosqueda, Sarai Velasquez, Carolina Molina, Valezka Murillo, Karen Gomez, and Rocio Murillo. I also benefited from the technical expertise of Andrew Zumkehr and Samuel Alvarez. I received valuable feedback on social movement dynamics when coteaching courses abroad (at the University of Costa Rica and at the National Autonomous University of Honduras) and while presenting my work in universities throughout Central America. I owe enormous debts to the activists I have interviewed over the years, mobilizing over issues varying from state repression to privatization, free trade, and environmental contamination. Two Fulbright Fellowships in 2008 and 2015 allowed me the time and resources to participate in international field research and to coteach courses on social movements.

My thinking about social movements has also evolved from collaborations with Mark Lichbach, Nella Van Dyke, Roxana Delgado, Allen Cordero, Chris Chase-Dunn, Eugenio Sosa, María Inclán, Maria Mora, Alejandro Zermeño, and Rodolfo Rodriguez. I am eternally grateful for my original collaborator and mentor, Linda Stearns. I would never have advanced as a scholar without Linda's guidance and time. I appreciate the hospitable environment of my sociology department and colleagues at UC Merced, which include Laura

Hamilton, Nella Van Dyke, Zulema Valdez, Sharla Alegria, Whitney Pirtle, Kyle Dodson, Tanya Golash Boza, Ed Flores, Irenee Beattie, Charlie Eaton, Marjorie Zatz, and Elizabeth Whitt. I appreciate the extra time Ed Flores took to look over parts of the manuscript and provide new insights.

UC Press representatives have been supportive from day one. I was thrilled when former acquisitions editor Seth Dobrin invited me to produce a work on social movements. Maura Rausner provided the perfect level of encouragement to finish the final manuscript. Sabrina Robleh offered constant technical advice in preparing the work. My copy editor, Jeff Wyneken, nicely cleaned up my prose and patiently awaited my corrections. In a world with such limited availability, I deeply appreciate the time the eleven anonymous external reviewers devoted to reading entire drafts of the manuscript and providing critical feedback. It is rare in sociology to have the opportunity to receive so much constructive commentary on one's work. The final product, undoubtedly, is vastly improved by having so many readers. I am also very much indebted to the hundreds of social movement scholars found in the bibliography, whose work I draw on throughout the book. An introductory social movement text would be impossible without the community of scholars that has produced a vast amount of literature to build upon. All misinterpretations of the work of others bears my responsibility.

Most important, I thank Andrea, for her constant support.

1 Social Movements

The Structure of Collective Action

The voluntary coming together of people in joint action has served as a major engine of social transformation throughout human history. From the spread of major world religions to community-led public health campaigns for reducing debilitating vector-borne diseases at the village level, collective mobilization may lead to profound changes in a wide variety of contexts and societies. At key historical moments, groups have unified in struggle in attempts to overthrow and dismantle systems of oppression and subordination, as observed in indigenous peoples' resistance to colonialism and in rebellions launched by enslaved populations. In the twenty-first century, collective action by ordinary citizens around the world could prove decisive in slowing down global warming and in supporting planetary survival. In short, the collective mobilization of people creates a powerful human resource that can be used for a range of purposes. In this volume we explore a particular type of collective action—social movements.

The study of social movements has increased markedly over the past two decades. This is largely the result of theoretical and empirical advances in sociology and related fields as well as an upsurge in collective action in the United States and around the world. The variety of mobilizations examined by students of social movements ranges from the anti-Trump resistance to anti-neoliberal and austerity protests in Asia, Africa, Europe, and Latin America. Already by 2011, global protests reached such a crescendo that *Time* magazine crowned the "Protester" as the "Person of the Year" (Andersen 2011). Then, in stunning fashion, citizens broke the record for the largest simultaneous demonstrations in the history of the United States, with the women's marches in 2017 and 2018. With so much social movement activity occurring in the twenty-first century, some experts predict we are moving into a "social movement society" (Meyer 2014) or a "social movement world" (Goldstone 2004).

On the basis of the best systematic evidence available from global surveys and "big data" collections of protest events over time (Ward 2016), social movement activity continues to be sustained around the world at heightened levels in the contemporary era (Dodson 2011; Karatasli, Kumral and Silver 2018). Indeed, over the past two decades groups engaging in social movement activities have not just proven to be impressive by their scale and intensity of mobilization, but have also transformed the social and political landscapes in the United States and across the globe. A brief sketch of some of the largest movements, including the anti-Trump resistance, immigrant rights, and movements for economic and climate justice, exemplifies these claims.

Women's March and Anti-Trump Resistance

The Women's March against the newly inaugurated Trump administration in early 2017 represented the largest simultaneous mass mobilization in US history, with the organizers, in the opening of their mission statement, explicitly stating a threat to the protection of rights, health, and safety as the primary motive for the unprecedented demonstrations.[1] Activists repeated the marches again in January 2018 with equally impressive levels of mobilization. The initiators of the mass actions strived for an intersectional strategy to unite women and others against structural exclusions along the lines of race, class, gender, and sexuality. The Women's Marches were held in hundreds of US cities and drew between four and five million participants (see figures 1 and 2), including people in dozens of countries outside the United States. The movement immediately evolved into the "Resistance" and has sustained mobilizations against subsequent exclusionary policies and public gestures by the Trump administration against immigrants, women, racial minorities, religious minorities, and LGBTQ communities (Meyer and Tarrow 2018).

Immigrant Rights

Between February and May 2006, the immigrant rights' movement burst on to the public scene in dramatic style with massive demonstrations and rallies in large and small cities in dozens of US states (Bloemraad, Voss, and Lee 2011; Zepeda-Millán 2017). The participants found motivation to take to the streets from new legislation (House Bill 4437) passed in the Republican-dominated U.S. House of Representatives that would make living in the United States without proper documentation a serious criminal offense for the undocumented, as well as for those aiding them. The impending negative consequences associated with this legislation mobilized

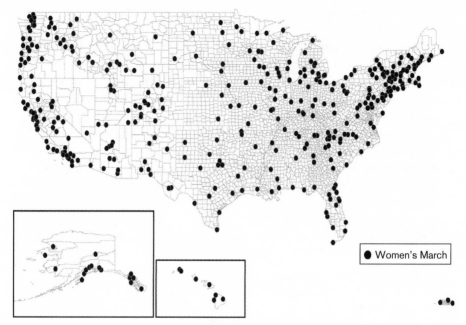

FIGURE 1. Locations of Women's March, 2017. Compiled by author from www. womensmarch.com/ in January 2017.

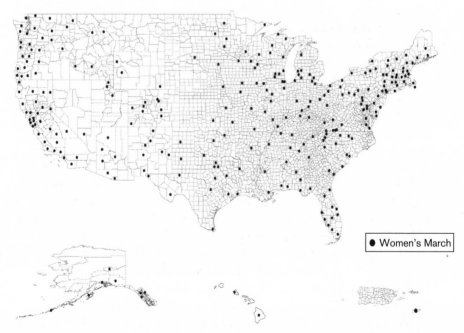

FIGURE 2. Women's March, 2018. Compiled by author from www.womensmarch.com/ in January 2018.

communities throughout the national territory, with several cities breaking records for protest attendance. The resources used to mobilize the movement included organizations of churches, radio stations, public schools, and an emerging pan-Latino identity (Mora et al. 2018). With some of the demonstrations drawing up to a million participants, Congress backed down and shelved the legislation in a stalemate between the House and the Senate. The power of mass collective action had prevented the implementation of a punitive law that potentially would have led to widespread disruption of working-class immigrant communities in the United States. A similar campaign emerged in the summer of 2018 against the Trump administration's policy of family separation of immigrants seeking asylum at the US-Mexican border, with protest events reported in over seven hundred cities.

Movements around the Globe for Economic Justice

Between 2000 and 2018, from the advanced capitalist nations of Europe and North America to large swathes of the developing world, citizens launched major campaigns against government economic cutbacks and privatization of social services and the state infrastructure—or what economists and sociologists call the economic policies of *neoliberalism*. Labor flexibility in France, austerity in Spain, Portugal, and Greece, and economic reforms in Argentina, Brazil, China, Costa Rica, and India all drew hundreds of thousands of people to public plazas and mass demonstrations demanding protection of their *social citizenship rights*—the basic right to a modicum of economic welfare provisioned by the state (Somers 2008).

The global movement for economic justice took off in the wealthy capitalist nations in the late 1990s and early 2000s with major protest events outside of elite financial summits in Seattle, Prague, Davos, Doha, Cancun, Quebec City, and Genoa. The mobilizations kept up steam by aligning with movements in the global South via the World Social Forum network. In July 2017 the global economic justice movement mobilized over one hundred thousand people to demonstrate against the G20 economic summit in Hamburg, Germany. Similar types of street demonstrations occurred in the United States over economic inequality between late 2011 and early 2012 with the occupation of public squares in the "Occupy Wall Street" movement. Privatizations of water administration, public health, telecommunications, and energy catalyzed some of the largest mobilizations in South America, Asia, and Africa over the past two decades. Taken together, there has been a recent upsurge of movements around the world struggling for more equitable forms of economic globalization (Almeida 2010a; Castells

2015; Almeida and Chase-Dunn 2018). On the dark side of politics, we also find that extremists and populist demagogues use the heightened inequities associated with economic globalization and free trade to mobilize right-wing and racist movements in the United States, South America, and Europe (Berezin 2009; Robinson 2014).[2]

Transnational Movement for Climate Justice

Since 2000 a worldwide movement has gained momentum in an attempt to slow down global warming. The "climate justice movement" seeks a global accord among the world's nations for an immediate and drastic reduction in carbon emissions. By 2006 the climate mobilizations had reached multiple countries on every continent. Climate justice activists use cyber networks and social media to coordinate with hundreds of nongovernmental organizations, concerned citizens, scientists, and environmental groups around the planet to hold public gatherings and demonstrations demanding governmental and industry action to reduce greenhouse gases. The global mobilizations usually take place in conjunction with annual United Nations-sponsored climate summits in order to place pressure on national leaders to act (including an enormous street march of four hundred thousand persons in New York City in 2014). Between 2014 and 2018 alone, the climate justice movement successfully mobilized thousands of protest events in 175 countries on multiple occasions—the most extensive transnational movement in history.

These four movements demonstrate the multiple facets of social movements discussed in the pages that follow. They all involve *sustained challenges seeking social change using resources to maintain mobilization*. All four movements first mobilized in reaction to real and perceived *threats to their interests*. Finally, and perhaps most germane here, the movements resulted in deep changes within the societies they operated in. The Women's Marches sent a powerful message that all attempts to deepen social exclusion by the newly elected Trump administration would be met with massive resistance. The immigrant rights movement forced anti-immigrant politicians to backpedal from their legislation as the mobilizations spilled over into a movement that fights for other immigrant rights issues, such as the right to education and employment for immigrant youth—the "DREAMers' Movement" (Nicholls 2014)—a comprehensive immigration reform act that provides a path to citizenship, and an end to the policy of family separation of asylum seekers. Economic austerity protests have swept several new left-wing political parties into executive power and parliaments in South America and southern Europe. The climate justice movement forced a long-awaited global treaty on carbon emissions at the end of the 2015 Paris Climate Summit.

DEFINING SOCIAL MOVEMENTS

The four movements portrayed above clearly exhibit properties of social movement activity. Throughout this text, we will work with the following definition: *A social movement is an excluded collectivity in sustained interaction with economic and political elites seeking social change* (Tarrow 2011). In such situations, ordinary people come together to pursue a common goal. Social movements are usually composed of groups outside of institutionalized power that use unconventional strategies (e.g., street marches, sit-ins, dramatic media events) along with more conventional ones (petitions, letter-writing campaigns) to achieve their aims (Snow and Soule 2009). The outsider status and unconventional tactics of social movements distinguish them from other political entities, such as lobbying associations, nonprofit organizations, and political parties (though these more formal organizations may originate from social movements). Most people participate in movements as volunteers and offer their time, skills, and other human resources to maintaining movement survival and accomplishing goals. Throughout this book, I will emphasize the *exclusion* of social groups from institutional, economic, and political power as a primary motive for engaging in social movement actions.

Social movements range from community-based environmental movements battling local pollution, to women's movements organized on a transnational scale attempting to place pressure on national governments and international institutions to protect and expand the rights of girls and women (Viterna and Fallon 2008). We will explore these different levels of social movement activity in the next chapter. The modern social movement form arose with the spread of parliamentary political systems and nationally integrated capitalist economies in the nineteenth century (Tilly and Wood 2012). Before the nineteenth century, collective action was largely based on local grievances at the village level and mobilization was sustained for shorter periods of time (Tilly 1978). Nonetheless, we observe important forms of collective mobilization throughout human history (Chase-Dunn 2016). The core movement elements of *sustained collective challenges* by *excluded social groups* attempting to protect themselves from *social, political, economic, and environmental harms* form the basis of our definition of social movements and drive the largest campaigns of collective action in the twenty-first century.

The Core Movement Elements

Sustained Collective Mobilization Social movements are collective and sustained over a period of time. How and why individuals come together to pursue common goals provides much of the content of this book. The larger the scale of collective action, the longer the mobilization should endure to be considered a "movement." Local neighborhood and community movements may last for only a few months or a year as they tend to have short-term and specific goals, such as preventing pollution from a nearby facility or demanding street lights for nighttime safety. Larger national-level mobilizations likely need to sustain themselves for at least a year to be considered a social movement. In contrast, a single demonstration or protest does not constitute a social movement. At the same time, collective actors must find ways to maintain momentum and unity. Preexisting organizations, social relationships of friends, neighbors, the workplace, schools, ethnic ties, collective identities, and a variety of resources assist in prolonging the mobilization process (see chapter 4 on movement emergence).

Excluded Social Groups Social movements are largely constituted by groups with relatively less political and economic power. Their exclusionary status provides the rationale for taking the social movement form (Burawoy 2017; Mora et al. 2017). Non-excluded groups benefit from more routine access to government and economic elites in terms of having their voices heard, and are *relatively* more likely to receive favorable resolutions for their grievances via petitions, elections, lobbying, and meetings with officials. Excluded groups (along racial, economic, citizenship, and gender lines, among many others) lack this routine access and may at times resort to less conventional forms of seeking influence to gain the attention of authorities and power brokers.

Social, Economic, and Environmental Harms A central motivation for social movement mobilization involves real and perceived harms. A critical mass of individuals must come under the threat of a particular harm, such as discrimination, job loss, or environmental health, that motivates them to unify and launch a social movement campaign, especially when institutional channels fail to resolve the issue at hand. Opportunities may also arrive to reduce long-standing harms, such as decades of discrimination or economic exploitation (Tarrow 2011). Social movement mobilization is much more likely to materialize when large numbers of people mutually sense they are experiencing or suffering from similar circumstances. This was precisely the case for the 2006 immigrants' rights protests discussed above. Millions of citizens and noncitizens came under a suddenly imposed threat of criminal prosecution for their undocumented status or for aiding nonlegalized immigrants. This led to mutual awareness among immigrant communities and to rapid mobilization (Zepeda-Millán 2017).

Throughout the text, I will emphasize these three core movement elements of (1) collective and sustained mobilization, (2) social exclusion, and (3) threats as key dimensions in characterizing social movement activity.

BASIC SOCIAL MOVEMENT CONCEPTS

As in most subfields of sociology and the social sciences there is a vernacular or jargon for discussing key social processes and terms. The field of social movements is no exception. As we progress deeper into the study of social movements in this book, new terms will be introduced and defined. To begin, some of the principal concepts used to discuss social movements are presented below.

Grievances and Threats   (demonstration)

An initial condition for social mobilization centers on shared grievances. In other words, people collectively view some facet of social life as a problem and in need of alteration (Simmons 2014). A wide variety of grievances have ignited social movement campaigns, including police abuse, racial and gender discrimination, economic inequality, and pollution. At times, communities experience grievances as "suddenly imposed," stimulating mobilization in a relatively short time horizon (Walsh et al. 1997). Recurring instances of suddenly imposed and shocking grievances were behind the anti–police abuse demonstrations in the United States between 2014 and 2015 following jury acquittals or dramatic videos that went "viral" on social media and the internet. These incidents catalyzed the Black Lives Matter movement into a new round of the struggle for racial justice in the United States (Taylor 2016).

At my home institution, the University of California, Merced, many students experienced the surprising presidential election results of November 2016 as a suddenly imposed grievance. The university is composed of a large majority of students of color, many coming from immigrant families. The following e-mail I received from a student the day after the elections demonstrates how the unexpected election results immediately led to some of the largest protests in the history of the new campus:

Good morning Professor Almeida,

As professor of the social movements, protests, and collective action class, I thought I'd inform you of the protest that occurred on campus last night. At about 11:00 pm, students on UC Merced classifieds on Facebook, posted that they would organize to speak up against the results of the presidential election. Students started getting together in the main entrance of the university, they advanced through the summits and the sierra terraces encouraging students to come out of their rooms. The students continued walking through scholars lane and finally gathered around the New Beginnings statue. It was there that the organizers informed the students that there would be another protest today at 10:00 am in front of the library. Afterward, the students walked back downhill chanting. . . . Students were also seen holding signs with words in Spanish such as "la lucha sigue" and "marcha". The crowd of students gathered once again in the summits courtyard, where the organizers re-announced the protest that will take place today and where the students continued their chants. A few trump supporters were seen during the protest, but the organizers reminded the students that "this is a peaceful protest". The entire protest lasted about two hours.

We will later discuss how grievances move from the individual to the group level. But even in this short e-mail we can see elements of the structure of collective action discussed throughout this book, including the role of Facebook and social media, everyday organizations such as the dorms, and the appeals used to bring more people into demonstrations. Another important issue related to grievances, explored in the chapter on theory (chapter 3), is whether people are responding to an intensification of grievances (*threats*) or to new possibilities (*opportunities*) to reduce long-standing grievances.

Strategy   (negonation)

The actual planning of demands, goals, tactics, and targets as well as their timing is part of an overall social movement strategy (Maney et al. 2012; Meyer and Staggenborg 2012). Once the collective action process moves from grievance formation to actual mobilization, social movements will likely formulate a set of *demands*. Demands are communicated to power holders as a means to negotiate and attempt to address and reduce the original grievances. Scholars also use the term "claims" interchangeably with movement demands. Demands or claims are often written in formal letters during negotiations, as well as displayed on banners and chanted in unison during protest rallies, or publicly stated during press conferences held by social movement leaders. Social movements increasingly express demands and claims via various social media platforms (e.g., Facebook, WhatsApp, Twitter). Demands may be communicated in very specific terms, such as raising the salaries of fast-food workers to a fixed wage amount (e.g., $15 per hour), as observed in recent strike campaigns in the United States.

Goals are generally conceived as broader than a set of demands (though they often coincide); for example, the larger goal of a "living wage" and "economic justice" for fast-food industry workers. Goals and demands are also categorized from reform minded to radical—from changing part of a government policy to calling for the complete transformation of a society, the latter acting as a common aim defining revolutionary social movements. We will observe in chapter 7 that goals provide a way to measure movement success in achieving social change in terms of specified objectives.

Social movements also employ a variety of *tactics*—a repertoire of actions from teach-ins and educational workshops to media events (such as press conferences) and street demonstrations. Tactics range from the highly conventional, such as petitions and letter-writing campaigns, to the highly unconventional and disruptive, such as "die-ins," sit-ins, and traffic obstruction. At times, tactics may escalate to the level of violent acts, as in the case of riots, revolutions, and terrorism. Classifying tactics into conventional, disruptive, and violent is a useful categorization scheme. It leads to interesting questions about the conditions shaping the type of tactic and its effectiveness in mobilizing people, influencing public opinion, and achieving stated goals.

As another component of their overall strategy, social movements eventually *target* institutions to present their demands. The targets are often multiple and commonly involve some part of the government such as city councils, school boards, state agencies, the courts, and congressional and parliamentary bodies, which may be the final arbiters of the conflict. Depending on the nature of the movement, a variety of targets may be drawn into the campaign, including the mass media and other institutions (schools, hospitals, churches, private industry).

Coalitions (حلف)

Collective actors often join with other groups to extend mobilization to other regions and sectors of society. When a collectivity aligns with at least one other group to engage in collective action, a *coalition* has formed. The formation of social movement coalitions raises intriguing research questions about their composition and consequences for mobilization (Van Dyke and McCammon 2010; Van Dyke and Amos 2017). At first glance, a coalition of multiple social groups (e.g., students, immigrant rights organizations, women's associations, environmentalists) appears to strengthen the level and size of mobilization by publicly exhibiting that several sectors of society are unified over a particular grievance or issue such as police abuse or a government's foreign policy in launching a military action. Large coalitions may be especially potent in struggles for democracy and human rights in authoritarian regimes by demonstrating that large segments of society oppose the prevailing lack of freedom and civil liberties (Schock 2005; Almeida 2005; 2008a). At other times, coalitions introduce new problems in sustaining collective action by trying to negotiate a consensus about strategy in terms of tactics, goals, and targets. This may lead to movement infighting and the rapid dissolution of mobilization.

Framing

The framing process incorporates many of the ideological and cognitive components of collective action (Snow et al. 2018). Chapter 5 is dedicated to the framing process and collective action frames. We will learn how movement leaders actively convey grievances to larger audiences in order to draw in more support for the movement and maintain commitments from movement participants. Movement ingenuity and creativity are put to the test in the way activists use existing cultural idioms and symbols to express social problems and motivate people into action.

The State

Throughout this work, I will use *the state* to refer to the government. The state may be local (e.g., city council), regional, or national. Social movements are deeply shaped by states, and at times movements have a profound impact in changing government policies and priorities. Different types of states often determine the possibilities for collective action and the forms they take. Repressive governments that do not allow citizens to form autonomous organizations or to assemble publicly place enormous obstacles for groups to initiate social movement campaigns. In some cases, governmental repression pushes groups into more radical demands and forms of mobilization. More-democratic states will likely tolerate social movement mobilizations and use softer forms of repression when trying to control or pacify mass dissent (e.g., manipulate the mass media, deny permits for demonstrations). Even at the local level in the United States there is wide variation among city governments and the amount of political space granted to excluded and marginalized populations.

Social Movement Organizations

Once social movements come into existence, they are likely to form organizations that support further mobilization (McAdam 1999 [1982]). We call these kinds of associations social movement organizations (SMOs) (McCarthy and Zald 1977; McAdam and Scott 2005; Minkoff and McCarthy 2005). The acronym SMOs has become so widespread in social movement studies that scholars often neglect to define the term. Examples of SMOs include the People for the Ethical Treatment of Animals (PETA), and the internationally active environmental organization Greenpeace. SMOs appear to be proliferating across national boundaries in the twenty-first century (Smith and Wiest 2012), a theme we explore in chapter 8.

These core social movement concepts are applied throughout this text. We can briefly start using these terms by returning to the Women's March and addressing the following questions: What were the grievances driving the largest mobilizations in US history? How would you describe the strategy of the organizers of the event? What were the central demands and goals of the marches? How would you classify the core tactic of the street march (conventional or disruptive)? What features did the organizers use in their framing strategies to bring millions out to protest? The maps in figures 1 and 2 illustrate where the women's marches occurred in the 3,007 counties of the United States. Why did some counties have multiple women's marches while many more counties failed to produce even one event? Chapter 4, on movement emergence, directly addresses this question.

MAJOR THEMES IN THE STRUCTURE OF SOCIAL MOVEMENTS

In the following chapters we explore in depth the multifaceted nature of social movements—the collective coming together of ordinary people to overcome exclusion and mount sustained campaigns for social change. We move from *methods* and *theoretical underpinnings* of social movements to the major subareas guiding the study of collective mobilization. These themes include *social movement emergence, collective action frames, individual recruitment and participation, the impacts of social movements,* and *the global spread of movement activities.*

Methods

While it might seem rather simple to identify a social movement on the basis of the concepts just outlined, systematically dissecting movement dynamics using social science methods is a challenging process. In the first part of chapter 2, I classify levels of social movement activity, from the microscale of everyday forms of resistance in small insular groups to the macroscale of mobilization spreading over entire societies and across countries. I next introduce the major techniques used in social movement research, including observation, interviews, newspapers, social media (Twitter, Facebook, WhatsApp, etc.), surveys, archives, and government statistics. Each method is directly linked to specific areas and dimensions of collective action, such as movement emergence and movement recruitment. Readers will be introduced to strategies on how to carry out collective action research, especially the appropriate techniques for collecting data for particular dimensions of social movement activity.

Theory

Chapter 3 introduces the main theoretical explanations for social movement dynamics. Theories provide guides that reduce the social world to the most important features driving social movement mobilization. We review early models of social movements that failed to account for the unequal distribution of power and resources in modern societies. The universe of contemporary movement theories will be examined, including rational actor, new social movement, and political process frameworks. The now-dominant political process approach centers on the larger political environment and how differentially configured political contexts shape the likelihood of social movement emergence, forms of mobilization, and movement outcomes. Special attention is given to the negative conditions driving collective action within the political process tradition as movements in the twenty-first century increasingly respond to environmental, political, social, and economic threats. With social movement theories in hand, readers will have the tools to scrutinize elite and mass media accounts of real-time social movements in terms of their origins, motivations, and consequences for changing society.

Movement Emergence

Chapter 4 examines how social movements are most likely to arise when a particular collectivity comes under threat or receives signals from the political environment that advantages may be forthcoming if groups decide to mobilize. In other words, either "bad news" or "good news" may motivate episodes of collective action (Meyer 2002). Under bad-news or threatening conditions, a community or population perceives that its situation will become worse if it fails to act and that it may lose collective goods (e.g., loss of land, rights, employment). In the good-news political environment, groups sense that they will acquire new collective goods if they act in concert (e.g., new rights, higher wages, greater environmental quality). Often, bad-news and good-news protest campaigns are triggered by government policies that signal to would-be challengers that the state is becoming less or more receptive to the issues most meaningful to the population in question.

Besides these motivations for movement emergence, some type of organizational base needs to be in existence to mobilize large numbers of people (McCarthy 1996; McAdam 1999 [1982]; Andrews 2004). These organizational assets may be traditional, such as solidarities based on village, religious, regional, or ethnic identities, or they may be associational, rooted in secondary groups such as labor unions, social clubs, agricultural cooperatives, educational institutions, and more formal social movement organizations (SMOs) (Oberschall 1973). Without preexisting solidarity ties and organizational links, either formal or informal, it is unlikely that threats or opportunities will convert into social movement campaigns. Hence, social movement scholars give special attention to variations in organizational resources across localities and over time in explaining social movement emergence (Edwards and McCarthy 2004; Edwards et al. 2018). More recent work in the resource mobilization subfield has expanded into sophisticated network analysis of the means by which a field of SMOs, potential participants, and sponsoring organizations are structurally connected to one another and how the variations in those structures affect social movement emergence (Diani and McAdam 2003; Diani 2015; Hadden 2015). The struggles of low-wage fast-food workers and the student movement against gun violence in the United States exemplify these dynamics.

Framing

Chapter 5 features the framing perspective and how it derives from the interpretive tradition in sociology, with a special concern for the ability of activists to construct social grievances (Snow et al. 2014; Snow et al. 2018). It is now largely understood that injustice and organizational resources alone do not explain the timing and location of social movement mobilization. Movement leaders and activists must construct norm violations, grievances, and experiences of oppression and injustice in socially meaningful and convincing ways that will motivate the targeted populations to participate in collective action (Snow et al. 1986; Snow and Benford 1988). In other words, social and political activists must "frame" the social world in such a manner that it resonates with rank-and-file movement supporters as well as sympathizers and fence-sitters. We explore the creative ways that movements employ cultural artifacts, such as popular music, to reach their intended audiences of adherents and potential sympathizers. The framing perspective incorporates the human agency components of the collective action process.

Movement Participation

Social movement recruitment and individual-level participation draw on microlevel models of collective action. Chapter 6 covers these individual-level dynamics in detail. Early explanations of social movement recruitment and participation emphasized the irrationality aspects of mass movements. Political movements of the unruly were viewed as fulfilling psychological deficits for movement participants—a kind of therapy to overcome sentiments of alienation and social strain inherent in fast-paced industrialized urban societies (McAdam 1999 [1982]). By the late 1970s and early 1980s, scholars began to look at more than just the beliefs and psychological profiles of movement participants. They also examined the microstructural context of mobilization, namely the social ties and networks of potential movement recruits (Snow et al. 1980; McAdam 1986). This newer empirical research found that movement participants were often highly socially integrated in their everyday lives and more likely to belong to civil society associations and clubs than those who did not participate in social movements. In addition, the connections individuals maintained with movement-sympathetic organizations and individuals made them much more likely to join a protest campaign, whereas those connected to organizations and individuals opposed to such activities were much more likely not to participate (McAdam 1986).

The most recent studies demonstrate how social networks interact with new political identities forged by political events (Viterna 2013). Further, movement mobilization occurs at a faster rate when entire groups and organizations are recruited en masse—a process termed "bloc recruitment"—as opposed to organizing single individuals one at a time (Oberschall 1973). Readers will develop a more pronounced understanding of the kinds of individual contexts, based on biography, ideology, networks, identities, and past collective action experience, that are more likely to condition one's choice to join social movement campaigns. Existing data sets on movement participation are also introduced, including state-of-the-art projects of collecting participant motivations in real-time protest demonstrations (Klandermans 2012).

Social Movement Outcomes

Perhaps the most important social movement arena involves movement impacts—the subject of chapter 7. What kinds of changes in the political environment can be attributed to the existence and actions of a social movement? What aspects of social change can be explicitly associated with the activities of a movement? Students of social movements examine various dimensions of social movement outcomes. The enduring changes associated with movements include impacts on individual movement participants, changes in the political culture, influence on state policies, and "spillover" into other social movements (Meyer and Whittier 1994; Whittier 2004). In comparison to movement emergence, there is less scholarly consensus on social movement outcomes (Jenkins and Form 2005; Amenta et al. 2010). Often it is difficult to decipher the particular contribution of a social movement to a specific outcome while attempting to control for nonmovement influences. Despite these scientific shortcomings, major movements of excluded social groups in the United States and elsewhere have improved their circumstances. Constituents represented by such movements obtained major policy changes because large numbers of people engaged in social movement struggles, including the women's movement, the African American civil rights movement, the Mexican American labor and civil rights movement, and the LGBTQ civil rights movement, among many others.

Global South, Authoritarian Regimes, and Transnational Movements

Chapter 8 focuses on movements in the global South and transnational movements (movements operating in more than one country). The majority of social movement studies concentrate on movements in industrialized democracies in the global North. However, a growing body of literature now exists on political contexts outside of the advanced capitalist states. The more stable forms of government in Western democracies allow for a greater upkeep of social movement organizations and more space to launch largely nonviolent campaigns. In nondemocratic and quasi-democratic nations (e.g., monarchies, dictatorships, military juntas, theocracies, authoritarian populism), where associational freedoms are proscribed and regular multiparty elections do not occur, scholars face challenges in explaining when social movements will arise and what forms they will take. One fruitful avenue investigates "cracks in the system," small political openings, or larger moves toward political liberalization in nondemocracies. These conditions often provide a conducive environment for a few activists in civil society to attempt to form civic associations and possibly even begin to seek small reforms. Other movements may be launched in institutions outside the purview of state control, such as religious institutions (mosques, religious schools, Catholic youth groups, etc.) or remote territories not completely controlled by the administrative state apparatus and army (Goodwin 2001). Foreign governments and movements may also support a fledgling movement in a non-democratic context.

The expansion of transnational social movements that link members and organizations across more than one country is a major global trend over the past three decades (Smith and Wiest 2012). Two noteworthy transnational movements in the early twenty-first century are international Islamic solidarity and the global economic justice movement. Internationally connected Islamic movements benefit from the concept of *ummah*—the larger community of believers that links the Muslim world beyond national borders (Lubeck and Reifer 2004; Roy 2006). With global migration flows and new communications technology, Islamic-based social movements easily mobilize internationally. Examples include transnationally organized insurgencies such as Al Qaeda or the Islamic State (ISIL). The *ummah* concept is also a powerful unifying force for nonviolent transnational antiwar and antidiscrimination movements in the Islamic world and diasporic communities, and it played a major role in the rapid diffusion of Arab Spring uprisings in 2011 against repressive governments.

The global economic justice movement (sometimes referred to by critics as the antiglobalization movement) is another major transnational movement that emerged in the late twentieth century. Supporters of this movement use global communications technologies to mobilize constituents. The global justice movement arose almost simultaneously with the expansion of the global internet infrastructure between the mid-1990s and the early 2000s. Several organizations in Europe and Canada, including the Council of Canadians, Jubilee 2000, People's Global Action, and ATTAC, began to work with nongovernmental organizations in the developing world to place pressure on newly emerging and older transnational governing bodies and economic institutions, such as the United Nations, the World Trade Organization (WTO), the International Monetary Fund, the World Bank, the Group of Eight (G8), and the European Union.

The demands of the global justice movement vary but tend to focus on economic justice, environmental protection, and the need for more transparency in decision-making among the elite transnational economic and political institutions mentioned above. Though the movement held several major protests in the late 1990s outside WTO and G8 meetings in Europe, a massive demonstration at the 1999 WTO meetings in Seattle, Washington, served as a breakthrough for the global justice movement. It was the largest sustained protest in an American city in several decades (Almeida and

Lichbach 2003). Global justice activists coordinated the arrival of participants from around the country and the world via the internet and organized the protests in the streets of Seattle with cell phones. Dozens of countries across the globe also experienced protests in solidarity with the actions in Seattle. The success of the Seattle mobilizations provided a template for organizing dozens of similar global days of action in the twenty-first century during major international financial conferences, World Social Forums, free trade meetings, and climate change negotiations, including the 2017 G20 Summit in Hamburg, Germany, and the 2018 G20 Summit in Buenos Aires, Argentina.

The Conclusion ends our long journey through the field of collective mobilization dynamics by summarizing key features of social movements we have considered in previous chapters. The collective knowledge of methods, theory, emergence, framing, and movement outcomes accumulated from previous chapters is applied to particular case studies of movements emerging in the 2010s and likely in the 2020s. New frontiers of social movement research are also presented, including recent global patterns in the use of social media technology in recruitment practices, as well as transnational movements such as climate justice.

2 How to Study Social Movements

Classification and Methods

The previous chapter defined and discussed social movements in basic terms. The present chapter explores the process of researching social movements. The exploration begins with a concise classification scheme of social movement activity from the micro- to the macrolevel. This categorization system runs from everyday forms of resistance to revolutions and transnational movements. The second half of the chapter covers the main types of methods used by social scientists, anthropologists, and historians to study social movements. Historical archives, surveys, observation, interviews, and content analysis along with document coding are all introduced. Each category of movement activity corresponds to different methodological tools (e.g., for "everyday forms of resistance" we use observation, interviews, and historical methods). Special attention will be given here to content coding of newspapers and protest event data (including strengths and biases) along with protest activity reported on activist websites, as these data collection techniques are some of the most common in contemporary social movement research.

Students and scholars investigating social movements make important social scientific discoveries, but they also document historical social change. This fact adds a "special mission" component to social movement research in that information systematically collected may also be of use to other social movements, historians, and the public in general. The chapter provides an introduction to the basic tools used to make these special contributions. In sum, readers will acquire knowledge of the primary classifications and methods employed in social movement studies.

SIX LEVELS OF COLLECTIVE ACTION
IN SOCIAL MOVEMENT RESEARCH

For conceptual clarity scholars find it useful to specify different levels of popular movement activity. The existing literature identifies at least six levels or types of movement actions. They include, in order of increasing scale, (1) everyday forms of resistance, (2) local grassroots movements, (3) national social movements, (4) waves of protest, (5) revolutionary movements, and (6) transnational social movements.

Everyday Forms of Resistance

Everyday forms of resistance involve acts of dissention and noncompliance by individuals or small groups against proximate sources of injustice. This level of microresistance is also referred to as "weapons of the weak" (Scott 1985). More-extensive coverage of this microlevel of collective action is provided here, as it is often underemphasized in social movement studies. These types of actions most often occur in situations of extreme oppression, such as enslavement, repressive agricultural systems, military dictatorships, colonial and foreign occupations, and concentration camps (Maher 2010; Einwohner and Maher 2011). The context is so overwhelmingly oppressive that open collective forms of defiance such as an organized protest or a strike would bring immediate harm, if not death, to the group initiating the resistance. This is the smallest level of oppositional activity. James Scott's (1985) ethnographic field research in rural Malaysia highlighted and popularized these "everyday" forms of resistance. Scott documented petty theft, village gossip, work slowdowns, noncompliance, and vandalism of farm equipment as exemplars of these forms of protest, previously underreported in the social movement literature. He also viewed them as more efficacious and pragmatic in comparison to more conventional forms of political organizing.

Scott also provides a rationale for why subordinate groups rarely engage in organized politics in his discussion of the "the dull compulsion of economic relations." He suggests that extreme economic barriers for many marginalized groups prevent them from openly defying their oppressive situation. Economic dependency is experienced to such a high degree that overt resistance would have tremendous negative consequences (e.g., economic hardship, physical punishment, hunger). The focus on economic dependency has also allowed scholars to analyze everyday forms of rebellion in relatively less oppressive contexts. Besides negative economic sanctions, subordinate social groups face other forms of coercion, such as

political and military repression. In general, marginalized groups participate in covert and anonymous micro-acts of defiance to avoid retaliation
from adversaries (Scott 1990).

Examples of the targets of everyday forms of resistance include landlords, field supervisors, wealthy villagers, abusive managers at worksites,
and threatening technologies. Scott also generalizes to other subordinated
social classes and times (e.g., the early nineteenth-century British working
class, the Mexican Revolution). In short, Scott contends that subordinate
groups at the microlevel are always resisting and negotiating the extraction
of surplus value in exploitative relationships in an attempt to slow down
the rate of abuse from superiors. This is a welcome contribution to our
understanding of how subordinate social groups resist domination by often
unobvious means.

Support for Scott's conclusions can be found in other contexts. Hossfeld
(1990) demonstrated that immigrant women working in Silicon Valley's
computer assembly plants inverted white male gender and racial ideology
to their small advantage, eventuating in longer breaks, promotions, and less
hazardous working conditions. Burawoy (1979: 171) reported individual
resistance in his participant observation of a machine shop in Chicago in
the practice of "chiseling," whereby workers transferred time saved from
one job to another. In northern Mexico, Peña (1997) observed that female
maquiladora workers engaged in work slowdowns ("*tortuosidad,*" or tur-
tle's pace) to resist abusive plant managers in assembly factories. Rollins
(1985) also shows a series of deference rituals invoked by domestic workers
in order to survive economically in the context of the psychological exploitation and domination of their privileged employers. Hank Johnston (2005;
2011), in his work on microresistance in Eastern Europe, adds the notion of
"speech acts" to our understanding of everyday forms of defiance. Johnston
provides a series of micro-acts of resistance. He shows that forms of speech
such as telling jokes in small groups about a repressive regime, graffiti, or
singing (or even humming) prohibited songs may plant the seeds in which
larger forms of solidarity begin to flourish.

Scholars highlight the use of everyday forms of rebellion in Africa as
well. Because of direct, harsh colonial rule in sub-Saharan Africa in the
early to mid-twentieth century, much rural defiance of the foreign imposi-
tion of cultivating agricultural commodities took the shape of everyday
forms of resistance in which peasants engaged in largely hidden types of
collective defiance. Again, these are contexts whereby open and sustained
social movement mobilizations are too high a risk and subaltern groups
must resort to less obtrusive and public forms of dissent. Allen Isaacman

(1993: 237) defines such situations of resistance in the African context as peasant attempts "to block or undercut the claims of the state or appropriating class." These daily forms of noncompliance often remain undocumented in official records. Such rebellious and clandestine acts included boiling cotton seeds before planting, in South Africa, Malawi, Tanzania, and Zaire; robbing tax collectors, in Angola, Ethiopia, Mozambique, and Zimbabwe; sabotaging farm equipment, in South Africa and Kenya; sharecroppers withholding part of their rice output, in the Gambia; planting cash crops late and in insufficient quantities (while intercropping subsistence foods), in Cameroon, Chad, Kenya, Malawi, Mozambique, Tanzania, and Uganda; and fleeing en masse when indigenous African communities (in a variety of locations) came under threat of forced labor or taxation (Isaacman 1993: 237–41).

In the first two decades of the twenty-first century, small groups in rural regions continue to engage in everyday forms of rebellion. A large proportion of these contemporary acts involve defiance of new rounds of natural resource extraction and land grabbing in the global South. Examples include small-scale collective actions against mining, the massive cultivation of biofuel crops (e.g., sugar cane, palm, soybeans), genetically modified plants, and rubber trees on native lands.[1] In urban areas, citizens sustain resistance to authoritarian rule with micro-acts of resistance. In the cities of Honduras in 2017, after the government declared a special state of emergency and military curfew following large-scale protests against perceived electoral fraud and glaring vote-counting irregularities, ordinary people banged on pots and pans outside their windows under the cover of darkness to maintain opposition within an increasingly repressive context. Pushing the boundaries of the definition of "weapons of the weak," some scholars in the twenty-first century even claim politically motivated internet and social media hacking, or "hacktivism," as a novel form of everyday disruption (Edyvane and Kulenovic 2017).

For those interested in protest escalation, however, the "everyday forms of resistance / weapons of the weak" approach only informs us that subordinate groups in a variety of contexts daily resist their mistreatment with the limited means available to them—usually in small groups at the site of production. Johnston (2005; 2011) contends a broader micro-macro link needs to be specified in order to understand how everyday resistance escalates into local grassroots movements. Scott (1985: 273) hints at a micro-macro link in these terms: "Such forms of resistance are the nearly permanent, continuous daily strategies of subordinate rural classes under difficult conditions. At times of crisis or momentous political change, they may be complemented by other forms of struggle that are more opportune. . . . They are the stubborn bedrock upon which other forms of resistance may grow." How everyday acts of resistance scale up into larger rebellions remains an open research question for future activists and students of collective action to address.

The greatest insight of the "weapons of the weak" level of contention is that it provides compelling evidence that subordinated groups are not simply ideologically manipulated or suffering from "false consciousness." Rather, they are involved in microcontention in the political sphere. Subordinate groups have their own normative structures or cultures of resistance that are more easily seen "backstage," away from the elite-dominated public sphere (Scott 1985; 1990). In summary, everyday forms of resistance provide a microlevel understanding of collective action, especially in situations of extreme oppression and exploitation.

Local Grassroots Movements

A local grassroots movement battles at the local or regional level for specified and limited goals (e.g., local pollution problem, unionization of a single workplace) and usually has a restricted supply of internal organizational resources. Such mobilizations appear closer to the definition of social movements in chapter 1 compared to everyday forms of resistance in that they are sustained over time. Local movements draw most of their support from individual volunteers in nearby communities. In many cases, their success in achieving stated goals relies heavily on the local movement's ability to form alliances with other groups, especially larger social movements (Almeida and Stearns 1998). More specified goals also give local movements greater prospects for success. In California, nonprofit organizations such as Communities for a New California (CNC) and Faith in the Valley have engaged in dozens of local-level struggles in poor and immigrant neighborhoods throughout the state. Since 2010, the CNC has worked with low-income communities in demanding basic neighborhood amenities such as sidewalks and city parks.[2] Residents struggling over the placement of big-box stores (such as Walmart) in their communities offer another example of local grassroots movements (Ingram et al. 2010; Halebsky 2009).

One of the most common forms of local grassroots struggle in the United States over the past thirty years can be found in the environmental justice movement. The movement took off in the 1980s after multiple communities around the United States became aware of and exposed to pollution in the vicinity of where people and families live, work, and play (Bullard 2000; Szasz 1994). A local pollution problem or environmental threat may drive local communities and neighborhoods to mobilize (e.g., lead poisoning in Flint, Michigan; risks associated with the Dakota Access Pipeline). In some cases it may be an industrial incinerator or hazardous waste site that initiates local mobilization. Other environmental justice struggles may be catalyzed by abandoned toxic storage sites, air pollution, or pesticide poisoning (Bullard 2005; Taylor 2014). These local movements continue to be active today, as in community battles over hydraulic fracturing ("fracking") with the gas and oil industry (Vasi et al. 2015; Auyero et al. 2018). The defining feature is that they are *local struggles* focusing on *local issues*, with volunteer membership deriving from nearby communities. Local grassroots movements also often name themselves after their own region, connecting their identities to a sense of place, as in the Mothers of East Los Angeles, the West County Toxics Coalition, and Concerned Citizens of South Central Los Angeles.

National Social Movements

National social movements represent broad struggles (enveloping much of the national territory) that involve formal organizations or federations of loosely affiliated networks (Tarrow 2011). National social movements possess internal resources and a wide range of goals directed at social and political reform and changing public attitudes. According to Tilly (1984), the national social movement arose concomitantly with the expansion of representative political systems in western Europe in the mid-nineteenth century. Geographic expansion and increasing administrative tasks made the state the locus for groups to press claims and express grievances.

Though the original home of social movement mobilization may be states with largely democratic polities, national social movements now appear throughout the globe in a variety of political and economic contexts. Through colonial expansion and anticolonial resistance, print and communication, and nation building, the modern national social movement form of exerting political influence and claims-making spread to world regions outside of the capitalist metropoles (McAdam et al. 2001; Markoff 2015a).

The national social movement is the most common form of movement studied and discussed. Exemplars include the civil rights movement, the women's movement, the environmental movement, the LGBTQ movement, the labor movement, and the disability rights movement, among many others. In the twenty-first century we see the rise of several other national social movements, such as the immigrant rights movement. When national social movements are successful and achieve some of their principal goals, major social change occurs. These positive outcomes may include extending voting rights and citizenship, access to healthcare, job security, and new laws protecting vulnerable groups, to name a few examples. In chapter 7 we give focused attention to social movement outcomes.

Long-enduring national social movements often mobilize in the form of *campaigns*. Large movements that last over several decades or even centuries tend to ebb and flow between periods of heightened activity and relative quiescence. The quiescence or "abeyance" period may be important for rebuilding the movement in hostile environments and preparing for the next round of mobilization (Taylor 1989). When major long-term national movements activate, their mobilizations often have a campaign-like quality focusing on a set of issues or goals. For example, in recent years the labor movement has supported campaigns for a living wage for service sector workers (such as the Fight for $15 campaigns), while the feminist movement led the campaign with other groups to coordinate the historic Women's Marches in 2017 and 2018.

Waves of Protest

Waves of protest occur when *multiple social movements* or social groups engage in sustained protest clustered in time and spanning a wide geographical boundary (e.g., national scale) (Tarrow 1989; 2011; Almeida 2008a; Della Porta 2013). During waves of protest, many sectors of society participate (e.g., students, public employees, industrial workers, farmers) and employ increasingly confrontational tactics. Thus, a wave of protest is a rapid expansion of social movement action in geographical scale, diversity of social groups participating, and amount of disruptive activity. First developed by Sidney Tarrow (1989), "wave of protest" is also interchanged by scholars with "protest cycles" or "cycles of protest." Waves are examined in a variety of contexts, including advanced capitalist industrialized democracies, repressive regimes, lesser developed countries, and earlier historical settings (Almeida 2014a). Protest wave research focuses on the emergence of waves, internal dynamics and diffusion within a cycle, and the political and cultural outcomes left in the aftermath of such large-scale contention.[3]

Examples of such cycles or waves range from peasant protest in nineteenth-century Asia (White 1995; Hung 2011) to protest waves in the 1960s and early 1970s in Japan (Broadbent 1998), Italy (Tarrow 1989), and the United States (Perrow 1979), antiauthoritarian protest in Eastern Europe in the late 1980s (Goodwin 2001), and nationalist dissent in the former Soviet Union (Beissinger 2001). Between 2000 and 2010, several major waves of protest broke out in Latin America over the neoliberal policies of privatization, free trade, economic austerity, and labor flexibility.

ntries experiencing major protest waves in this period include Argentina, Bolivia, Costa Rica, Ecuador, El Salvador, Guatemala, Honduras, Panama, and Paraguay (Silva 2009; Almeida 2014b).

The leading theoretician of protest cycles, Sidney Tarrow (1989; 2011), hypothesizes that waves of protest have a parabolic pattern. That is, political institutions open and resources expand in a way that encourages protest activity to increase for one or a few social movements, such as student movements in universities, and then quickly spread to other groups (such as industrial workers, the church, and public employees) by providing them with new occasions to act and highlighting the vulnerability of particular state and economic agencies. The scale of protest peaks with new interpretive frames, tactical innovation, and diffusion to new groups. Over time, protest eventually descends through a mixture of institutionalization, government reform, state repression, and participant exhaustion. These stages represent the "cycle" of a protest wave.

Tarrow's inverted U-shape hypothesis of protest wave trajectories has empirical support within the experience of advanced democratic polities (e.g., Koopmans 1993; Kriesi et al. 1995) but needs to be examined in other political and national contexts (McAdam et al. 2001). Collective action researchers have recognized the multiple paths that cycles of contention may follow. The direction of these paths depends on particular political contexts (i.e., level of democratization), the interaction between movements and the state, as well as competing movements. Tarrow (2018) views the United States as entering a cycle of contention (i.e., a wave of protest) since late 2016 with the rise of Trumpism and the multiple movements that constitute the "resistance," including the activist group Indivisible with nearly six thousand local chapters nationwide (Brooker 2018). Indeed, Kauffmann (2018) reports, using Crowd Counting Consortium data, that nearly twenty-five thousand protests involving between fourteen and twenty-one million Americans have taken place since President Trump took office in January 2017—more social movement activity than at the height of protests in the late 1960s.

Recent research emphasizes that protest waves may be triggered by negative conditions such as state repression (Brockett 2005; Chang 2015) or unfavorable economic policies (Auyero 2002). One fascinating question for students of collective action centers on the possibility that a protest wave—under special conditions—may escalate or radicalize into a revolutionary movement (Brockett 2005; Almeida 2008a). The recent examples of protest waves in the Arab Spring countries of Libya, Syria, and Yemen that radicalized into revolutionary mobilization and civil war give credence to this perspective (Alimi 2016).

Revolutionary Movements

Revolutionary movements seek the overthrow of the existing political regime and institutions of governance as a primary goal (Goodwin 2001; Goldstone 2014). No longer are challengers interested in securing new policies and protecting existing benefits. Rather, they see a complete replacement of the government and its practices as desirable. Revolutionary movements often emerge from movement interaction with a repressive and illegitimate state (Goldstone 1998; Almeida 2003; 2007a). This dynamic interaction leads to the formation of cross-class challenger coalitions (Foran 2005). Between the 1950s and 1980s, revolutionary mobilization in Africa, Asia, and Latin America most commonly involved direct attacks on coercive bodies of the state—the type of strategy promoted by the Argentine revolutionary Ernesto "Che" Guevara. In the twentieth century, revolutionary parties, organizations, ad hoc coalitions, and "vanguards" often aided or directed movements seeking the seizure of political power.

In the last century and increasingly in the current era, revolutionary movements cluster together in time and by region. In the aftermath of World War II, multiple revolutionary movements occurred in Africa and Asia as part of a set of anticolonial struggles (Goodwin 2001). Another clustering of revolutions took place in Latin America in the 1960s and 1970s, following the successful Cuban Revolution (Wickham-Crowley 1992; 2014). The Latin American revolutionary upsurge extended into Central America through the early 1980s, with the grouping of revolutionary movements in El Salvador, Guatemala, Honduras, and the triumph of the Sandinista Revolution in Nicaragua. We observed this clustering once again in the late twentieth century with the Eastern European revolutions between 1989 and 1991. The trend continues in the twenty-first century with the "Color Revolutions" in former Communist states in the early 2000s, and the Arab Spring uprisings in 2011.

Before the 1990s, social movements and revolutions were treated as separate political processes, with specialists focused in one field or the other (Goldstone 1998). In more recent years, the study of social movements and revolutions has become blurred. As our example regarding the radicalization of a protest wave into a revolutionary movement suggests, revolutionary mobilization can be viewed as a particular type of social movement in which the primary goal of overthrowing the government sets it apart from other, more conventional social movements (Goodwin 2001). To complicate matters even more, some groups of scholars contend that a revolutionary movement does not require the violent seizure of power. This emerging scholarship

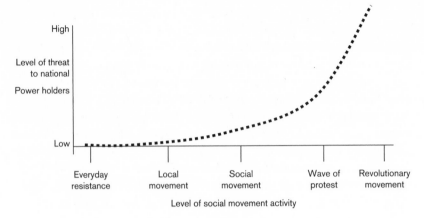

FIGURE 3. Escalating Levels of Movement Activity.

views many "people power" movements achieving the goal of overthrowing the government through mass *nonviolent* resistance, as in the cases of the Philippines against Marcos and the racist apartheid regime in South Africa in the 1980s; the Eastern European and Colored Revolutions; and the Arab Spring, in the cases of Egypt and Tunisia (Schock 2015b; Nepstad 2011; Chenoweth and Stephan 2011). This is largely because most states now maintain the infrastructural power to control their territories and effectively suppress armed rebellion (Goodwin 2001). At the same time, nonviolent action allows for a broader participation of civil society sectors in mass demonstrations and the potential to oust authoritarian rulers (Schock 2005).

The scholar of third world revolution, John Foran (2005), takes this debate even further. He finds that revolutions can also occur through democratic elections. If a political party comes to power via the ballot box and immediately implements radical structural changes, such as land redistribution and the nationalization of natural resources and core industries, Foran classifies the process as a revolution. He views cases such as the rise of Salvador Allende in Chile in 1970 and Hugo Chávez in Venezuela in 1999 as examples. The electoral triumphs of Evo Morales in Bolivia in 2006 and Rafael Correa in Ecuador in 2007 roughly fit his model as well.

The five levels of social movement activity summarized above can be placed on a continuum of escalating political contention from the least intensive to the most intensive (see figure 3). Everyday forms of resistance only disrupt routines in small settings of extreme oppression (and sometimes only symbolically). Local grassroots movements are directed at elites at the levels of towns, cities, and counties. Local movements rarely grab the attention of national power holders. National social movements begin to draw the attention of national governments since they are organized on a much broader scale and target the state or large institutions. Stable democracies (where regular competitive party elections are held) can usually tolerate national social movement activity without a major political crisis. Nondemocratic regimes will likely feel threatened by national social movements and move to suppress them via a variety of strategies, from harsh repression to co-optation.

Waves of protest bring large numbers of groups into protest across multiple sectors and regions of a country. Mass discontent from several social movements in a wave of protest garners substantial attention from national governments—both democratic and authoritarian states. Revolutionary movements, by definition, seek the overthrow of existing governments and represent the highest threat to power holders. Revolutionary movements are historically rare (Goldstone 2014) and much more likely to occur in nondemocratic political contexts (Goodwin and Rojas 2015).

Transnational Social Movements

A final class of social movement activities operates at the international level. Transnational social movements are mobilized in at least two nations and often dozens more. While revolutionary movements can be classified as the most *intensive* form of mobilization, transnational movements are the most *extensive*. Transnational movements can be traced back to at least the eighteenth century in political movements demanding national constitutions and democracy across Europe and the Atlantic (Markoff 2015a). In the nineteenth century, movements mobilized in multiple countries against slavery and for voting rights for women, while labor movements also forged ties across national boundaries (Keck and Sikkink 1998). In the late twentieth century, we observed a steep rise in transnational movements with new global internet communication technologies (ICTs) coupled with rising planetary concerns for social problems affecting people worldwide, such as human rights, economic justice, and global warming (Castells 2015; Bennett and Segerberg 2013; Smith and Wiest 2012). Because of the use of ICTs, the variation among transnational movements is substantial. Indeed, this variety of movements can be observed across some of the largest contemporary transnational movements, which range from the Islamic State of Iraq and the Levant (ISIL) to the largely pacific movement for climate justice.

Figure 4 maps out the transnational protests in one of the early transnational campaigns for global economic justice—the World Trade Organization

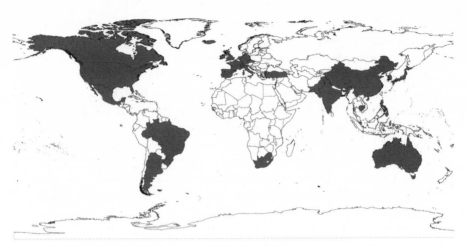

FIGURE 4. World Trade Organization Protests, 1999 (Almeida and Lichbach 2003).

(WTO) Ministerial Conference in Seattle in late 1999. Activists converged on Seattle for a week of protests against free trade globalization over concerns ranging from environmental protections to the weakening of labor standards (Smith 2001). At the same time, solidarity protests and demonstrations took place around the world (represented by shaded countries in the map) (Almeida and Lichbach 2003). This would become the template for mobilizing simultaneous transnational protests for global economic justice in the twenty-first century, as well as transnational campaigns against foreign military intervention and for climate justice. Figure 4 also leads to many puzzling research questions for students of social movements. The most fundamental question is why some countries recorded a protest or demonstration against the WTO while many more did not. What patterns emerge among the protesting and nonprotesting countries? By the conclusion of this chapter, readers will have more ideas on how to investigate this question through a variety of research methods. And by the end of chapter 8, readers may have plans for a study design incorporating theory and methods to carry out a research project on transnational movements.

Identifying the level of social movement activity provides a starting point to understand collective action dynamics and likely outcomes. Particular methods and research strategies are also employed to grasp the varying levels of social movement activity. Table 1 summarizes these escalating forms of collective mobilization. With this classification scheme, students of social movements can better identify what kind of collective action they are observing and may form expectations about the level of

TABLE 1. Levels of Social Movement Activity

Level of Movement Activity	Core Characteristics	Examples
Everyday forms of resistance	Small acts of resistance by small groups under extremely oppressive conditions	Work slowdowns (e.g., foot dragging) on plantations systems; humming national anthem while under foreign military occupation
Local grassroots movements	Community groups struggling over a local grievance and targeting local political and economic elites	Local mobilization against polluting facilities such as landfills, incinerators, hog farms; neighborhood struggles for parks, sidewalks, and street lights
National social movements	Nationally organized struggles with broad goals for social change composed of many SMOs	Women's movement, civil rights movement, environmental movement, immigrant rights movement
Waves of protest	Multiple social movements and groups acting close together in time with a heightened level of protest across the national territory	Protests in the United States in the 1960s and early 1970s, 2017–18; Argentina 1997–2002; Bolivia 2000–2005; Honduras 2009–11; Syria 2011–12; Spain 2011–14; Greece 2010–14
Revolutionary movements	Movements that seek the overthrow of the government and the seizing of state power as the primary objective	French, Russian, Chinese, Mozambican, Sandinista, and Iranian Revolutions, Arab Spring
Transnational social movements	Movements that are organized in multiple countries and coordinate their actions	Human rights movement, climate justice movement, international terror networks

mobilization, the context of the struggle, and the likely range of outcomes that are possible.

METHODS AND TOOLS OF RESEARCH

Social movement scholars employ the same conventional methods as other subfields of sociology and the social sciences in general. In addition, researchers in several disciplines in the humanities, such as history, ethnic studies, and social anthropology, also study social movements and use similar research tools, including observation, interviews, oral history, and historical archives. In this section we explore the primary methods used to understand social movements, and the particular dimensions of collective action each technique uncovers.

Interviews

Interviews with movement leaders and participants provide one method to understand social movement dynamics. They provide "one of the primary ways researchers actively involve their respondents in the construction of data about their lives" (Blee and Taylor 2002: 92). Interviews with movement leaders may be especially insightful in how movements strategize in terms of tactics, targets, and goals. Movement leaders also can offer indispensable information about the history of the movement and referrals to other key participants to interview (e.g., "snowball sampling"). Gaining access to interview social movement leaders often involves already knowing movement participants or critical "gate keepers" that can vouch for the researcher. When movements unfold in real time, leaders may be suspicious of journalists and scholars attempting to secure interviews with participants.[4]

Interviews may lead to other sources of information as well, including movement archives and other relevant organizations involved in a campaign. Certain kinds of movements are not covered in news media outlets or documented in historical archives, and one of the only means to establish basic components of what took place requires systematically questioning those people in and proximate to the struggle (Della Porta 2014). This would certainly be the case for the "weapons of the weak" types of resistance discussed above (and also for local grassroots movements). Only by interviewing communities and survivors subjected to extreme acts of subjugation would it be possible to document some of the microforms of disobedience used. Related, many rural social movements of the past lacked written documentation. One example that brings several of these limitations together is the study of the 1932 worker-peasant revolt and subsequent massacre in El Salvador, by Jeffrey Gould and Aldo Lauria-Santiago (2008). These two social historians carried out more than two hundred oral history interviews with massacre survivors and their families in western El Salvador in the late 1990s and early 2000s, including senior citizens and children of the victims. Their interview data uncovered how social interaction between town and rural workers took place before the uprising, making the mass revolt even possible when the government turned much more repressive. In short, through the interview process (combined with archival materials), Gould and Lauria-Santiago reconstructed a popular revolt that represents one of the largest uprisings in Latin America during the Great Depression and one of the greatest governmental acts of ethnocide against indigenous peoples in the Western Hemisphere in the twentieth century.

Interviews usually range between thirty minutes and several hours. Researchers most commonly have a series of well-thought-out questions in advance (an interview protocol) that they ask to multiple movement participants and those around the movement (Blee and Taylor 2002). The interview protocol is based on the researcher's understanding of the movement as well as prevailing social movement theories that guide causal explanations of the area of interest. Interviewing is a skill. Some of the best interviews result from allowing the subject some flexibility and following up on intriguing responses about movement dynamics that were not originally known. Scholars also need to be equipped with techniques to avoid the respondent's dominating the interview by giving lengthy responses that do not address the issues of research interest. Dahlerus and Davenport (1999) document in detail many of the concerns encountered in interviewing former social movement participants, in their excellent self-account of research on reconstructing the struggle of the Black Panther Party in the late 1960s and early 1970s.

Observation

Another major research strategy involves field observation of social movements. This is precisely the method that James Scott used to uncover everyday forms of resistance in Southeast Asia (Scott 1985; 1990). In collective action research, this method often involves *participant observation*, whereby the investigator is also active in the movement under study "as the movement is happening" (Lichterman 2002: 120). Researchers collect data at one or multiple sites by compiling extensive field notes from their observations over several months or even years. The field site may be a particular social movement organization (SMO), labor union, or other location where collective action is emerging or ongoing. Such a research method involves a high level of trust between the investigator and movement participants. Participant observation is particularly useful in revealing strategies, ideologies, and emotions within social movements. These fundamental elements of movements are often difficult to identify or extract from other methods. Participant observation and ethnographies of social movement dynamics also provide vital information about the "backstage of mobilization" not observed in the more frequently studied protest events (Balsiger and Lambelet 2014).

Some of the best scholarship on farmworker mobilization on the West Coast of the United States comes from participants and organizers (Ganz 2009; Pawel 2010; Bardacke 2012; Sifuentez 2016). Marshall Ganz, for example, spent over sixteen years (1965–81) working as an organizer for the United Farm Workers. Through his field notes and other documentary evidence, he produced a pathbreaking book on the ingredients for successful organizational strategy by leadership teams that come from the communities they are attempting to mobilize (Ganz 2009). Local struggles or local chapters of larger movements, such as municipal-level aspects of the Occupy Wall Street movement, also lend themselves to participant observation better than more macro levels of collective action (King 2017). Much of our intimate knowledge of local environmental justice struggles comes from the use of participant observation techniques (Lichterman 2002; Shriver et al. 2008). Flores (2018) uses participant observation techniques to demonstrate the redemptive powers of social movement participation in local movements against punitive laws banning the formerly incarcerated from employment opportunities.

Researchers even combine interviews and direct observation in field research to explain the critical question of *nonmobilization* in the presence of severe grievances and threats. Auyero and Swistun (2009) used ethnographic techniques to understand why residents of an environmentally contaminated poor neighborhood on the outskirts of Buenos Aires failed to mobilize. With their "cubist" ethnographic methods (emphasizing multiple points of view), the authors interviewed and observed a variety of relevant local actors, from community inhabitants to doctors, lawyers, public health administrators, governmental officials, and representatives of the adjacent polluting industrial plants. Throughout the study, the researchers demonstrated how sentiments of confusion and uncertainty prevailed in the shantytown, eventuating in scant collective action and continued suffering.

Surveys

Surveys provide a standardized set of questions most often used for quantitative research in the social sciences. Movement scholars may implement the survey among social movement organizations or individuals to collect systematic information on movement dynamics. For instance, Andrews et al. (2010) surveyed a sample of Sierra Club chapters to demonstrate leadership processes in social movements. Most often surveys are used at the individual level. One of the most common uses of surveys involves querying people about their level of participation in social movement activities.

Researchers generally implement surveys on social movements in two ways—surveys of general populations and surveys directed at particular social movements. General population surveys draw a random sample of the entire population of a country or a region and ask respondents a series of questions about their interest in politics, along with many more questions about biographical and demographic background (age, education, gender, employment, etc.). Usually a few of the questions are geared toward various forms of political participation in the past year (voting, signing a petition, contacting a politician, and protest). The General Social Survey in the United States is formatted this way for information about protest participation over the past year.[5] In most years, about 5 percent of the United States population reports participating in a protest demonstration. Other US scholars have used national surveys on civic participation, such as the American Citizen Participation Study (Schussman and Soule 2005; Lim 2008).[6] Social scientists have also implemented these types of general surveys in other world regions on a repeated basis to observe trends over time. These regional surveys include the Latin American Population Project, the Latin American Barometer, the Euro Barometer, and the African Barometer (Pilati 2011). On a global scale, students and researchers have investigated social movements with the World Values Survey, which uses the same standardized questionnaire and design in dozens of countries on every continent. The World Values Survey allows scholars to assess long-term trends in individual protest throughout the world (Dodson 2011). Many students and faculty have access to these data sets through university subscriptions or through online open access.

The national-level surveys offer excellent tools to uncover the variation among individuals in protest behavior in general. They can answer such questions as, Do people who vote for the Republican Party protest more than those who vote Democrat? Are those who are currently unemployed more likely to engage in protest than those who have stable employment? Nonetheless, national-level surveys have limits. National surveys usually only incorporate one module set aside for a few questions about protest and civic participation. General social surveys often do not ask about the type of movement that one participated in or the specific issue that was protested. Hence, they lack the kind of contextual information that many scholars of social movements seek to understand, such as particular kinds of movements and protests (e.g., labor strikes, immigrant rights demonstrations, Tea Party mobilizations). In order to elicit this type of contextual information scholars implement another type of survey aimed at specific social movements.

Most survey research in social movements is designed to focus on particular types of movements, such as environmental groups, the women's movement, and immigrant rights. By focusing on a particular movement, researchers can develop research designs that match the most important conditions around a particular struggle. One of the most common research designs centers on understanding the differences between individuals recruited to a specific social movement and individuals that stay at home. Scholars begin by identifying a pool of people composed of movement sympathizers. From this point they sample the sympathetic population and end up with data on those who participated in the movement and those who did not. The survey protocol includes a number of questions about possible correlates of participation, from ideological beliefs and membership in civic organizations to friendship networks (see chapter 6 on individual movement participation for in-depth coverage of these issues).

Archives and Secondary Data

Social movement researchers also use historical archives and secondary data to analyze social movements. Historical archives can be used to reconstruct movements of the past—from earlier decades to earlier centuries (Markoff 2015b). Ho-fung Hung (2011) used centuries of Chinese archives to show how the form of protest changed in China among different dynasties, from taking protests to local power holders, to traveling to regional capitals to deliver petitions. Historical archives may provide written records of movement activities from police records, news clippings, movement propaganda and newsletters, or diaries of movement leaders and participants. For example, one of the prized documents for scholars interested in retracing the United Farm Workers movement led by Cesar Chavez and Dolores Huerta in the 1960s and 1970s is the union's newsletter *Malcriado*.[7] These types of sources are used by qualitative researchers such as historians and by historical and comparative sociologists as well as quantitative researchers if there is enough information to systematically code events such as protests.

Secondary data means information collected by some other researcher or agency often not for the purpose of studying social movements. Government records, such as the Census, are one source of secondary data. The Census provides basic information across geographical units, such as population size, household income, employment, and ethnic composition of communities. Other kinds of government data may be compiled by the agriculture department or the labor department, such as the number of labor strikes per year and in which particular industries they are occurring

(Cohn 1993). Secondary data may be especially useful for quantitative studies analyzing mobilization across regions or over time.

Protest Event Analysis

One prominent method in social movement studies is protest event analysis (PEA). This technique involves systematically counting the number of protest events and their forms (e.g., conventional, disruptive, violent). PEA is a variant of content analysis methodology (Rucht et al. 1999; Koopmans 2002); it is a content analysis of texts (Hutter 2014) that provides information on "distinct collective action pursuing an explicit goal by the use of confrontative, disruptive or even violent means" (Rucht and Ohlemacher 1992: 77). Practitioners of protest event analysis divide the process into two stages. The first stage involves the selection of articles from a newspaper or multiple news sources, such as those digitally archived in LexisNexis Academic Universe and NewsBank.[8] The second stage entails coding and content-analyzing the selected newspaper articles from a predesigned protocol. The coding protocol distinguishes the varying types of protest over time, their frequency, the participating groups, the objects of popular claims (i.e., targets), and geographical location.

Table 2 provides an example of a coding protocol.[9] From here, researchers identify temporal and spatial trends in protest and the forms they take. Students of collective action can focus on a particular movement (immigrant rights) or on an entire wave of protest using such a coding scheme. The coding protocol in table 2 was used to code a daily newspaper in El Salvador between 1962 and 1981 for protest events. The project identified 4,151 protest events and was used to demonstrate two protest waves in El Salvador. By using this strategy (Almeida 2003; 2008a), the researcher demonstrated how social protest escalated from nonviolent demonstrations into a revolutionary movement as the government sought to violently suppress the protest waves.

Another major initiative using protest event analysis in the United States is the Dynamics of Collective Action project housed at Stanford University. The research team collected over twenty thousand protest events by coding daily editions of the *New York Times* between 1960 and 1990.[10] These protest event data have yielded at least a dozen pathbreaking studies.[11] The publications from the event data show the influence of protest on congressional voting and legislation (McAdam and Su 2002; King et al. 2007; Olzak et al. 2016) and on stock price fluctuations (King and Soule 2007), and the overuse of police in African American demonstrations (Davenport et al. 2011). Such coding schemes can also be used to demonstrate the geographical distribution

TABLE 2. Coding Rules for Protest Event Data

Protest event: an action or claim by a group of three or more persons outside of the government at a given point in time against economic and/or political elites and institutions.

Time

Date of Event: Reported day event occurred (day, month, year). Also separately record the date the event is reported in the press, page number, and newspaper.

Geography

Location: City, state, and county where event occurred. National events such as nationwide strikes are coded as "national."

Numbers

Number of Participants: Record exact number if explicitly stated. Infer adjectives "many," "numerous," etc.

Groups

Party Responsible: Name of the organization or movement in which persons are engaging in the protest event.
Social Sector Participating: Record either students, teachers, urban workers, peasants, market vendors, service sector employees, public employees, professionals, church groups, or others participating in the protest event.

Nonviolent protest

Strike: All work stoppages by employees on farms, factories, service sector, or government. Also include students refusing to attend school. Strike is at the level of the plant, not the industry.
March/Demonstration: A protest event that involves movement of a group through a public place—usually in some form of line, making claims on a nearby target.
Petition/Delegation: Presenting political demands in a written form or through a group meeting with authorities.
Rally/Public Gathering: A group gathering in public, making or discussing political claims in one physical space.
Public Statement: Making a political claim through a newspaper, press conference, or other means of mass communication.

Propaganda: The distribution of political literature such as flyers, bulletins, or broadcasted messages.

Spray Paint: Spray-painting political symbols and slogans in public places.

Disruptive protest

Sit-In: The physical occupation of public space by a group making political or economic claims.

Barricades: Using some type of object(s) to obstruct traffic or the encroachment of security forces.

Occupation of Church: A takeover of a church or church-run facility by a group of people.

Occupation of Work: A takeover of a workplace by employees.

Occupation of Government Building: A takeover of a government administration building by a group of persons.

Occupation of Market: A physical takeover of a market building/place by a group.

Occupation of Foreign Embassy/Building: A takeover of a foreign embassy or building by a protest group.

Land Seizure: Occupation of land by a group.

Occupation of School: A takeover of an educational institution by students, teachers, or parents. Also, occupation of individual academic departments within a university.

Cut Power: The turning off of electrical energy by government power workers.

Violent forms of protest

Armed Attack: Firing weapons in a political event, such as attacks on security forces and political assassinations.

Arson/Vandalism/Sabotage: The burning or destruction of government and private property by politicized groups (e.g., burning buses, destroying utility lines).

Occupy Radio/TV: The forced takeover of a radio or TV station in order to broadcast a political or economic claim.

Kidnapping: The forceful removal of a person from their home, work, or other location by a politicized group.

Bomb: The detonation of explosives by politicized groups.

Occupation of Town: A forced takeover of a town or central plaza/city hall by a politicized group.

Two-Way Clash: An exchange of gunfire between politicized groups and security forces, but only when it is initiated by the government or it is unclear who initiated the attack.

Claims making

Type of Demand: E = economic demands, which extend or defend existing material benefits to claimants. P = political demands, which involve the authority to make decisions concerning the extraction and distribution of social values and resources. O = other, noneconomic or nonpolitical demands.

(continued)

TABLE 2. *(continued)*

Target of Protest: Pr = president of the republic; Pa = parliament/legislative assembly; G = national government ministry, office, or personal representative; L = local government; C = capitalist, owner of private party/farm, private business; M = manager of private firm or public institution; S = security forces such as police, army, national guard, and other law-and-order units; O = other. Record multiple targets.

Violent/nonviolent protest

Violent/Nonviolent Protest: Violent events involve the intention to damage property or injure persons. Nonviolent events do not intend to damage property or harm persons. Violence = armed attack, two-way clash, occupy town, occupy radio, bomb, rob, arson/vandalism, kidnap.

SOURCE: This protocol is a modified version used by Almeida (2008a) for research on protest waves in El Salvador. It was modeled on Tarrow's (1989) coding scheme of protest waves in Italy.

of protest across political units such as cities, counties, or even nations (Auyero 2007; Almeida 2014b; Biggs and Andrews 2015).

One of the most common sources of information for protest event analysis is newspapers. Newspapers have three properties that make them especially attractive to social movement researchers: (1) continuity, (2) scope of coverage, and (3) reliability (Koopmans 1999). The *continuity* of newspapers relates to their coverage over long periods of time. Depending on the newspaper, this may include coverage over several decades, or even a century or more for outlets such as the *New York Times* and the *London Times*. This means we can document the rise and fall of a social movement over time by counting the number and size of protest events. The advantage of the wide *scope of coverage* of newspapers allows for the capturing of all kinds of social movement activity, including the women's movement, LGBTQ mobilizations, civil rights, youth movements, and protests by a wide variety of groups. Combining the properties of continuity with scope of coverage, a student of social movements can demonstrate the outbreak of a wave of protest by documenting a heightened period of social movement activity with the participation of multiple groups. Finally, newspapers have a certain level of *reliability* and standardization in that the same types of stories and events are reported in the same way repeatedly. Even given all of the shortcomings of newspapers, they remain, compared to most alternatives, the most reliable, long-lasting, and consistent sources to study protest over long periods of time and over multiple geographical regions.

There are also three major biases in newspapers that researchers must address. They are biases of (1) intensity, (2) proximity, and (3) ideology (Koopmans 1999). The *intensity* bias deals with the level of magnitude of a protest event. Newspapers and reporters more likely cover protest events that are large in size, violent, or disruptive, or that involve the police and arrests. *Proximity* relates to protests that occur geographically close to a major newspaper or to where a journalist is dispatched. This means that social movements in cities receive more coverage than movements in rural areas. If a researcher decides to study a particular movement that is active in a particular region, it may be best to use the newspapers of the region. For example, the *Los Angeles Times* would be a better source of information for social movements on the West Coast than the *New York Times*. Newspapers also maintain an *ideological* bias based on the editorial board and ownership. Conservative newspapers would likely give more coverage to conservative movements such as the Tea Party, antiabortion, and mobilizations by the Christian Right. Liberal newspapers would likely provide more coverage of left-leaning movements such as labor unions and environmental activism. And newspapers are better for collecting data on the "hard" news than the "soft" news (Earl et al. 2004). The hard news includes where the protest occurred, the number of people involved, and what kind of protest action occurred (the who, what, where of protest). Newspapers tend to do a poor job of reporting the "soft" aspects of movements, such as the motivations, "framings," and ideologies of the participants. This is where interviews and observation complement newspaper-based information—a research strategy referred to as "triangulation."

An emerging issue in the twenty-first century is the use of other forms of data, such as activist websites, Twitter feeds, Facebook posts, and other social media (Almeida and Lichbach 2003; Earl and Kimport 2011; Gaby and Caren 2012; Bennett and Segerberg 2013; Carty 2015). In our example of the 2017 and 2018 Women's Marches in chapter 1, scholars have already made estimates of the size of each individual street march by using online newspapers, Twitter feeds, and Facebook posts (Berry and Chenoweth 2018).[12] Social movement scholars are faced with an immense amount of information with the rise of ICTs and new social media. Figure 5 illustrates the kind of data we can capture, or "scrape," from a few webpages.[13] It shows the Occupy Wall Street movement actions in late 2011.

Through protest event analysis, researchers are able to map the entire mobilizations of the Occupy movement in the United States from just two websites! Progressive activist websites (such as countlove.org) are now even overcoming the biggest shortcoming of web-based protest event data by

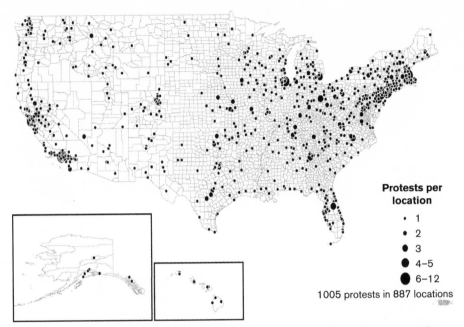

Protests per
location

•   1
•   2
●   3
●   4–5
●   6–12

1005 protests in 887 locations

FIGURE 5.   Occupy Wall Street Protests 2011. Created by author from publicly available data at www.theguardian.com/news/datablog/interactive/2012/sep/17/occupy-map-of-the-world and http://directory.occupy.net/.

providing linked news stories for each event, empirically documenting that the event actually occurred. These internet-based data lead to several research questions: Why did protest erupt in some cities and counties and not in others in the Occupy movement? What are the characteristics of cities and counties with Occupy protests compared to cities where no demonstrations materialized? The subsequent chapters address these compelling issues.

Mixed Methods

While the above section presented some of the most common methods employed in social movement studies, in larger research projects, such as dissertations, book manuscripts, or multiple publications, students of collective action often employ multiple or "mixed methods." Practitioners refer to this approach as "triangulation" (Snow and Trom 2002). Ayoub et al. (2014: 71) contend that "triangulation has critical benefits in that the logics of distinct methods are understood to complement each other, as opposed to substituting for one another." Hence, in order to better understand social dynamics in multiple dimensions (e.g., type of grievances and magnitude of mobilization), investigators may employ multiple methods in the ~~~~~ study, such as combining interviews with protest event analysis (Almeida 2008a; 2014b). For example, Ayoub's study (2016) of the transnational LGBTQ movement in Europe utilized legislative and SMO data sets, participant observation, surveys, and semistructured interviews. In his reconstruction of student hunger strikes in the early 1990s to save ethnic studies programs on multiple campuses in California, Armbruster-Sandoval (2017) used in-depth interviews with former hunger strikers, protest event coverage in newspapers, archival data, the participants' own archives, and activist newsletters (e.g., MEChA periodicals).

CONCLUSION

This chapter introduced methodological issues in the study of social movements. A classification scheme of movement activity was presented in order to understand the different levels of social and political life in which people and groups coordinate joint action—from everyday forms of resistance to revolutions and transnational movements. The second half of the chapter familiarized readers with the various methods used in the study of collective action, concluding with the triangulation of methods used in many projects. In the next chapter we turn to the theoretical approaches used to explain the rise of social movement activity.

Besides advancing contributions to social science on the dynamics of how people come together to push for social change, the investigation of collective action may also serve humanistic purposes. Contemporary and future activists can use information from past research not only to strategize effective campaigns; they can also draw from earlier struggles for inspiration to motivate new rounds of popular mobilization. This is the special mission or responsibility for collective action researchers to keep in mind when conducting work.

ADDITIONAL RESOURCES ABOUT SOCIAL
MOVEMENT METHODS

Della Porta, Donatella, ed. 2014. *Methodological Practices in Social Movement Research*. Oxford: Oxford University Press.
Klandermans, Bert, and Suzanne Staggenborg, eds. 2002. *Methods of Social Movement Research*. Minneapolis: University of Minnesota Press.
Rucht, Dieter, Ruud Koopmans, and Friedhelm Neidhardt. 1999. *Acts of Dissent: New Developments in the Study of Protest*. Lanham, MD: Rowman & Littlefield.

3　Theories of Social Movement Mobilization

The previous chapter focused on the methods of social movement research. We examined how to classify different levels of collective action and various approaches to collecting systematic information on the multiple dimensions of movement activities. In this chapter, we shift from concrete tools for observing social movements to more abstract theories explaining their origins and trajectories. Theories reduce the social world into the most important causal dimensions in explaining empirical patterns and outcomes. Scholars strive for parsimony in their explanations of the dynamics of social change. For social movements, we employ conceptual frameworks to understand specific subfields such as movement emergence, ideology, recruiting networks, and movement outcomes, which I elaborate in subsequent chapters. At the same time, there are theoretical perspectives within studies of social movements that have set the parameters for the entire field.

This chapter begins with a brief discussion of how different types of theories and models are used to explain particular components of the mobilization process. A short presentation of the evolution of the paradigmatic social movement frameworks is followed by sustained attention to the political process model—arguably the dominant model of contemporary social movement research. The chapter provides an overview of both political opportunity ("good news") and threat ("bad news") versions of political process theory (Meyer 2002; 2004) and the importance of organizational infrastructures for mobilization (McCarthy 1996; Andrews 2004; Edwards et al. 2018). The chapter concludes with brief introductions of emerging theoretical perspectives, including approaches examining emotions, multiple institutions beyond the state, intersectionality, and even right-wing movements (such as the alt-right).

EARLY GENERAL SOCIOLOGICAL THEORISTS

The early general sociological thinkers offered preliminary insights into our understanding of large-scale transformations and the social cleavages driving collective action. Karl Marx and Friedrich Engels (1978 [1848]) viewed the spread of industrial forms of capitalism as creating an unprecedented demographic shift in worker density for the laboring classes to launch collective forms of resistance against exploitation and the distribution of the social surplus. Émile Durkheim (1984) observed that the increasing institutional differentiation of an incipient industrial society created the need for the kinds of associations that would not only serve social integration purposes but also contribute to internal solidarity of occupational groups such as labor unions (Emirbayer 1996). Durkheim also highlighted mutual awareness and the generation of emotional energy in face-to-face encounters that could sustain collective action (Collins 2004). Max Weber (1978) provided valuable insights on the types of rationales and the binding social ties that motivate joint social action, as well as the advantages of structuring collective mobilization along bureaucratic lines (Gamson 1990 [1975]). Nonetheless, as Connell (2007) has pointed out for sociology in general, these "founding fathers" are not usually directly incorporated in contemporary social movement research, with the exception of Marx and variants of neo-Marxism, especially in the global South.

W.E.B. Du Bois co-founded one of the most important social movement organizations (SMOs) in the United States—the NAACP. He also presciently theorized that the "color line," racial oppression, and decolonization struggles would serve as the axes for social movement struggles in the twentieth century and beyond (Morris 2015). Charlotte Perkins Gilman's sociological writings in the 1910s on the lack of compensation for women's labor set the stage for second wave feminism over issues of comparable worth and against employment discrimination based on gender (Finlay 2007). These early statements by major sociological thinkers provide guidelines to consider the general parameters of social movement mobilization.

Today the subdiscipline of social movements is much more specialized than conceived by the early influential sociological theorists Du Bois, Durkheim, Marx and Engels, Perkins Gilman, and Weber. Students of social movements develop explanatory schemes for different levels of analysis and different components of the mobilization process. For example, in order to understand at the microlevel why individuals join social movements, we use social network, framing, organizational, and collective identity theories (see chapter 6). Scholars use framing theories for movement ideological appeals (chapter 5) and organizational perspectives for movement emergence and diffusion (chapter 4). When studying social movement outcomes (i.e., whether a movement succeeds or not), students of collective action employ theories about coalitions, strategies, and the nature of the political environment (chapter 7). For large-scale social change, such as waves of protest or revolutions, scholars develop macrotheories of major societal conflicts among elites, economic crisis, state repression, and changing forms of state policy and political rule (chapter 8). While we use different kinds of theory to understand specific subareas of social movements, some of the most influential approaches are those that explain multiple levels of collective action.

EVOLUTION OF SOCIAL MOVEMENT THEORY

The original theories of social movements were developed largely to explain the emergence of collective action. These prominent theories fall into three traditions: classical theory, resource mobilization, and political process frameworks (McAdam 1999 [1982]). *Classical theories* dominated studies of social movements from the late nineteenth century through the 1960s.[1] The *resource mobilization* perspective ascended in the 1970s and 1980s and transitioned into *political process theory*, which continues to influence scholarship to the present, with several challengers on the horizon.

Classical Theories

Although elements of the classical theories still find some resonance in the collective behavior research tradition, especially the study of fads, panics, and human responses to disasters and terrorist attacks (Aguirre et al. 1998), they have fallen out of favor in the study of more politically oriented movements. Nonetheless, there are some elements of the classical tradition that continue to influence current thinking on the nature of mass mobilization. McAdam (1999 [1982]) and Buechler (2011) provide some of the best summaries of the classical tradition in social movement research. The classical theories focus on system strains or breakdowns in society that lead to psychological distress and eventuate in social movements (Smelser 1962; Buechler 2004). There are several variations of classical theory, including mass society theory, status inconsistency, collective behavior, and relative deprivation (see McAdam [1999 (1982)] for an overview of these perspectives).

One concern of classical theorists (such as Gustave Le Bon, Robert Park, and Herbert Blumer) centered on crowd dynamics (Buechler 2011). Hence, the earlier thinkers in this tradition developed their frameworks of collective action by examining crowd behavior, especially the norms and social pressures that influence individuals to behave in particular ways that emerge when large groups come together in public (congregating outside of a rock concert or a sporting event). Other versions of classical theory concentrate more on the alienating elements associated with rapidly industrializing and urbanizing societies. From this perspective, traditional community ties of kinship and village erode in modernizing societies while the mass public faces chronic crises of economic and technological change. These rapid changes and loss of community push individuals into joining mass movements to compensate for the multiple social and psychological strains they endure (McAdam 1999 [1982]).

A unifying theme of classical theories centers on the view that the political system is pluralistic, with power distributed widely throughout society and with multiple points of institutional access (Lukes 2005). Classical scholars portrayed social movement mobilization as *irrational* because modern political systems were open to adjudicate grievances (McAdam 1999 [1982]). Citizens can petition, vote, or meet with authorities to resolve community problems. Taking to the streets in mass marches, and other noninstitutional tactics, appear futile and unnecessary under a responsive polity structure, in the view of the classical theorists. Hence, there is little acknowledgment of social and political exclusion—a core defining feature of social movements in this text. Popular mass media and elite depictions of protest demonstrations often draw from classical theory perspectives to stigmatize social movements as irrational and without legitimate demands (Marx Ferree 2005).

Resource Mobilization and Resource Infrastructures

A new generation of scholars advanced social movement theory by observing the wave of global protests in the 1960s and early 1970s. The protests included issues of civil rights, anti-war, antiracism, feminism, gay rights, disability rights, ecology, and anticolonial struggles. In contrast to classical theories, emerging scholarship increasingly viewed social movements as *rational actors* and contended that political power is concentrated in the hands of economic and political elites. Groups of ordinary people excluded from institutional centers of power desire a mechanism to pressure elites for social change and address major social grievances. Scholars increasingly viewed the use of unconventional strategies by less powerful groups, such as street demonstrations, rallies, boycotts, and strikes, as a rational means to exert influence on power holders and the government. Movements of the 1960s and 1970s fought for voting rights and equal rights for women and people with disabilities, and against legalized racism, legalized discrimination, and foreign military interventions in the global South. The school of thought analyzing these struggles came to be known as resource mobilization theory, with a focus on the resources excluded social groups could pool in attempts to sustain mobilization against powerful interests (Jenkins 1983; McCarthy and Zald 2002; Edwards and Kane 2014).

Resource mobilization perspectives made several contributions to the theory of social movements. Early versions of resource mobilization emphasized both the professionalization of SMOs and the external resources provided to movement challengers by more privileged groups (McCarthy and Zald 1977). Resource mobilization theory also directed scholarly attention to "conscience constituents" or groups and individuals that might support a social movement even though they receive no direct material benefit from its success (McCarthy and Zald 1977). This insight advances understandings of allies and solidarity within social movement campaigns—including civil society support from the global North to transnational movements in the global South. The resource mobilization perspective has evolved in recent decades. Scholars now highlight the role of indigenous organizations and other parts of the resource infrastructure that increase the likelihood that a social movement will surface (Edwards et al. 2018).

Scholars have long established that collective action most likely emerges out of preestablished institutions and organizations (McAdam 1999 [1982]; Morris 1984; McAdam 2003). Why is this the case? As a collective process, social movements require some level of trust and solidarity among participants in order to act in concert and sustain mobilization. Modern societies are characterized by high levels of individualism and lack of deep community relations). Preexisting organizations partially overcome these shortcomings of atomization in the contemporary world. Parent-teacher associations, gardening groups, recreational soccer and softball teams, nonprofit organizations, community choirs, childcare centers, and student and religious organizations provide communal locations for social interaction and feelings of solidarity and mutual support (Small 2009). Segments or factions within these kinds of groups may be the first to mobilize in a social movement because social ties are already solidified. Notice also that these are largely nonpolitical everyday-life associations and groups not explicitly established for social movement mobilization (McCarthy 1996; Gould 2005). Imagine how much easier it would be to try to convince fellow students in your study group or soccer team to join a protest rally than it would be to go door to door in a variety of neighborhoods where you barely know the residents or do not know them at all. From this kind of knowledge students of social movements can begin to understand why we expect mobilization to materialize in regions (neighborhoods, cities, states, countries) where many organizations and social institutions already exist versus regions that lack organizational and civic vitality. Within this perspective of preexisting groups, traditional associations along communal lines of village, kinship, ethnic, or religious ties may also increase the rate of mobilization (Oberschall 1973).

Other resources include the human capital of the people attempting to organize social movements. Marshall Ganz (2009) has referred to the tacit organizational skills of community leaders as "strategic capacity." He finds that attempts at social movement mobilization are more likely to be successful when intrinsically motivated leaders work in a diverse team, have previous organizing experience in the communities they serve, and adapt from new information received in the environment. He developed this resource-based perspective after working over sixteen years as an organizer with farmworkers in California's Central Valley. Others have confirmed that those with previous organizing experience can offer a major boost in launching a movement campaign (Van Dyke and Dixon 2013; Rodriguez 2017). Another resource may come from alliances with outside groups. These may come in the form of establishing a coalition—a partnership with another group's organizations. For example, a crisis of pesticide poisoning or chemical contamination of the water supply in a low-income community may call for special assistance in order to mobilize effectively. If the polluted community forms an alliance with an environmental advocacy organization that maintains lawyers and scientists on its staff, the community may experience more efficacious mobilization by linking the pollution to health outcomes and developing legal action for compensation. Chapter 4 on movement emergence introduces more detailed dimensions of the resource infrastructure.

Social Construction and Collective Action Frames

Resources and organizational infrastructures alone are not sufficient to sustain social movement activity. Movement leaders must convincingly guide and motivate potential supporters to join campaigns of collective action. They must place grievances in an appropriate cultural context. This social construction process is referred to as *framing* (Snow et al. 1986). Three core ideological tasks for movement leaders include diagnostic, prognostic, and motivational framing (Snow and Benford 1988). *Diagnostic framing* refers to the ability of would-be activists to define social problems and attribute blame (Snow and Corrigall-Brown 2005). Leaders also need to engage in *prognostic framing* by generating a plan of action or strategy. Finally, *motivational framing* involves making appeals to mobilize that resonate within the cultural milieu of the populations targeted for collective action. Organizers need to effectively convey and carry out all three core framing tasks in order to ensure the emergence of cooperative and joint action for social change. Economic justice activists provide one recent historical example of a powerful framing strategy in the use of the "99%" (e.g., ordinary people) against the "1%" (e.g., the economic elite) in the Occupy Wall Street movement. Chapter 5 discusses these ideational processes in more detail, including examples of the employment of collective action frames from a variety of cultural resources.

Political Process Theory

Political process theory has served as the most influential perspective on explaining social movement dynamics over the past three decades. The political process perspective reached ascendancy by partially incorporating resource infrastructures and framing processes into its analytical framework. Indeed, some describe the theory as a "sponge" soaking up the causal universe of potential explanations for social movement mobilization (Gamson and Meyer 1996). The influence of political process theory provides the rationale for giving it extensive attention in this chapter. Beyond resources and framing, the surrounding political and economic environment serves as the core of political process theory. This larger environment shaping the potential for collective action tends to appear in two forms as outlined by David Meyer: (1) good news, characterized by political opportunities, and (2) bad news, characterized by threats (Meyer 2002).

Good News "Opportunity Model"

The good-news environment literally emits positive cues to would-be challengers. If people organize and mobilize in the present, they increase their chances of winning new benefits and advantages (McAdam 1999 [1982]; Goldstone and Tilly 2001). This good news is referred to as "opportunities" or "political opportunities" in the study of social movements (Tarrow 2011). Five specific opportunities have been found to be especially important in encouraging social movements (McAdam and Tarrow 2018):

1. Institutional access

2. Conflict among elites

3. Changing political alignments/elections

4. Relaxation in governmental repression

5. Multiple centers of power within the regime

Institutional access refers to an opening in the political system for excluded social sectors, which may benefit specific groups. Institutional access may either be symbolic or involve substantive policy changes. Governmental leaders at times make public statements that encourage disempowered groups to launch mobilizing drives. The president of a nation may give a speech signaling she is open to change in a particular sphere of social life, such as the right of workers and employees to earn a living wage—enough salary to meet a person's or family's most basic needs for food, housing, schooling, and health. The speech may give hope to low-income workers and motivate them to mobilize to push the government and policy makers to enact a living-wage law in their city, county, or state. An example of a state policy acting as institutional access would be a governmental decree instituting land reform in a country where a substantial percentage of the population lives off the land for subsistence. Often land is concentrated in the hands of a small privileged class of landowners producing agricultural commodities (coffee, cotton, sugarcane, bananas, etc.) for export markets (Edelman et al. 2016). When governments decide to assist poor farmers by enacting agrarian reform, peasants and groups living off the land feel inspired to mobilize and begin occupying idle lands (Enríquez 1991; Wolford 2010). In short, institutional access occurs when governments and policy makers begin to make symbolic gestures or enact decrees that potentially favor marginalized populations, thus providing an opening for groups to mobilize and try to gain new advantages.

Another piece of "good news" for excluded social groups may occur when political and economic *elites engage in conflict with one another.* This creates general instability and vulnerabilities in the political system, allowing groups to mobilize (Almeida and Stearns 1998). When elite groups quarrel with one another, one faction may align with social movements. In the 1960s in California, agricultural elites (large commercial farm owners) conflicted with governmental elites over new laws to protect Mexican American and Filipino American farmworkers from exploitive and dangerous conditions in the fields. When US senator Robert Kennedy visited farmworkers in the Central Valley of California in 1966 and advocated for better living and working conditions, it emboldened rural communities to redouble their efforts and it infuriated landowners who had long controlled politics in the region.[2]

Changing political alignments, especially among political parties and their constituencies, may also favor social movements. In recent years, the Democratic Party has taken relatively favorable stances toward immigrant rights and paths to citizenship as a means to increase the size of its constituency. Between 2007 and 2016, these actions provided a relatively more favorable political opportunity for immigrant rights movements to mobilize after mass protest events in 2006, especially after the Obama administration's Deferred Action for Childhood Arrivals (DACA) decree and the passage of the California DREAM Act (Zatz and Rodriguez 2015).[3] The rise of the anti-immigrant policies of the Trump administration has now pushed immigration policy in the opposite direction. Even *competitive elections* provide opportunities for excluded social groups to mobilize. During electoral campaigns politicians and political parties are more susceptible to popular demands and may need to incorporate them into their platform to be elected. At the local level, social movements at times elect their own candidates to office, when mobilizing a few thousand people may be sufficient to win elections in small and medium-sized towns.

Another political opportunity involves a *government relaxing its level of repression* against civil society (McAdam 1996; Tarrow 2011). When the US federal government and Supreme Court began to issue orders for racial desegregation in the southern United States in the late 1950s, it provided relatively more space for African Americans to collectively mobilize for more changes, including voting rights, even in the face of white reactionary violence at the local level (Andrews 2004). In the mid-1960s the repressive threat of mass deportation for immigrant farmworkers in California lessened as the Bracero program ended and there was a labor shortage. Farmworkers used this relaxation in repression to mobilize at an unprecedented rate and achieved a rural labor union of over one hundred thousand affiliates by the mid-1970s (Ganz 2009). In countries with authoritarian and military governments, periods of political liberalization, where the government allows more freedom, often lead to attempts at organizing civil society (Almeida 2008a).

A final opportunity involves *multiple centers of power* within a society. These provide multiple occasions to mobilize since excluded groups have more options for where to apply collective leverage (McAdam and Tarrow 2018). If the legislature turns down a movement's attempts at seeking an amelioration of grievances, the movement can take the struggle to the courts.

When all five of these "good news" opportunities occur simultaneously, we expect especially strong mobilization, perhaps reaching a wave of protest. Even one or two opportunities, however, are enough to stimulate social movement activity. Figure 6 illustrates the relationship of political opportunities, resource infrastructures, and framing to sustained mobilization in the good-news model of social movements. In summary, the opportunity perspective offers a framework in which the political environment opens in

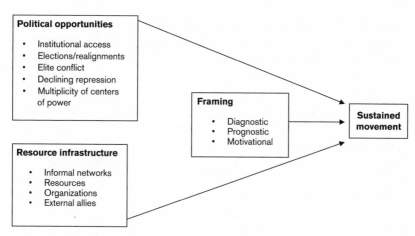

FIGURE 6. Good-News "Opportunity" Model of Collective Action.

a positive manner that encourages groups to mobilize and attempt to gain new advantages.

Bad News "Threat Model"

Another type of political environment also produces attempts at collective mobilization. The bad-news environment is characterized by negative conditions that encourage collective action. If mobilization is not undertaken, conditions will deteriorate for the population in question. Social movement scholars refer to these negative conditions as "threats" (Tilly 1978; Jasper 1997; Goldstone and Tilly 2001). Threats tend to heighten already existing grievances and create new ones for affected communities (Pinard 2011). Just as specific political opportunities in the good-news model produce incentives for social movement mobilization, so do threats in the bad-news model. There are four structural threats that consistently drive defensive collective action (Almeida 2018):

1. Economic problems
2. Environmental/public health threats
3. Erosion of rights
4. State repression

Economic Problems   One of the principal forces generating social movement activity resides in the deterioration of the material conditions of life. A variety of economic problems have the potential to motivate groups into campaigns of collective action. Some of the most potent economic problems include mass unemployment / general economic crises, government austerity, and threats to subsistence and rural livelihood (Reese 2011; Caren et al. 2017). In recent years the United States witnessed several national-level protests over economic problems. These include the Occupy Wall Street movement, movements for a living wage, the Poor People's campaign, and antiglobalization mobilizations. Elsewhere, in Asia, Africa, Europe, and Latin America, sustained mass protest campaigns have focused on economic austerity (i.e., government budget cutbacks), structural adjustment, privatization, and free trade (Almeida and Chase-Dunn 2018). These economic measures, taken together, represent neoliberal policies. In some cases, neoliberal economic policies have generated the largest social movement activities in decades, as in Argentina, Bolivia, Brazil, Ecuador, Costa Rica, Nicaragua, Panama, Paraguay, El Salvador, India, Nigeria, Bulgaria, Mexico, China, Spain, Portugal, and Greece.

In rural areas of the world, economic problems come in the form of subsistence survival (Scott 1976). When families and communities in the countryside lose their land because of encroaching commercial agriculture and farming, they may be pushed into defensive collective action in the form of peasant and cooperative movements that demand sufficient land to maintain their livelihoods. In the twenty-first century, a new round of global "land grabbing" is taking place, pushing rural communities into collective action (Edelman et al. 2016).

Environmental and Public Health Threats   Ecological and public health threats also come in a variety of forms. Community-based pollution from landfills, industrial establishments, or pesticides can generate citizen action to improve local environmental quality (Cordero Ulate 2009). Such environmental contamination is also a threat to public health. As discussed in chapter 2, between the 1980s and the 2010s in the United States, local grassroots movements mushroomed to fight lead poisoning, hazardous waste storage sites, air pollution, and dozens of other environmental hazards (Bullard 2005; Szasz 1994). These battles were largely fought at the municipal level and came to be known as the environmental justice movement (Edwards 1995). Often the mobilizations occurred in working-class communities of color where the struggle also confronted environmental racism, as these communities faced a disproportionate amount of pollution (Taylor 2014; Pellow 2017). Other public health threats such as HIV/AIDS created one of the most attention-grabbing national social movements in the United States in the late 1980s, with groups such as ACT UP unleashing dramatic mobilizing events such as "die-ins" and other provocative disruptive tactics to get the government and medical authorities to take concerted action to address the public health epidemic and its victims (Gould 2009).

Another major environmental threat pushing groups to organize around the globe involves global warming and climate change. The threat of a planet heating up beyond the level of ecological survival has generated a transnational movement to pressure governments to reduce carbon and other greenhouse gas emissions. Since the mid-2000s, climate change activists have pieced together global days of citizen action that stretch across all continents, and mass marches that have reached up to four hundred thousand participants, such as in New York City in September 2014, and Washington, DC, in April 2017. Climate change is undoubtedly the environmental hazard with the most extensive reach, placing life on the planet in precarious circumstances. Many other environmental threats at the local level also may activate attempts at collective action, such as unfavorable community reactions to mining and the extraction of natural resources, or economic infrastructure projects, including hydroelectric dams, international tourism zones, and other megadevelopment initiatives (McAdam et al. 2010). As the twenty-first century unfolds, environmental and public health threats increasingly trigger social movement activity.[4]

Erosion of Rights   Another negative condition that motivates collective action occurs when a substantial subset of the population perceives a loss in their rights as citizens. One of the most potent threats to existing rights is when governments take away democratic elections by canceling them or holding them in a fraudulent manner. Such state actions instantly strip large segments of society from their suffrage rights and often lead to large demonstrations demanding the restoration of the constitutional order. Just the mass perception of election irregularities has the potential to lead to mass mobilization, as in the 2006 Mexican presidential elections and the 2009 Iranian national elections. In late 2017 electoral irregularities in the Honduran presidential elections led to mega protest marches and roadblocks and barricades across the national territory (Sosa 2018).

Other kinds of deteriorations in rights can also generate protest campaigns. Especially forceful in creating mass discontent are policy changes that are perceived to reduce the rights of particular groups. Pending legislation over firearms, abortion laws, and welfare benefits provide just a few examples of policies that create incentives for social movement mobilization in order to prevent or pass the measure in question. Mobilization around the erosion of rights appears much more likely when the population

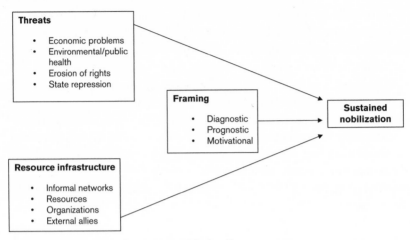

FIGURE 7. Bad-News "Threat" Model of Collective Action.

has become accustomed to the rights over several decades or longer and is suddenly faced with their loss. Indeed, the historic Women's Marches in 2017 and 2018 (discussed in chapter 1) were largely catalyzed by the threat of losing rights in the incoming Trump administration.

State Repression When governments (via the army, police, security forces, or other state-sponsored agents) repress citizens through violence and intimidation, attempts at collective defiance are probable. In the most extreme cases, government massacres of citizens, either in their communities or during actual peaceful public demonstrations, create "backlash" effects whereby the outrageous act of state violence creates new rounds of assertive popular mobilization (Francisco 2005). If such governmental repression continues on a consistent basis, this repressive threat may direct collective action itself onto a more radical or revolutionary trajectory as mobilized civil society finds that the overthrow of the government remains the only strategy to end the violence and abuse of human rights. In other words, state repression may contribute to escalating collective action from a protest wave to a revolutionary movement.

Other forms of repressive threat such as police abuse, racial profiling, and "stop and frisk" policies also drive communities into defensive collective action campaigns. Such forms of threat played a decisive role in the Black Lives Matter movement in the United States and other community campaigns (Taylor 2016) as well as ethnic-based riots in the United States, France, and Britain. Figure 7 summarizes the threat or "bad news" model of sustained mobilization.

A final consideration in the bad-news model of mobilization centers on a more precise characterization of the threat in question. Scholars working in this tradition find that issues such as the *severity, length,* and *credibility* of the threat also need to be addressed. When economic, environmental, political, and repressive threats are severe, sustained, and credible, attempts at collective action are more likely (Einwohner and Maher 2011). In addition, others have emphasized the *breadth, visibility, source,* and *timing* of threats. In this perspective, negative conditions induce collective protest when the threat is wide in scope (affecting multiple groups or large numbers of people), highly visible, occurring from a single source to focus blame, and impending over time to provide an adequate period to organize resistance (Zepeda-Millán 2017).

Hybrid Environments: Opportunities and Threats Combined

In the scenarios above, pure models of good-news and bad-news environments were presented. In many other political and economic circumstances, threats and opportunities may be acting *simultaneously.* For example, a state or city may face severe air pollution while at the same time benefit from a new government office dedicated to reducing air pollution. In this hypothetical case, a community suffering from air pollution has incentives to mobilize from both environmental threat (bad news) and institutional access (good news). Another scenario of a hybrid environment might occur during a period of mass unemployment and divided elites. Unemployed workers may be able to mobilize around economic threat and take advantage of the conflict between political and economic elites to win demands. Hence, it is important to consider a number of combinations of opportunities, threats, resource infrastructures, and framing strategies in the real world of politics that excluded groups confront on a daily basis.

Additional and Related Theoretical Perspectives

Students of social movements use several other theoretical perspectives to comprehend social movement mobilization. These alternatives include (1) rational choice, (2) multi-institutions, (3) new social movements, (4) emotions, (5) intersectionality, and (6) explanatory schemes for right-wing mobilization.

Rational Choice   Rational choice theories focus at the individual level of collective action providing a microperspective on movement dynamics. Borrowing principles from microeconomics, rational actor models predict individual participation in collective protest events. The perspective builds an elaborate causal scheme based on incentives. Individuals will join in a social movement if they calculate that they will be made better off from their participation. They have to believe their contribution will make a difference, and they need to highly value the benefits achieved. For example, a worker will join a labor strike if he is confident it will succeed and result in higher wages. Rational choice scholars, however, condition the above participation in collective action on the "free rider" problem (Olson 1965). They ask how you can convince individuals to participate in a movement if they will still receive the benefits without participating (Lichbach 1995). The answer comes in a set of selective economic incentives to induce participation and reduce the costs (Olson 1965). Critics within the rational choice perspective point out that there are other incentives for participation besides strict material benefits and sanctions. Such alternatives include sentiments of solidarity, interdependence, efficacy, and collective identity among members of the group engaging in a collective struggle (Opp 2009). Other critics find that one may join a social movement because she has a loyalty to the group, irrespective of the prospects for success.

Multi-Institutional Theories Multi-institutional theories acknowledge that social movements target other entities beyond the state (Armstrong and Bernstein 2008). Power is dispersed across multiple institutions. Political process theory largely focuses on the government as the main target or arbiter of movement demands. Recent scholarship has focused on social movements targeting other major institutions and organizations in society, such as corporations, the educational system, religious institutions, medical establishments, and international bodies, among many other nonstate targets (Van Dyke et al. 2004; Walker et al. 2008; Soule 2009; Bartley 2018).

One of the larger student movements to emerge in the 1990s in the United States was against sweatshops, in which students largely targeted large corporations such as Gap, as well as universities (Einwohner and Spencer 2005). University students pressured the corporations to improve working conditions for low-paid workers in export processing zones in the Caribbean, Latin America, and Asia (Armbruster-Sandoval 2005). They protested outside of retail stores in malls, held boycotts, and interrupted stockholder meetings. On campus, they worked to confirm that university apparel was certified by the International Labor Organization as produced in a factory with labor rights. Other struggles outside the state include the battle of women for leadership positions in religious institutions, such as the Catholic Church (Katzenstein 1998).

New Social Movements and Collective Identities   By the 1980s a renewed flourishing of popular mobilization by a variety of social sectors and groups came to be called *new social movements*. The movements included struggles over ecology, LGBTQ rights, feminism, disability rights, and ethnic and cultural identity. Scholars labeled the movements as "new" since they did not fit the traditional definition of social movements fighting largely for economic and material benefits. Some versions of new social movement theory viewed the innovative groups as an outcome of a *postmaterialist* society (Ingelhart 1977), where social conflict moves to the terrain of values, beliefs, and identities. Industrialization in the advanced capitalist countries of North America, Europe, Australia, and Japan has reached a stage of development and stability whereby movements mobilize less around the traditional cleavage structures of class and party, and focus on newer issues such as peace, nuclear disarmament, and the protection of immigrants (Kriesi et al. 1995).

More recent new social movement scholarship emphasizes the postmaterialist elements less and instead concentrates on the grievances and issues of specific collectivities, such as LGBTQ movements, ecology movements, and a variety of youth movements and subcultures. One essential contribution of this perspective centers on the recognition that a larger variety of social movements has emerged around the world since the 1970s. These newer social movements also face social exclusion in a variety of contexts and institutions, pushing them into social movement mobilization.

The focus on collective identities presents another fascinating dimension of new social movements. Participation in social activities also provides a venue for individuals to share in their personal identities with a group of like-minded others forming a collective identity. This collective identity may convert into an activist identity when the group participates in movement mobilization (Jasper 1997). Pan-ethnic collective identities may be especially potent for racial and ethnic minority groups to align in larger coalitions. Okamoto (2014) documents the rise in pan–Asian American activism in the 1970s and 1980s in response to occupational segregation and discrimination. The role of collective identities is also taken up in chapter 4 on movement emergence, and in chapter 6 on movement recruitment.

Emotions   A novel theoretical perspective at the microlevel involves emotions and social movement mobilization (Goodwin et al. 2001; Jasper 2018). Scholarship downplayed the role of emotions for several decades with the fall of classical theories by the 1970s. The earlier theories viewed emotions in a pejorative framework, whereby they steered collective action down an irrational path. Nonetheless, by the late 1990s and early 2000s, scholars increasingly incorporated the role of emotions in fomenting collective action along with the other structural dimensions discussed in the political process model. These studies range from developing a typology of emotions to subsequent predictions on how they motivate individuals to act (Jasper 2018). The perspective also investigates movement leaders attempting to tap into specific emotions to generate or sustain mobilization among adherents, bystanders, and the larger public. Indeed, Jasper (1998) provides a list of seventeen emotions shaping social movement mobilization, including hostility, love, solidarity, suspicion, trust, anger, grief, outrage, shame, compassion, cynicism, defiance, enthusiasm, envy, fear, joy, and resignation. These emotions may be used either to ignite social movement participation (particularly moral shocks that generate sentiments of outrage, anger, indignation, and resignation) or to sustain mobilization over the longer term within a movement (especially those feelings that create a mood of love, loyalty, respect, and trust). Randall Collins (2001) has also theorized the positive roles emotional energy plays in collective events by sustaining feelings of solidarity.

Intersectionality Theory   An emergent framework in the 2010s in relationship to social movements focuses on the mobilization of people across multiple identities and systems of oppression (Terriquez 2015a; Terriquez et al. 2018; Collins and Bilge 2016; Rojas 2017; Chun et al. 2013). Still in its early stages as applied to social movements, the theory addresses how people come together in coalitions that are impacted by multiple forms of inequality. The historic Women's Marches of 2017 and 2018 explicitly used an intersectionality framework to bring multiple groups into the massive mobilizations, especially highlighting gender, race, and sexuality in the mobilization appeals and mission statement of the organizers (Fisher et al. 2017; Berry and Chenoweth 2018). Intersectionality acts as a powerful tool of resistance in unequal societies that are stratified along multiple social dimensions (Valdez 2011). Luna (2016) has taken such an approach by observing the different strategies of building coalitions among women of color from varying racial and ethnic backgrounds. She finds intersectionality alliances are highly complex and interactive with the ongoing need to establish and maintain solidarity based on similarities while simultaneously negotiating each group's lived experiences. We are likely on the cusp of an outpouring of new research on intersectional alliances as real-world events and race/ethnicity scholars push activists and students of social movements to rethink the conditions and relationships that bring people together in defiant collective action (Bracey 2016; Pulido and Lara 2018).

Power Devaluation Theory and Right-Wing Movements There is much less theoretical scholarship on right-wing mobilization as there is for more progressive movements. Movement thinkers have developed theoretical perspectives to explain right-wing mobilization. The power devaluation model provides one example. The power devaluation perspective, developed by McVeigh (2009) to explain Ku Klux Klan mobilization in the 1920s, contends that when groups with previous social and economic privileges perceive or experience a decline in status, they collectively mobilize around nationalism, patriotism, and exclusion. McVeigh (2009: 39) explicitly finds a loss of power in three arenas as most forceful in catalyzing rightist mobilization: (1) devaluation in economic power, (2) devaluation in political power, and (3) devaluation in social status. These three conditions lead to attempts at right-wing framing using racial superiority and anti-immigrant propaganda in mobilization appeals—increasingly via social media in the twenty-first century (Caren et al. 2012). Van Dyke and Soule (2002) use a similar perspective to show the growth of right-wing militia groups in the United States in the 1990s. They demonstrate with fine-grain county- and state-level analyses that militia movements are more likely to be found in regions with high unemployment, deindustrialization, and a threatened loss of patriarchal status. According to preliminary scholarship, these are the same kinds of conditions that mobilized the Trump presidential campaign between 2015 and 2016 (Autor et al. 2016; Monnat 2016; Gest 2016; Bobo 2017). Hence, this presents an intriguing line of theoretical inquiry regarding the relationship between social movement mobilization and electoral mobilization. Martin (2013) also finds that the wealthiest economic sectors take up protest campaigns against progressive forms of taxation when those are perceived as policy threats to their interests.

SUMMARY

Social movement theories guide studies of the overall dynamics of social movements, highlighting the most relevant factors in the causal universe driving collective action. Beginning with early sociological thinkers such as Du Bois, Durkheim, Marx, Perkins Gilman, and Weber, theories have evolved and become more refined to address specific aspects of the mobilization process. A new wave of scholars viewing collective action as rational by excluded groups supplanted classical movement theories from the mid-twentieth century. Contemporary social movement theories emphasize opportunities, threats, resource infrastructures, and framing strategies. New frontiers in social movement theorizing ask questions about collective identities, especially intersectional identities, in mobilizing heterogeneous populations in unequal societies. Innovative frameworks also incorporate the role of emotions and the targeting of institutions beyond the state. Students of right-wing movements employ variants of social movement theory to explain conservative backlash mobilizations that attempt to stifle progressive social change and promote policies harmful to vulnerable groups.

4 Social Movement Emergence

Interests, Resource Infrastructures, and Identities

The previous chapter on movement theories provided abstract models on the core frameworks explaining collective action dynamics. This chapter examines the most investigated dimension of collective mobilization: when and where social movements are most likely to surface. The first sections focus on three arenas shaping the formation of social movements: common interests, organizational building blocks, and group identities. The chapter concludes by discussing diffusion processes after a movement begins to establish itself. In other words, it addresses how protest campaigns spread and multiply across cities, states, and even nations. The struggle of fast-food workers in the United States completes the chapter as a compelling case to demonstrate the dynamics of movement emergence.

The classical theories discussed in the previous chapter offered some of the first attempts to explain movement emergence. Recall that the classical theories largely focused on a set of vague system strains creating varying forms of social psychological tensions that resulted in collective action (Buechler 2004). This group of theories lacked empirical evidence for how individual psychological stress converts into collective protest—which is a large gap left to explain (McAdam 1999 [1982]). Fortunately, alternative frameworks for examining the rise and diffusion of social movements have developed into a rich literature over the past few decades. One of the path-breaking investigations that advanced the understanding of movement emergence was Piven and Cloward's (1979) study entitled *Poor People's Movements*. Their research retained some elements of classical theory while advancing our understanding that movements are rational and goal oriented while using noninstitutional mobilizing strategies.

The basic thesis of Piven and Cloward states that excluded social groups rarely have the opportunity to mobilize to improve their circumstances (a

63

proposition that is currently highly debated). From here, they outline the basic conditions necessary for the emergence of collective mobilization by marginalized communities. In most times and places, less powerful people find themselves under some form of political and economic domination that includes loyalty to the values, beliefs, and rituals of the prevailing structures of governance—or what the Italian socialist Antonio Gramsci (1971) refers to as *hegemony*. Under this system of everyday domination, excluded groups find themselves embedded in their daily routines and habits with few prospects of conditions improving, eventuating in sentiments of fatalism.[1] Moreover, Morris and Braine (2001: 22) state that "these cultures of subordination arise because oppressed populations devise survival strategies that enable them to cope with adverse social conditions they encounter on a regular basis." Despite these obstacles, when major societal crises erupt via a severe economic downturn, rapid technological change, or major demographic shifts, the system of social control tends to deteriorate. Under such circumstances, ordinary people become dislodged from their habitual routines and begin to question the legitimacy of authorities.

The breakdown of everyday life and quotidian routines (via unemployment, economic stress, and uncertainty) pushes groups in similar situations into acquiring a collective consciousness (Snow et al. 1998). This community change in collective beliefs centers on people acquiring a sense of efficacy and the ability to improve current circumstances via sustained protest mobilization campaigns. In other words, people begin to believe change is possible through massive protest actions. Piven and Cloward (1979: 12) termed this change in collective beliefs "transvaluation," and McAdam (1999 [1982]: 48–50) refers to a similar process as "cognitive liberation." These mass protest campaigns disrupt the status quo for economic and political elites and provide leverage for excluded groups to push forward their demands. Piven and Cloward examined unemployed and industrial workers in the 1930s along with the civil rights and welfare rights movements in the 1960s and early 1970s as their historical case studies. It is interesting to observe in the United States a similar upswing in social movements, in the context and aftermath of the 2008–9 Great Recession, with immigrant rights movements, Black Lives Matter, Occupy Wall Street, living-wage campaigns, and the anti-Trump marches (Milkman 2017).

As observed in the diagram below, the Piven and Cloward model includes components of classical theory but also elements of political process theory. It is a hybrid theory of movement emergence marking the transition from classical theories (with the emphasis on societal breakdown and system strain) to contemporary emergence theories with a focus on the rational interest of excluded groups to use disruptive actions to achieve common goals. This theoretical advancement influenced a new generation of scholars over the next several decades in terms of collective consciousness, economic threats, and the use of disruptive protests. These advances also come with criticisms. For instance, the Piven and Cloward emergence model not only downplays the role of formal organizations in collective action, but contends that organizations *demobilize* social movements. Below we look at contemporary perspectives on the key building blocks of social movement emergence. We will detail the conditions driving the emergence of social movements over time and across geographical space by using many of the concepts introduced in the previous chapter, with a specialized focus on (1) common interests, (2) organizational building blocks, and (3) group identities.

PIVEN AND CLOWARD MODEL OF MOVEMENT EMERGENCE

System Crisis → Breakdown of Routines → Collective Consciousness → Disruptive Protest

COMMON INTERESTS

In order to convert individual grievances into collective action, a sense of common interests needs to be established. Many early theories of movement emergence failed to connect individual-level deprivations and strains to larger group processes. As discussed in chapter 3, the political process framework states that either a good-news or a bad-news environment may provide the incentives to initiate a protest campaign (Meyer 2002). The good-news environment begins with the core concept of political opportunities. Recall that political opportunities include institutional access, elite conflict, changing political alignments, a lessening in repression, and multiple centers of power in a regime (McAdam and Tarrow 2018). The main point is that when a community or group perceives a positive change in their political environment (i.e., good news) that favors the issues or demands they are concerned with, members may initiate a collective action campaign to win new benefits or advantages. For example, once the California Assembly and Senate reached a near supermajority of Democrats in 2014, a movement campaign was launched (called "Ethnic Studies Now") to establish ethnic studies curricula in high school classrooms in public school districts throughout the state. The measure was passed by the state legislature in 2016.

The bad-news environment provides a set of negative incentives (threats) that may stimulate collective action. Four principal threats include economic problems, environmental/public health crises, erosion of rights, and state repression (Almeida 2018). A new or increasing threat such as water pollution making the public ill could drive an attempt at local social movement mobilization. In summary, common interests may be amplified by the good news of increasing opportunities or the bad news of mounting threats.

Nonetheless, positive or negative incentives need to be experienced collectively in order to create *common interests*. Individuals and groups living under similar social circumstances enhance the likelihood that opportunities or threats will be understood in similar ways. When similarly situated groups face good news or bad news, the potential and scale of common interests widen if people are already embedded in organizations and communities, as solidarity is heightened and communication flows rapidly (Gould 1995). Hence, would-be social movements benefit from other kinds of resources to act on their common interests.

ORGANIZATIONAL AND RESOURCE INFRASTRUCTURES

Organizations

Once organizations are up and running, they have a tendency to endure and remain resilient. They offer perhaps the most valuable resource to would-be collective actors. Social movements are more likely to emerge from already existing organizations and institutions. As McAdam (2003: 285) notes, "Most social movements develop within established social settings . . . established social settings provide insurgents with the various resources (e.g., recognized leaders, communication channels, networks of trust, etc.) needed to launch and sustain collective action." Each of these elements is vital for starting mobilization. Leadership teams provide salient knowledge and experience from past collective action. Those leaders who are intrinsically motivated (as opposed to being motivated by material rewards) have been found to be more effective organizers (Ganz 2009). Organizations and preexisting groups also provide a bounded setting to communicate and build an oppositional consciousness (Morris and Braine 2001). A common fate is much more easily achieved within an organizational setting (Gould 1995).

A wide variety of organizational forms with a range of purposes exists in civil society (Clemens 1997; Clemens and Minkoff 2004). Two types of organizations are especially useful in providing the resources for social movement emergence: *activist organizations* and *everyday organizations* not originally established for collective action. Leaders create activist organizations for the explicit purpose to coordinate social movement campaigns. Activist organizations include groups such as Greenpeace, People for the Ethical Treatment of Animals, United Farm Workers, Service Employees International Union, and MEChA (Movimiento Estudiantil Chicanx de Aztlán), to name just a few. Many of these social movement organizations (SMOs) formed from previous struggles and maintain their existence over long periods of time. SMOs constitute a field of organizations that can be tapped in order to launch a new mobilization drive. This is how workers at times can initiate a rapid strike campaign or how women's rights groups mobilize simultaneously when threatened by new unfavorable policies. Social movement labor unions (Martin 2008) and feminist groups (Van Dyke 2017) already in existence allow for this kind of swift emergence in collective action. In new protest campaigns without preestablished SMOs, in order to sustain mobilization over the long term, activists may establish more explicit social movement organizations during the heat of a struggle (McAdam 1999 [1982]).

Everyday organizations are explicitly set up to meet goals other than those of collective action (Gould 2005). Such organizations include nonprofit social service organizations, nongovernmental organizations (NGOs), religious institutions, educational institutions (high schools and universities), agricultural cooperatives, neighborhood committees, recreational sports clubs[2], and many other kinds of nonactivist ordinary organizations. In specific times and places, these common organizations may provide the mass base to an emerging social movement, especially in regions without many activist organizations or at points in history when a new type of movement is surfacing on the political landscape. For example, at the height of protest against free-market reforms in Latin America in the early 2000s, local regions with a higher density of NGOs in Bolivia, El Salvador, Guatemala, and Nicaragua registered more protest events (Boulding 2014; Almeida 2012; 2014b). These organizations mobilized people in marginalized urban and rural communities that have been abandoned by other organizations, including the government. NGOs usually do not spend time mobilizing people for protest actions. Instead, they provide services and resources to underserved communities (healthcare, training, counseling, etc.). Nonetheless, under special circumstances they mobilize people in campaigns for social change.

Another example of the mobilizing potential of everyday organizations comes from the public school system. The campaign to ban the purchase of military assault weapons received an enormous boost in the wake of the massacre at Marjory Stoneman Douglas High School in Florida in 2018.

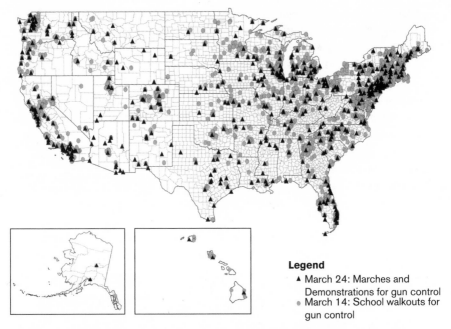

FIGURE 8.   Gun Control Protests, 2018. Constructed from countlove.org and www .womensmarch.com/.

Student leaders at the high school immediately used social media to connect with thousands of high schools and middle schools across the United States. They effectively used the everyday organization of the public schools to launch over three thousand student walkouts and eight hundred mass marches one month following the massacre, with the goal of stricter gun control policies (see figure 8). On the basis of the visual pattern in figure 8, the school walkouts on March 14 likely explain the city location of the street marches and rallies that occurred ten days later on March 24, 2018. Without the everyday organizations of the public schools, the gun reform movement would be much weaker as a force of mass mobilization and public pressure. Also, in recent years in the United States, teachers have used strikes and street demonstrations and coordinated these actions at the level of the public schools to protect their pensions and increase their low salary and staff allocations (and school supplies) in Arizona, Colorado, Illinois, Kentucky, North Carolina, Oklahoma, and West Virginia. Arguably, the mass base of the 2006 immigrant rights movement relied on student walkouts in the public schools. Hence, public schools serve as central locations from which collective action may emerge (in the United States and around the world).

The acknowledgment of the role of preexisting activist and everyday organizations in generating collective action opens up many interesting questions as to when and where social movements will begin to appear as well as the pace of mobilization. Social movement experts tend to believe that collective action will likely first emerge in regions with already-existing organizations (both activist and everyday organizations) or where large portions of the population are actively participating in civil society organizations. Preestablished organizations and institutions provide occasions for "bloc recruitment" whereby entire segments of the organization may be drawn into an incipient social movement campaign (Oberschall 1973; McAdam 1999 [1982]). As mentioned in chapter 3, this organizational mechanism accelerates the rate of mobilization by avoiding the recruitment of individuals one by one.

Additional organizational dynamics related to movement emergence include the network relationships between units. If organizations are already connected via overlapping memberships, affiliations in larger umbrella groups, or participation in coalitions, information can travel quickly and preexisting obligations may activate interorganizational solidarity to contribute resources (Van Dyke and Amos 2017). Simply counting the number of network ties between everyday and activist organizations may predict the likelihood and strength of mobilization. Indeed, Osa (2003) showed that after weaker mobilizations in Poland against the authoritarian regime in the 1960s and early 1970s, network ties between oppositional organizations increased in density by the late 1970s, leading to the formation of "Solidarity" (a federation of labor unions and other civil society groups), unprecedented mass mobilization on a national scale, and the eventual collapse of the regime.

Despite the multiplicity of benefits provided by organizational resources for movement emergence, a series of criticisms remains. One of the most influential critics of organizations for mass mobilization is the German political scientist Robert Michels. Michels (1962) viewed that even progressive political organizations, such as the socialist German Social Democratic Party, would evolve to become more conservative over time. Michels characterized the process as marked by a few leaders taking control of the organization and using it for their own ends to secure survival instead of mass empowerment via movement mobilization. Piven and Cloward (1979) also viewed formal organizations as leading to movement demobilization as movement leaders are co-opted into NGOs, government bodies, political parties, and lobbying organizations. The deep distrust of formal and hierarchical organizations continues in the twenty-first century, including the mobilization of new social movements that prefer more horizontal, informal, and participatory forms of coordination (Clemens and Minkoff 2004). Such movements can be observed in feminist reading circles, the horizontalist neighborhood committees and recuperated factories in Argentina, the Occupy movement in the United States, the Indignado youth of Spain, and the various forms of contemporary anarchism such as Black Bloc and Antifa (Mason 2013; Wood 2015). Even given the desire by some collective actors to maintain flexible and horizontal networks, movements require some degree of organization and coordination to sustain themselves over time (Snow and Soule 2009).

Other Components of the Resource Infrastructure

Beyond organizations, other resources may promote social movement emergence. While the listing of potentially beneficial assets to promoting collective action could be infinite, previous studies highlight some of the most crucial resources. Indeed, Edwards and Kane (2014) mention material, human, cultural, socio-organizational, and moral resources as contributing to sustained mobilization. We can collapse this grouping into three major nonorganizational resources that include human capital, social capital, and strategic capital. In the tradition of the French sociologist Pierre Bourdieu (1986), we can think of "capital" as multidimensional with the tripartite classification of human, social, and strategic forms.

Human capital involves the skills of the population susceptible to mobilization. A variety of human skills, from public-speaking ability to communications technology, provide advantages for mobilizing over communities that lack these talents. Such skill sets are also partially context specific. Community leaders need to know what kinds of speeches will be persuasive to the excluded groups they are attempting to mobilize. For example, "potential [movement] participants are more likely to accept frames that fit with their existing beliefs, their sense of empirical credibility, their own life experiences, and the narratives they use to describe their lives" (Jasper 1997: 75). Talented and persuasive public speakers assist by performing these mobilization appeals effectively (a topic of chapter 5). Social media experts need to understand the level of technology within the population and to employ targeted messages to key individuals and organizations. Many other human skills may assist as well, such as scientists and lawyers in movements seeking to organize against environmental contamination (Almeida and Stearns 1998; Brown et al. 2012).

Social capital has been defined as levels of trust and cohesiveness within communities. Neighborhoods where the residents know one another and hold frequent community events tend to be more accountable to one another (Putnam 2000). Where people are in more frequent interaction, critical information is exchanged that would otherwise be less accessible (Small 2009). Recent studies of rural populations in India, China, and sub-Saharan Africa frequently report that informal trust networks along kinship and village lines are more associated with collective action than are more formal organizations (Krishna 2002; Bratton 2008; Lu and Tao 2017). For these reasons we expect more social movement activity to surface in zones with higher levels of social capital. Oberschall (1973) emphasized such communal groups as playing a decisive role in collective action.

Another crucial resource beyond organizations is *strategic capital.* Scholars define strategic capital as a community's experience with collective action. Those groups that have organized in the recent past have a greater ability to mobilize in the present and future. As Aldon Morris (1984: x) succinctly states in reference to African American collective struggles: "The tradition of protest is transmitted across generations by older relatives, black educational institutions, churches, and protest organizations. Blacks interested in social change inevitably gravitate to this 'protest community,' where they hope to find solutions to a complex problem. Once the contact is made the newcomer becomes a link in the tradition. Thus the tradition is perpetually rejuvenated by new blood."

Activists and communities know where and how to mobilize the population based on experiences. Indeed, the massive 2006 immigrant rights movement in the United States at first appeared as a spontaneous reaction to the congressional bill (HR 4437) that threatened noncitizens' legal status. Closer research demonstrated that in many of the locations the protests were preceded by an "Immigrant Freedom Ride" campaign in 2003 led by labor and immigrant rights organizations (Bloemraad et al. 2011). Okamoto (2003) has also demonstrated the resource of prior protest activity in sustaining Asian American collective action. In another example of the power of community mobilization know-how, Almeida (2014b) demonstrated that some of the largest campaigns against neoliberalism (privatization, free trade, and austerity) in Central America reported more protest events in localities that had previously mobilized against economic reforms in the recent past. Scholars that study indigenous peoples' mobilization in Mexico with data sets of protest events over time and across large portions of the national territory also contend that villages with past experience in mobilizing for their rights are more likely to launch new rounds of collective resistance than communities with less history of struggle (Inclán 2008; Trejo 2012).

Strategic capital also evolves through learning and adapting by discarding tactics and strategies that fail, while retaining successful organizing templates. This includes coalitional strategies. Even though a vast social movement literature shows the power in numbers via the coordination of large coalitions (Van Dyke and Amos 2017), movement leaders often learn the hard way in trying to launch a protest movement campaign in a single sector by a single group. They discover via trial and error that coalition strategies are more effective, and strive to reach out to other groups in subsequent rounds of mobilization (Almeida 2008b).

All three types of resource capitals (human, social, and strategic) are fungible—they can be used for multiple purposes (Almeida 2003: 350; Edwards and Kane 2014). This makes human, social, and strategic capital especially valuable for people and communities seeking to organize themselves in social movement campaigns. Such resources can also be extended to other forms of collective action, such as public health campaigns, disaster relief, and international migration (e.g., migrant caravans).

COLLECTIVE IDENTITIES

A fundamental characteristic of social movements centers on a sense of togetherness or "we-ness" and "one-ness" of a group (Snow and McAdam 2000). New social movement theorists largely made this contribution to social movement emergence (Melucci 1988; Touraine 1985). One way this process takes place is through personal and collective identities. Personal identities involve one's sense of self. Collective identities provide sentiments of group belonging. Collective identities can be especially strong when they are consonant with individual identities (Jasper 1997). Taylor and Whittier (1992: 105) provide a precise definition: "Collective identity is the shared definition of a group that derives from members' common interests, experiences, and solidarity." Collective identities may maintain boundaries based on ethnicity, region, neighborhood, citizenship status, class, gender, religion, sexual orientation, or many other traits. The collective sense of belonging enhances sentiments of solidarity as the group in question seeks new benefits or protects itself from increasing threats. Collective identities are also built on the shared definition of the situation by members of the groups (Johnston et al. 1994).

Verta Taylor and Nancy Whittier (1992: 111) also note that "for any subordinate group, the construction of a positive identity requires both a withdrawal from the values and structures of the dominant, oppressive society and the creation of new self-affirming values and structures." This particular perspective offers a powerful insight on how communities can overcome the intractable forms of domination described above by Piven and Cloward. In other words, it offers an avenue of agency and active resistance to prevailing forms of hegemony and systems of exclusion. At other times, sudden events like school shootings, environmental catastrophes, or government repression may cause rapid shifts in identities. For example, Jocelyn Viterna (2013) found that rural women in El Salvador in villages facing extreme human rights abuses by the military in the early 1980s shifted their identities from working mothers and daughters to revolutionaries as they joined insurgent forces to overthrow a government that sponsored the killing of their families. Once collective identities have been politicized and the community engages in collective action, the collective identity may be transformed into an activist identity promoting future rounds of mobilization (Jasper 1997; Horowitz 2017).

Much of the identity-building exercises occur outside the view of the public and social movement scholars. In meetings, neighborhood gatherings, ceremonies, and other internal events, communities and groups build collective identity by sharing experiences, singing songs together, and generally enhancing fellowship by highlighting commonalities (Zermeño 2017). Well-trained community organizers describe this process as "capacity building," which takes place over several months or years (Wood and Fulton 2015). Collins (2004) views such gatherings as crucial "interaction rituals" where deep bonds of solidarity are created and the participating individuals become infused with emotional energy. These collective identity construction processes are best investigated with ethnographic field research techniques discussed in chapter 2. At times, expressions of collective identity break out into the public sphere via annual collective actions such as May Day demonstrations, Cesar Chavez and Martin Luther King Jr. Day celebrations, International Women's Day marches, gay pride parades, and other commemorative events (Armstrong 2002; Inclán and Almeida 2017). One of the most important contributions of leaders, activists, and artists resides in their ability to produce powerful symbols to reinforce collective identities and strengthen bonds of fraternity. The sense of collective belonging is essential for launching a movement campaign and nurturing its growth.

DIFFUSION: HOW SOCIAL MOVEMENTS SPREAD

Once movements emerge, a closely related question is how they spread across regions, including neighborhoods, cities, states, and nations. This is the area of the *diffusion* of social movement mobilization. Scholars often document a common tactic, collective action frame, or goal to trace the diffusion process.

This may include a strike wave, rioting across cities, student walkouts, or a campaign with the goal of a living wage. One of the main facilitators for the spread of social movements centers on the existence of similar conditions in multiple locations. Students of organizations, networks and social movements refer to this process as "structural equivalence" (Strang and Soule 1998). A recent example in the United States can be found in the mobilizations over the Occupy Wall Street movement. Between September 2011 and February 2012, students and activists erected hundreds of protest encampments in cities across the United States in a case of rapid diffusion (Gould-Wartofsky 2015). The protests spread quickly as the common demand focused on reducing income inequality in the context of the Great Recession (see figure 5 near the end of chapter 2). The movement in most locations used the collective action frame of the "99%" against the "1%" as a dramatic call to address the maldistribution of wealth in the country that has intensified in recent decades (Piketty 2014). Scholarship has found that the Occupy Wall Street movement was more likely to spread through traditional organizational lines, such as universities, as well as social media conduits, especially Facebook pages (Vasi and Suh 2016). The idea that similar circumstances in multiple regions (or structural equivalence) encourage movement expansion offers intriguing lines of inquiry for social movement studies. In particular, how do people become aware of social movement campaigns that have yet to reach their own region? To answer this question we explore more precise mechanisms and conduits for the diffusion of collective action.

Three prominent mechanisms for the multiplication of social movement activity are direct, indirect, and mediated diffusion (Kolins Givan et al. 2010). *Direct diffusion* occurs through ties between organizations, leaders, and informal groups. This takes place through overlapping memberships, participation in larger federations of organizations, or proximity to major trade and transportation routes. *Indirect diffusion* derives from the spread of social movement activity by shared cultural understandings and structural equivalence. The mass media and social media make unconnected groups aware of one another and set the conditions for imitation of movement tactics by similarly situated groups that were previously unaware of the tactic. For example, analysts also find that the repressive threat of arrests of participants in the early Occupy Wall Street encampments created more social media attention and outrage on Twitter and Facebook, which in turn facilitated the spatial diffusion of Occupy protest events to new cities (Suh et al. 2017). The final mechanism of *mediated diffusion* occurs through a broker that connects otherwise disconnected organizations and individuals (Vasi 2011).

APPLYING MOVEMENT-EMERGENCE TOOLS:
THE "FIGHT FOR $15" CAMPAIGN

Figures 9 and 10 provide an opportunity to systematically apply the concepts and processes of movement emergence detailed above to a contemporary social movement: the struggle of fast-food and other service workers to earn a living wage. After years of living-wage campaigns in the 1990s and 2000s targeting local, national, and federal levels of government, one of the largest labor unions in the United States (Service Employees International Union, or SEIU) decided to launch a campaign focusing on the salaries of fast-food restaurant workers. The campaign had precursors such as SEIU's "Fight for a Fair Economy Campaign," the efforts of the Change to Win labor coalition, the Occupy Wall Street movements, and over a decade of innovative service sector union organizing in Los Angeles County. The campaign began in November 2012 when several dozen fast-food employees in New York City walked out during working hours. The movement gained enormous momentum in 2013, and by the end of the year it had mobilized rallies, walkouts, and protests in well over one hundred cities in the United States. The collective actions became known as the "Fight for $15," with chants such as "No justice, no grease." The core demand focused on a fifteen-dollar hourly wage. By 2014 and 2015 the Fight for $15 campaign reached hundreds of towns and cities. The movement organized by choosing strategic dates and holding all of the protest events on the same day as simultaneously coordinated events. The movement sustained energy into 2016 and 2017 with simultaneous one-day actions covering even more locations around the country. By 2018 the movement coordinated with the new Poor People's Campaign for economic justice. The Fight for $15 has become one of the largest social movements in the United States in the second decade of the twenty-first century, along with Black Lives Matter, immigrant rights, Occupy Wall Street, the anti-Trump resistance, youth against assault weapons, and climate justice.

With low-wage work and few benefits found throughout the fast-food industry, the national days of protest campaigns spread quickly across the United States, where the common demand focused on raising hourly pay to a level where employees could meet their basic daily needs and expenses. The protests stretched across all the familiar chains from McDonald's to Wendy's, KFC, Burger King, and Taco Bell. Workers in uniforms and their allies held rallies in front of the restaurants, marched down major city streets, demonstrated at international airports, and even blocked roads at times. The national days of action were largely nonviolent but at times

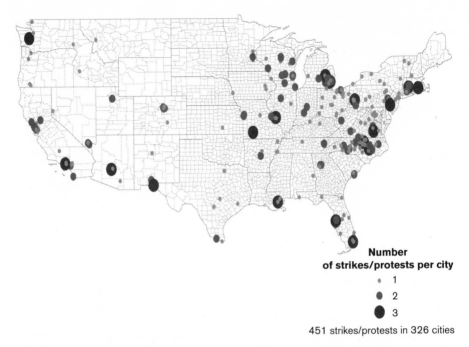

**Number
of strikes/protests per city**

• 1

● 2

● 3

451 strikes/protests in 326 cities

FIGURE 9. Fast-Food Worker Protests, 2013–2015. Constructed by author from www
.ibtimes.com/fast-food-worker-strikes-these-are-100-cities-where-fast-food-workers-will-
walk-job-1495758 http://fightfor15.org and http://thinkprogress.org/economy/2014/05/15
/3438218/map-fast-food-strikes-may/.

disruptive, with the intervention of law enforcement. For example, the
November 29, 2016, day of actions resulted in hundreds of arrests across
several cities.

Figures 9 and 10 provide geographical information on where the fast-food
protests occurred on some of the days of the largest mobilizations (December
5, 2013, May 15, 2014, November 10, 2015, April 4, 2016, and September 4,
2017, when low-wage fast-food workers and their allies launched a national
day of strikes, protests, and rallies).[3] The maps illustrate the distribution of
the fast-food protests across the 3,007 counties in the United States. What do
these protest campaigns tell us about movement emergence and diffusion?
We can address this question with our understanding of common interests,
resource infrastructures, and collective identities.

We can start with *mutual interests*. For decades, real wages in the United
States have not kept pace with the rate of inflation, making life especially
difficult for low-wage workers and their families (Rolf 2016). The fast-food
industry is one sector where the problem of low wages has reached a crisis

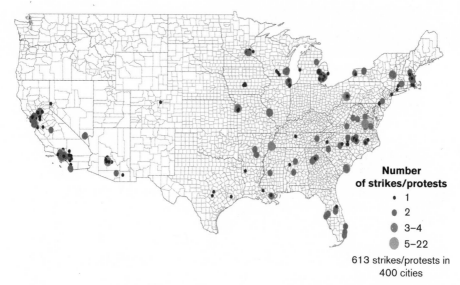

Number
of strikes/protests
• 1
● 2
◉ 3–4
⬤ 5–22
613 strikes/protests in
400 cities

FIGURE 10.   Fast-Food Worker Protests, 2016–2017. Constructed from http://fightfor15.org.

point. Employees in this industry share a direct and common material interest in increasing their wages for household survival. Fast-food industry workers make similar wages and likely have a sense of comparable circumstances. This creates conditions of structural equivalence across the industry with workers from Portland, Maine, to San Diego, California, in a similar economic situation. Long-term economic threats of the rising cost of living while wages remain stagnant provided the negative conditions motivating mobilization. If food-service workers failed to organize in the present, they would likely witness a continual decline in their standard of living. A macrolevel political opportunity at the beginning of the campaign was having a Democratic president in the White House who showed signs of sympathy toward the movement. Indeed, in a rapid reversal of this opportunity, upon taking office in 2017, the Trump administration appointed antiunion members to the National Labor Relations Board, and the SEIU has reportedly cut funding to the Fight for $15 campaigns.[4]

The fast-food workers' campaign also benefited from *resource infrastructures*. Luce (2017) notes that the fast-food worker protests and strikes between 2012 and 2017 built on the earlier living-wage movement that took off in 1994 in dozens of municipalities across the nation. By 2009, 125 cities and counties had passed a living-wage ordinance (Luce 2017: 870). Activists coordinated these local-level campaigns by piecing together a variety of coalitions composed of labor unions, community-based organizations (e.g.,

ACORN), faith-based organizations, students, and clergy. This *strategic capital* of previous mobilizing experience would be used to support the fast-food mobilizations in the 2010s. From the maps in the two figures one might hypothesize that more fast-food worker mobilizations occurred in the counties and regions with an earlier living-wage campaign.

Also directly related to the resource infrastructure would be the SEIU labor union, which initiated the fast-food worker strike campaign. The SEIU union dispatched labor activists to dozens of cities. Other cities have active SEIU chapters in other service sectors outside of the fast-food industry (e.g., healthcare, property services/maintenance, public service). From this organizational view, the pattern of fast-food protest activity should be associated with where the SEIU labor organization has a geographical presence. More recent social movements have offered support to the fast-food worker struggle, including Black Lives Matter. Hence, we would expect fast-food strike activity to emerge in those regions where the Black Lives Matter movement is most active.

Common identities also likely played an important role in the fast-food worker protest mobilizations. The structural equivalence conditions mentioned above for low-wage fast-food workers also would contribute to forming strong collective identities along the lines of employment status as well as benefiting from ethnic and interethnic solidarity in those communities with high concentrations of Latinx, Black, Asian American, and immigrant workers. In regions where activists were able to forge intersectional identities by unifying low-wage workers along the lines of race, class, gender, and sexuality (Chun et al. 2013), they may have developed stronger solidarities to risk participation in the face of job dismissal. Indeed, on April 4, 2017, the Fight for $15 joined forces with Black Lives Matter on the forty-ninth anniversary of the Reverend Martin Luther King Jr.'s assassination. The two groups coordinated protests in over thirty cities to simultaneously battle racism and economic exploitation. Students of collective action would want to explore the preexisting multiracial and intersectional coalitions in place on the eve of the Fight for $15 campaign to inquire if such conditions increased the likelihood of mobilization in some localities over others.

The Fight for $15 also *diffused rapidly*, reaching hundreds of cities by 2014 and 2015. The spread of the protest also likely followed the activism of organizations and movements on the ground such as SEIU and Black Lives Matter. Once the campaign was up and running, national coordinating meetings were held in Chicago and other cities. Those cities with representatives at the national coordination meetings also were a likely source of direct diffusion of the movement. Structural equivalence and the success of pulling off the first national days of protest in 2013 also provided an effective model for emulation in cities that had not yet been reached by the protests. The simultaneous mobilizations were reported in real time on official Fight for $15 Twitter and Facebook accounts, potentially reaching hundreds of thousands of nonmobilized fast-food employees. Even inspiring a small fraction of the more than three million nonmobilized fast-food workers via social media could make a huge difference in subsequent national days of protests.

Beyond the core movement-emergence dimensions of interests, resource infrastructures, and identities, other related conditions should also be considered in understanding the geographical dispersion of the fast-food workers' movement. These would include demographic factors such as population size and the number of fast-food establishments in a city or county. The more fast-food employees in a region, the more likely that some will decide to participate in the struggle for a fifteen-dollar hourly wage. Regional labor histories would also need to be taken into account. Labor-based mobilization would be much more difficult in "right to work" states and regions with other hostile policies toward labor unions (Dixon 2008).

SUMMARY

This chapter introduced the processes of movement emergence and diffusion. While human agency and determination provide the first steps toward launching a collective action campaign, common interests, organizational and resource infrastructures, and collective identities shape the possibilities of sustaining mobilization. These dimensions are unevenly distributed over geographical space and time. Organizers can actively work to overcome these uneven distributions by building common interests and identities as well as appropriate resource infrastructures. Activists may marshal these tools of agency to sustain campaigns that confront structural economic and political power that prefers the status quo. The living-wage movement and the Fight for $15 national days of action offer recent examples of how it is possible to mobilize collectively and attempt to overcome the tremendous obstacles of economic exclusion in modern societies by spreading and sustaining a movement.

5 The Framing Process

The previous chapter introduced the main conditions associated with movement emergence and diffusion. Besides the brief attention given to oppositional consciousness and collective identities, chapter 4 largely emphasized structural and material factors such as interests, organizations, and resource infrastructures. The present chapter introduces the framing process, which focuses on cognitive dynamics (what is in people's heads) in the act of promoting social movement mobilization.

The discussion of framing provides an analytical means to study the ideological components related to social movement mobilizing. Framing involves the battle over ideas. Imagine the uphill struggle excluded social groups face in trying to organize in the ideological arena and overcoming the colonization of the public sphere (or even of people's minds) by a globalizing culture emphasizing individualism, consumerism, and apathy (Habermas 1989; Castells 2013). Recall from chapter 3, on theoretical approaches, that opportunities, threats, and resource infrastructures alone are not sufficient for social movement emergence—people's beliefs are equally important. Students of social movements usually employ the verb "to frame" to give agency to collective actors attempting to control their own discourse and narratives (Snow and Soule 2009). Framing work involves the active interpretation of grievances to broader audiences, including adherents, bystanders, the general public, targets, and adversaries (Snow 2004). Scholars also use the term "collective action frame" as a noun to illustrate particular frames associated with different movements or changes over time. The concept of framing within social movements was largely developed by David Snow, Robert Benford, and their collaborators (Snow et al. 1986; Snow and Benford 1988; Benford and Snow 2000; Snow

2004; Snow et al. 2014) as they built on Erving Goffman's work on frame analysis in microlevel interpersonal interactions (Goffman 1974).

When scholars use the term "frame," they figuratively mean that movements seek to focus public attention within the interior of a picture frame and mark off what is relevant from what is irrelevant (Snow 2004). This includes activists centering audiences on the plight and grievances of the social movement while avoiding other distractions not related to those grievances. Activists need to interpret the structural conditions and threats a population confronts in meaningful ways in order to motivate people into action and justify the strategies they are taking. These processes of converting good news and bad news into frames to encourage and guide collective action cannot be taken for granted. Often activists lack the capacity to frame current conditions into appropriate models for mobilization and fail to initiate movement activities (Snow and Corrigall-Brown 2005) or to attract influential allies (Bob 2005). In order to be convincing, frames and ideological appeals need to resonate with local cultural beliefs, symbols, and norms. This chapter addresses how activists frame their struggles. It covers several core framing tasks of movement leaders and cultural activists. Such discussions provide a means to understand the ideological components of social movements and assess their effectiveness. Such exercises also evaluate how various audiences, like the general public and potential sympathizers, receive mobilization messages. Framing shapes not only movement emergence but also movement outcomes (see chapter 7). Below, after we define key framing components, the case of protest music is given extended attention as an exemplar of a channel for creating and disseminating movement frames.

DEFINING FRAMES

A collective action frame is an interpretive schema that "simplifies and condenses the 'world out there' by selectively punctuating and encoding objects, situations, events, experiences, and sequences of actions within one's present or past environment" (Snow and Benford 1992: 137). Drawing on the work of Antonio Gramsci and Erving Goffman (Snow et al. 1986), the concept involves the construction and shaping of the social world in a manner consonant with encouraging and sustaining movement participation. In order for a movement to be potent, it must have a viable collective action frame. Social movements proffer ideas that emphasize shared injustices and underscore experiences of oppression in a fashion consistent with widespread cultural beliefs in an attempt to engender and maintain active resistance (Tarrow 2011). This active interpretation reinforces beliefs, collective identity, and solidarity among already committed movement members, evokes sympathy from potential supporters, and calls the attention of a broader population to a situation that is unjust and in need of change (Klandermans 1988). The agency attributed to movements in the framing perspective moves scholarship away from the classical and collective behavior theories mentioned in chapter 3, whereby analysts placed the emphasis on the psychological dispositions of individuals waiting to be attracted to a social movement that tapped into their anxieties (Snow 2004). In the framing process, much of the work on constructing social reality derives from movement activists and leaders as opposed to individuals targeted for movement participation and sympathy.

Examples of collective action frames include the "return to democracy" frame that emerged in Chile in 1983 during the Days of Protest against the Pinochet regime (Noonan 1995), and the "autonomy" and "workerism" frame in the wave of student and worker militancy that shook Italy between 1965 and 1975 (Tarrow 1989). When we consider major historical social movements in the United States, some of the defining collective action frames that immediately come to mind include "civil rights" for the black freedom struggle of the late 1950s and 1960s, and "We are the 99%" versus the "1%" for the Occupy Wall Street movement. Some frames become so potent and modular that multiple movements adopt them. This was precisely the case for the "civil rights" frame, as several other movements of the late 1960s and early 1970s used a similar frame, including second wave feminism, disability rights, LGBTQ rights, Asian American rights, Latinx rights, and even environmental rights. Snow and Benford refer to these widely applicable frames as "master frames," especially when they provide ideological coherence to an entire wave of protest (Snow and Benford 1992; Tarrow 2011). In the contemporary period, immigrant-based movements have also adopted "the rights" master frame (Bloemraad et al. 2016).

In developing a collective action frame, a movement conjures up historically significant events, shared experiences, and martyrs and vilifies oppressive target groups and social structures. To subsist and reproduce, collective action frames require active work and flexibility by movements. Researchers tend to consider movement documents and press, public demonstrations, statements by leaders, and mass media presentations as ways in which the collective action frame is conveyed to a broader population (McCammon 2012; Rohlinger 2015). Most of the literature on framing, however, is theoretically driven, with relatively few empirical investigations (Klandermans 1988; McAdam et al. 1996: 6) before the past two decades. By the early

2000s, Snow (2004) documented seventeen major publications that used empirical data to examine framing processes. Social media that are readily and publicly available, such as Twitter feeds and Facebook, and used by contemporary social movements, offer an increasingly promising line of empirical research on framing strategies (Earl and Garrett 2017; Abul-Fottouh and Fetner 2018).

FRAME ALIGNMENT STRATEGIES AND CORE FRAMING TASKS

Scholars use a number of terms to dissect the complex process of framing. While at first seeming abstract, analytically evaluating ideological appeals offers organizers crucial insights on how to convert grievances into compelling stories and narratives on why potential participants and the public should empathize with a movement. In early elaborations of the framing perspective, David Snow and his colleagues concentrated on four frame alignment processes that bring individual beliefs into congruence with a social movement (Snow et al. 1986). Table 3 list these four alignment processes.

The basic frame alignment processes demonstrate the work that activists must take on in order to reach large numbers of people, and the challenges they encounter in the process. Social movement leaders need to bridge or connect their frames to multiple groups across wide geographic spaces that are similarly situated in terms of grievances (i.e., structural equivalence). Cultural activists also need to sharpen the focus of the frame to particular grievances and events within appropriate cultural parameters that will emotionally move target populations with their messaging. In order to bring multiple groups into broader coalitions, the focal movement may need to incorporate other elements into its frame, as observed in the historic Women's Marches in the United States in 2017 and 2018.

Finally, because social movements are oppositional in nature, prevailing cultural circumstances may not allow their framing strategies to gain much traction. Such situations may call for the daunting task of frame transformation. Such rare historical occurrences may even be externally generated. This was precisely the case for dozens of countries around the world following the Second Vatican Council of the Catholic Church in the early 1960s. The church changed its doctrine to focusing on the poor and changed elite religious practices to allow the participation of lay persons in organizing rituals. In Latin America, the Second Vatican Council radicalized and transformed into a frame of "liberation theology," where local parishes organized a plethora of social movements in the late 1960s and 1970s

TABLE 3. Frame Alignment Strategies

Frame Alignment Strategy	Function
Frame bridging	Bringing previously unconnected sentiment pools into interaction with one another under an overarching frame (similar to the process of movement diffusion but at the cultural level, bringing similarly situated groups together)
Frame amplification	The clarification and invigoration of an interpretive frame that bears on a particular issue, problem, or set of events (highlighting particular grievances to bring out cultural values and strong emotional responses)
Frame extension	Extending the boundary of a frame to bring in the issues of other groups (often necessary when forming movement coalitions)
Frame transformation	"New values may have to be planted and nurtured, old meanings and understandings jettisoned, and erroneous beliefs or 'misframings' reframed" (p. 473) (e.g., radically changing religious practices and rituals that emphasize fatalism to encourage active movement participation in order to achieve social change in the present)

SOURCE: Snow et al. (1986).

guided by the idea that God demands the church to give preferential treatment to the poor of the region (Gutierrez 1973; Smith 1991).[1]

Snow and Benford (1988: 199), drawing from Wilson (1973) and Klandermans (1988), have further specified the framing process by delineating three core framing tasks: (1) diagnostic, (2) prognostic, and (3) motivational. Most contemporary work employs these categories to assess the efficacy of the framing process by a variety of movements. All three core framing tasks need to be implemented in order to successfully translate grievances and social problems into collective action.

Diagnostic framing involves a diagnosis of some event or aspect of social life as problematic and in need of alteration. Besides diagnosing social problems and properly defining them, activists must also convincingly attribute blame to agents causing the problem (Snow and Corrigall-Brown 2005). Both specifying the problem and attribution are crucial in this first phase of the core framing tasks. When the cause of the grievance derives from multiple sources, collective attribution becomes much more difficult and may even place the would-be movement in peril of even launching (Zepeda-Millán 2017). *Prognostic framing* offers a proposed solution to the diagnosed problem, which specifies what needs to be done. At this stage of the framing process, activists devise actual strategies for action. *Motivational framing* acts as a set of moral appeals to engage in collective action. Motivational framing draws heavily on emotionally laden pleas and strongly held cultural beliefs to push populations into action.

The diagnostic and prognostic framing tasks are directed toward achieving consensus mobilization—getting potential participants on the same page in terms of problems, targets, and strategy (Klandermans 1997). The third task, which concerns action mobilization, provides the motivational impetus for participation. This tripartite scheme of core framing tasks—diagnostic, prognostic, and motivational—provides a concise means for analyzing the multiple and interrelated ideational dimensions of social movements. In this theoretical framework, injustices are defined, as well as their causes; solutions are proposed; and mechanisms for activating potential participants are employed. Snow and Benford (1988) contend that movements need to pay adequate attention to each of the three core framing tasks. The more energy expended by movements on each of these tasks, the stronger the mobilization effort. Diagnostic and prognostic framing work in conjunction with motivational framing by identifying problems, assigning them causes, and offering strategies for their resolution. Motivational framing seizes on the mobilization potential they create through direct moral appeals and inducements (moral, solidary, and material) that encourage movement participation. Klandermans (1988) hypothesizes that motivational framing more likely targets committed supporters, and over time movements should focus increasing energy on this third core framing task once shared grievances and strategies for action are firmly established.

Snow and Benford (1988) also alert activists to two remaining concerns within the framing process: *frame centrality* and *frame vulnerabilities*. Frame centrality addresses the question of how important the grievance or social issue is on the hierarchy of issues that the public considers, or for the group targeted for mobilization. If the population is less aware or less troubled by the issue, the movement may need to engage in more educational work, such as holding teach-ins, workshops, and training sessions (with a heavy emphasis on diagnostic framing) instead of trying to mobilize protest events. This would be a scenario of low centrality. If the population to be mobilized is already acutely aware and deeply concerned about the issue, then activists may go directly into engaging in prognostic and motivational framing tasks detailed above. Public opinion surveys and polls (when available) provide one means to gauge and detect the level of frame centrality. Some locally based organizations even carry out their own needs-assessment surveys at the neighborhood or municipal level to identify the problems most pressing to communities in order to develop grassroots campaigns.

Frame vulnerabilities arise when a collective action frame overextends or comes under attack from outside groups (Snow and Benford 1988). Activists may overreach in the frame extension process in building a wider coalition. At some point in the coalitional negotiations, by incorporating other viewpoints and themes, the original frame may become watered down or lost in the multiple issues presented in a coalition platform (e.g., racism, gender discrimination, economic injustice, and environmental destruction). The other major dynamic that may make a frame susceptible is an assault from countermovements and their own frames, which may be diametrically opposed to the original movement's frame. Common contemporary examples include framing by movements for women's reproductive rights and movements to end gun violence attacked on the ideological plane by countermovements. Hence, movements facing counter-frames face an uphill struggle compared to collective challenges that lack strong ideological opposition (Benford and Hunt 2003).

Revolutionary Frames

In recent years there has been a marked shift from structural explanations of movement processes to explanations integrating more cultural concerns. A contributor to this change in emphasis is the work of John Foran (2005), which places the concept of "political cultures of resistance and opposition" in a central theoretical position in explaining revolutionary outcomes. The idea is similar to the framing perspective but it is used primarily to analyze revolutionary movements. Foran contends that oppositional political cultures vary historically and from place to place in their ability to shape the kinds of class alliances necessary for a revolutionary transfer of power (Foran 2009). By "political cultures of resistance and opposition," Foran (1997) means "the plurivocal and potentially radical ways of understanding one's circumstances that various groups within a society sometimes articulate to make sense of the political and economic changes they are living through. . . . Such cultures tap everything from historical memories of past conflicts to inchoate sentiments about injustice, to long-standing religious idioms and practices, to more formal elaborated political ideologies" (208–9). Hence, for revolutionary movements, scholars often draw on the idea of political cultures of resistance and opposition, while for social movement struggles they tend to use the language of collective action frames.

TABLE 4. Empirical Evidence of Framing Strategies

Type of Data Source	Type of Framing Most Commonly Found
Protest signs,[a] banners, and chants of demonstrators in collective events	Diagnostic and motivational
Activist websites, Facebook, social media feeds	Diagnostic, prognostic, motivational, bridging, extension
Speeches by movement leaders	Diagnostic, prognostic, and motivational (with an emphasis on motivational)
Protest songs	Diagnostic, prognostic, and motivational, bridging, extension, centrality
Other forms of activist art (murals, dance, poetry, etc.)	Diagnostic, prognostic, motivational, centrality
Flyers, pamphlets	Diagnostic, prognostic, motivational, bridging, extension

[a] Northeastern University Art and Design faculty and students have launched "Art of the March," an interactive archive of over six thousand protest signs that were created for the historic Boston Women's March on January 21, 2017. Designers, software developers, and archivists collaborated with the research team to create various digital means to examine, sort, and annotate the documents and images, resulting in this first public view of the entire collection (http://artofthemarch.boston/). Such a database would be an excellent resource for framing studies of the Women's Marches.

From Foran's definition of oppositional cultures we observe the conjuring up of "historical memories of past conflicts" in many cases. These include the use of Emiliano Zapata and the Mexican Revolution in the current struggles of the Zapatista indigenous peoples movement in Chiapas, or the invocation of Augusto Cesar Sandino and Farabundo Martí in revolutionary movements and political parties in Nicaragua and El Salvador, respectively (Selbin 2010). Revolutionary leaders and cultural activists transmit past struggles, injustices, martyrs, and heroic acts to populations in the present via oral testimony, especially through protest music, which can reach rural and semiliterate groups. We also see "long-standing religious idioms and practices" utilized in revolutionary movements around the world, including Islamic-based movements and those inspired by liberation theology Catholicism.

Table 4 reduces the abstraction of the framing literature by providing concrete data sources where students of collective action actually observe and empirically analyze movement framing tasks in a systematic fashion. Protestors themselves carry frames in the banners, signs, and chants found in demonstrations. When photography and video are used, these elements may be captured by activists and by researchers (Doerr and Milman 2014). Activist websites also provide a wealth of framing information along with more publicly available social media platforms such as Twitter feeds and Facebook pages. Some analysts even use sophisticated web scraping technologies to extract massive amounts of information ("big data") from internet and social media sites (DiGrazia 2017). Current social movement research is just beginning to capture the potential of these data sources for framing studies (Mosca 2014; Ince et al. 2017).

Observing and recording the speeches by movement leaders provides another avenue into collecting information on framing strategies. For larger historical movements, the speeches by key movement leaders may be archived as written texts in libraries (such as from Alice Paul, Dorothy Day, Fannie Lou Hamer, Mahatma Gandhi, Nelson Mandela, Cesar Chavez, Martin Luther King Jr., Dolores Huerta, Evo Morales, and Berta Cáceres). Movement displays of art and graffiti may offer insights into framing strategies of particular movements (see Jobin-Leeds and AgitArte [2016] for art examples produced by contemporary movements in the United States). In repressive regimes, graffiti in highly visible public places may be one of the only tactics for expressing a collective action frame, as discussed previously with everyday forms of resistance (Johnston 2011). Finally, protest music offers another powerful and multidimensional way of conveying frames to wide audiences that remains in people's heads long after the song or rally concludes (Eyerman and Jamison 1998; Roscigno and Danaher 2004; Roy 2010; Rosenthal and Flacks 2012). The following section delves further into the use of protest music as a crucial means of framing.

CASE STUDY OF PROTEST MUSIC

Popular music and songs offer one of the more underexplored arenas of social life where activists and cultural producers engage in framing processes (Van Dyke and Taylor 2018). While the documentary evidence is strong that music has served critical functions in resistance movements, from slave rebellions (Cruz 1999) to workers' movements (Roscigno and Danaher 2004; Roy 2010) and civil rights struggles (Carawan and Carawan 2007), music has been given less attention in the framing literature. In another historical example from participant testimony and archival evidence, we know that music played a central role in sustaining the five-year-long United Farm Workers strike in California in the late 1960s that later empowered the larger Chicano movement (Broyles-Gonzalez 1994) as well in movements against racism with the

Two Tone ska movement in Britain. The lyrics and rhythms of protest music can easily be analyzed from a framing perspective.

One of most powerful contemporary examples of protest music as an integral part of the framing process comes from Central America. In the late 1960s and early 1970s, the countries of the region (Costa Rica, El Salvador, Guatemala, Honduras, and Nicaragua) came under the influence of rock music from the global North, such as the Beatles, the Rolling Stones, and Credence Clearwater Revival. Local groups emulated the styles of the British and North American rockers until these were partially displaced by protest musicians from the global South. By the mid-1970s, protest music in Spanish from South America gained influence in Central America. The South American protest-music movement is known as *la nueva canción* (the new song). Some of the most notable musicians and groups in this movement included Quilapayún, Inti Illimani, Victor Jara, Violeta Parra (from Chile), Mercedes Sosa, Quinteto Tiempo (from Argentina), Ali Primera, Soledad Bravo, Lilia Vera (from Venezuela), Daniel Viglietti, Los Olimareños, Alfredo Zitarrosa (from Uruguay), and Carlos Puebla, Silvio Rodriguez, and Pablo Milanes (from Cuba). Mexico also produced several musical artists and groups in this era, such as Amparo Ochoa, José de Molina, and Judith Reyes. The movement strived to draw on traditional and indigenous rhythms with poetic songs that denounced economic injustice, state repression, and foreign intervention in the region. The music reached Central America via group tours, radio, and the diffusion of professional recordings on vinyl and cassette.

Arguably, the most influential protest group in Central America in the 1970s was the Venezuelan ensemble Los Guaraguao. In 1973 Los Guaraguao recorded a version of Ali Primera's "Techos de Cartón" (cardboard roofs) and renamed it "Casas de Cartón" (cardboard houses). It became an immediate hit in Central America, and disk jockeys gave it airtime on commercial radio stations, as well as on Catholic radio. The song tells the plight of a slum dweller living in a cardboard house. Slums grew rapidly in the 1970s in Latin America (Castells 1983) and continue to be a major problem in the global South in the twenty-first century (Davis 2007). The song appears below in its entirety.

LAS CASAS DE CARTÓN

Qué triste se oye la lluvia
en los techos de cartón.
Qué triste vive mi gente
en las casas de cartón.

Viene bajando el obrero
casi arrastrando sus pasos

por el peso del sufrir.
Mira que mucho ha sufrido
mira que pesa el sufrir.

Arriba deja la mujer preñada
abajo está la ciudad
y se pierde en su maraña.

Hoy es lo mismo que ayer,
es un mundo sin mañana.

Que triste se oye la lluvia
en los techos de cartón.
Que triste vive mi gente
en las casas de cartón.

Niños color de mi tierra
con sus mismas cicatrices
millonarios de lombrices
y por eso . . .
que triste viven los niños
en las casas de cartón.

Que alegres viven los perros,
casa del explotador.

Usted no lo va a creer
pero hay escuelas de perros
y les dan educación
pa' que no muerdan los diarios,
pero el patrón
hace años muchos años
que está mordiendo al obrero.

Que triste se oye la lluvia
en los techos de cartón
que lejos pasa la esperanza
en las casas de cartón.

THE CARDBOARD HOUSES

How sad does the rain sound
on the cardboard roofs.
How sad do my people live
in the cardboard houses.

The worker goes down the road
barely lifting his feet
because of the weight of suffering.
Look how hard he has suffered
look how heavy is the suffering.

Above on the hill he leaves his pregnant wife
below is the city and he gets lost in its maze.

Today is the same as yesterday,
a world without tomorrow.

How sad does the rain sound
on the cardboard roofs.
How sad do my people live
in the cardboard houses.

Children the color of my land
with the same scars
millionaires of parasitic worms
and for this . . .
how sad the children live
in the cardboard houses.

How joyful the dogs live,
in the exploiter's house.

You are not going to believe it
but there are schools for dogs
and they provide them education
so the dogs do not bite the newspapers,
but the boss
for years and years
has been biting the worker.

How sad the rain sounds
on the cardboard roofs.
How far away hope passes
in the cardboard houses.

The song circulated throughout Central America in the mid-1970s. The musical artists performing the song were aligned with social movements in Venezuela. The song's lyrics largely carry out the functions of *diagnostic framing*. They emotionally dramatize the plight of the urban poor in Latin America in general. The lyrics begin by setting a somber mood of how sad the rain sounds on the roofs of cardboard houses. The next stanza describes a worker meandering down from the slums into the city practically tripping from the weight of his own suffering. The song then turns even darker with the comment that for the worker "today is the same as yesterday, a world without tomorrow," and concludes by emphasizing that "hope" is "far away." The song also makes a reference to the lack of access to healthcare and sanitation with the mention of children, sadly residing in cardboard houses, as "millionaires of parasitic worms." In the final stanzas, the song shifts from defining social problems of extreme poverty, sanitation, and inadequate housing to a class analysis attributing blame to the rich. The lyrics juxtapose the suffering of the worker and children in the slums with the neighborhood of business owners, and how the "exploiters" are so wealthy they send their pet dogs to school to learn not to chew up the daily newspaper.

The influence of the song cannot be overstated. The majority of the adult population of Central America even today is likely familiar with "Las Casas de Cartón." Indeed, in an open-ended survey question by the author of over one thousand 2014 May Day participants in El Salvador and Honduras (discussed in chapter 6), respondents more frequently reported "Las Casas de Cartón" as their favorite protest song over any other song (21% in El Salvador, and 13.6% in Honduras). It is interesting how the song discusses the conditions of inequality in the abstract and does not offer prognostic or motivational frames (probably explaining why the song was initially permitted on commercial radio even under authoritarian regimes). Prognostic and motivational framing would be left to the cultural work of local musicians who aligned with social movements in the region in the late 1970s. "Casas de Cartón" did tap into a period of economic slow-down in the region after a relatively prosperous decade of growth in the 1960s. The cost of living and inflation increased markedly in the mid-1970s. In El Salvador social movements such as the Unión de Pobladores de Tugurios formed over the conditions in the slums and shantytowns, and many of the mobilizing grievances of the mid-1970s centered on economic issues such as rising prices.

By the mid-to-late 1970s, dozens of protest musical ensembles emerged throughout Central America; in most cases (with the exception of Costa Rica), they supported social movements seeking the overthrow of military governments. In contrast to the emulation of rock groups from the global North in the early 1970s, many of the new musical ensembles gave themselves indigenous names and identities such as Mazehual and Kin Lalat (in Guatemala), and Yolocamba Ita, Tepehuani, and Mahucutah (in El Salvador). Nicaragua experienced a particularly powerful protest musical movement with groups like Pancasan and the Mejia Godoy brothers (Carlos and Luis Enrique), and the groups sang songs similar to "Casas de Cartón," such as "Juan Terremoto," "El Cristo de Palacaguina," and "Quincho Barrilete." By the late 1970s and early 1980s, the repression intensified throughout the isthmus (Brockett 2005). In correspondence to the military repression, the protest musicians redoubled their efforts and called on local populations to resist, as this song from El Salvador illustrates:

DIOS SIGUE EXIGIENDO LA LIBERACIÓN

Aunque acallen la voz, seguiremos gritando,
Seguiremos cantando por la libertad

Aunque maten al pueblo, seguiremos de nuevo,
Nos organizaremos por la libertad

Coro: *Por las fabricas, en las milpas, por tugurios y escuelas Dios sigue*
    gritando, Dios sigue exigiendo,
"La liberación," "La liberación"
Dios sigue gritando, Dios sigue exigiendo,
"La liberación," "La liberación

Aunque torturen al preso y quebranten sus huesos,
Seguiremos tu ejemplo por la libertad

Aunque maten al cura, seguiremos a Cristo,
Las bienaventuranzas de la libertad
Por las fabricas, en las milpas, por tugurios y escuelas Dios sigue
    gritando, Dios sigue exigiendo,
"La liberación," "La liberación"
Dios sigue gritando, Dios sigue exigiendo,
"La liberación," "La liberación

Aunque acercan cantones, y desalojen las fabricas,
No desistiremos por la libertad

Aunque reciben las armas del extranjero,
No tendremos miedo por la libertad

Por las fabricas, en las milpas, por tugurios y escuelas Dios sigue
    gritando, Dios sigue exigiendo,
"La liberación," "La liberación"
Dios sigue gritando, Dios sigue exigiendo,
"La liberación," "La liberación

GOD CONTINUES DEMANDING LIBERATION

Even though they silence the voice, we will continue shouting,
We will continue singing for freedom

Even though they kill people, we will begin anew,
We will organize ourselves for freedom

Chorus: Through the factories, in the cornfields, through the
    shantytowns and schools, God continues shouting, God keeps
    demanding,
"Liberation," "Liberation"
God continues shouting, God keeps demanding,
"Liberation," "Liberation"

Even though they torture a prisoner and break his bones,
We will continue your example for freedom

Even though they kill a priest, we will continue to follow Christ,
The blessings of freedom

Through the factories, in the cornfields, through the shantytowns and
    schools
God continues shouting, God keeps demanding,
"Liberation," "Liberation"
God continues shouting, God keeps demanding,
"Liberation," "Liberation"

Even though they surround the villages and dislodge the occupied
    factories,
We will not stop for freedom

Even though they receive arms from abroad,
We will not be afraid for freedom

Through the factories, in the cornfields, through the shantytowns and
    schools
God continues shouting, God keeps demanding,
"Liberation," "Liberation"
God continues shouting, God keeps demanding,
"Liberation," "Liberation"

This song was likely circulating in El Salvador in the period around 1979 (because of the level of repression and the reference to the occupied factories).[2] The social movements were strengthening in the context of massive state repression by a military government. Songs such as this were performed or broadcasted on the Catholic radio, in schools, churches, and Christian base communities, providing one of the few channels to build an oppositional consciousness (Morris and Braine 2001) and sustain and reinforce collective action frames outside of the surveillance of the security forces—especially when people left activities with the songs and lyrics humming in their heads. The above song performs several *diagnostic framing* tasks. It discusses multiple acts of brutal repression and human rights abuses (killing priests, torturing prisoners, invading villages, etc.). The perpetrators—the military government and its allies—are not explicitly named in the song; it was unnecessary at this stage in the struggle, as the security forces were killing dozens if not hundreds of people per month.

Just as forceful as the diagnostic frame is the *prognostic frame* of how the resistance will continue to organize in a broad coalition (with the mentioning of multiple sectors—shantytowns, schools for teachers and students, cornfields for the peasant sector, and factories) despite massive state violence. Indeed, a wide multisectoral struggle is likely the only means to withstand opposition to dictatorship (Schock 2015b). A single sector alone (e.g., the educational sector) is not sufficient. Finally, perhaps the most haunting component of the song is the *motivational framing* whereby God himself is invoked, demanding participation in the struggle for national liberation in a population where 95 percent subscribe to Catholicism (during the high point of liberation theology). The repetition of the chorus, "God continues shouting, God keeps demanding liberation," helps explain why so many may risk their lives and remain active in a movement that faces so many repressive threats.

In the 1970s and 1980s, cultural workers and artists in Central America performed hundreds of original protest songs similar to the two above. The artists interpreted the grievances of the period in ways that resonated with the populations they targeted, using Catholic symbols, popular and local working-class jargon and humor, and composing songs in familiar and often danceable rhythms such as *cumbias, rancheras, merengue,* and *salsa.* It remains the task of contemporary anthropologists, ethnomusicologists, sociologists, historians, and students of social movements to document and preserve these precious cultural artifacts of rebellion and compelling empirical examples of the movement framing process.

FRAMING IN THE NEOLIBERAL ERA

Tarrow (2013) has argued that the language of contention shifts and evolves in different historical settings. This is clearly the case with Latin American protest music. After the violent conflicts and revolutions of Central America simmered down by the early 1990s, the region transitioned to neoliberalism and *relatively* more democratic governments controlled by financial elites in place of military dictatorships (Robinson 2003). In this new era, the protest music survived with many of the same songs from the 1970s and 1980s blasting out of speakers during May Day marches and commemorative anniversaries (e.g., the Nicaraguan Revolution; the 1944 Revolution in Guatemala; the martyrdom of Monsignor Romero in El Salvador). Between 1990 and the current period, one of the grievances driving the largest mobilizations has centered on the policies related to economic liberalization and neoliberalism (Almeida 2014b). These policies include free trade, privatization, austerity, subsidy cuts, wage freezes, and labor flexibility. And once again, the protest music and cultural artists innovated and adapted to the (neoliberal) era with protest songs, both in social movement campaigns against economic liberalization measures and in electoral contests that support antineoliberal political parties. In order to attract new generations of youth, contemporary protest musicians augment the traditional rhythms of *corridos, rancheras,* and *cumbias* with rap and reggaeton, and change the lyrics to some of the most popular songs of commercial musical stars, such as Juanes and Daddy Yankee. Below is an example of a protest song that accompanied the campaign against the Central American Free Trade Agreement (CAFTA) in Costa Rica—one of the largest social movements in the modern history of the country (Raventos 2013).

DERROTEMOS AL TLC EN COSTA RICA

Costa Rica tiene en su territorio
la gente de un Pueblo que es grande en su historia
que sabe que es libre que tiene cerebro y dirá que No

Pues con el tratado perdemos la tierra perdemos la gracia de la libertad

Juntemos los ticos nuestras voces todas votemos unidos No al TLC

Juanito Mora mira desde el cielo él es el testigo. Pues de nuevo Walker pretende estas tierras que siempre ha querido para esclavizar

Perdemos el ICE, perdemos la CAJA perdemos semillas, agua y libertad

Nos dicen mentiras, sí tendremos sed hay gato encerrado No al TLC[3]

WE WILL DEFEAT CAFTA IN COSTA RICA

Costa Rica has in its territory
the people of a Nation that is great in their history
that know they are free, that have a brain and will say No

Since with the free trade treaty we lose our land, we will lose the benefits of freedom

Ticos/Costa Ricans shall get together with all our voices and vote united No to CAFTA

Juanito Mora looks eagerly from heaven, he is our witness. Because once again William Walker aspires to take these lands that he has always wanted to enslave

We lose ICE [telecommunications and electrical power], we lose social security [healthcare], we lose seeds, water, and freedom

They tell us lies, we will be thirsty, there is a scam going on, No to CAFTA

The above song appeared late in the social movement campaign against the Central American Free Trade Agreement in Costa Rica (Raventós Vorst 2018). After four years of mass mobilizations, general strike attempts, and other creative protests, the movement forced the government to hold a popular referendum on CAFTA in late 2007 (Almeida 2014b). It was the first referendum in the history of the country. The song surfaced in mid-2007 to rally the population to vote no on CAFTA in the referendum as part of a larger and organized cultural movement that accompanied the anti-CAFTA protest campaign.

The musical artist clearly engages in the core framing tasks of diagnostic, prognostic, and motivational framing. The *diagnostic framing* can be found in the predicted problems and threats that the free trade treaty proposes. In the context of one of the strongest welfare states in the global South (Edelman 1999), the lyrics remind citizens that they will lose access to basic utilities (the ICE) and healthcare (the CAJA) if the treaty is approved (because of privatization). Over 80 percent of the Costa Rican population maintains medical coverage by the state. The song also reminds los Ticos (Costa Ricans) that there were earlier invasions from North America, such as when William Walker led a military expedition in the mid-nineteenth century into northern Costa Rica and southern Nicaragua in order to expand slavery from the southern United States. Costa Ricans united other native Central American armies in Honduras, Nicaragua, and El Salvador to defeat Walker in a military campaign under Juanito Mora's direction as president of Costa Rica. The *prognostic frame* is straightforward and simple, urging the population to vote no on the referendum in a united and collective fashion. Several *motivational frames* are used, especially at the opening of the song. The Costa Rican population is positioned as a proud people that have "a brain" and "know what it means to be free" and will not be fooled by this new treaty propagated by outsiders lacking in national commitments.

Such songs endure into the 2010s with the deepening of neoliberalism and even democratic reversals. For example, several protest songs were immediately created during the protests against perceived electoral fraud in Honduras in 2017 and 2018 (Sosa 2018) and massive state repression in Nicaragua in 2018. Protest songs continue to proliferate from Argentina (with groups such as Santa Revuelta supporting the unemployed *piquetero* movement) to Mexico and North America. Much more work remains on the multiple dimensions of framing and music.

THE DARK SIDE OF FRAMING

This chapter ends on a less optimistic note by considering the framing by racist and backlash movements. So far, the discussion has centered on the use of framing by excluded social groups seeking progressive social change to improve current circumstances or avoid impending threats. Others have examined the role of framing by right-wing movements and political parties. These "discursive opportunities" may lead to increases in right-wing tacks and hate crimes (Koopmans and Olzak 2004). The rise of right-wing electoral political parties in the United States and Europe over the past twenty years gives such entities a public voice to advocate for anti-immigrant, xenophobic, and pronationalist/nativist agendas. With the legitimacy of elected positions and representation in government, reactionary framing of social problems, which includes blaming the most vulnerable groups in society (Bobo 2017), gives those views an outlet in mainstream mass media sources such as television and newspapers, which are then reamplified through social media platforms. With growing representation in European parliaments and influence in US politics (Gest 2016), such parties provide a protective cover for even more extremist groups to carry out hate crimes and other extraparliamentary actions.

SUMMARY

Understanding framing processes offers a critical missing link between structural conditions of inequality and grievances on one side, and the emergence and diffusion of collective action on the other. Activists need to interpret pollution outbreaks, discrimination, and labor exploitation in compelling ways to affected populations in order to initiate a social movement campaign. Once framing work begins, movement leaders must draw on appropriate cultural tool kits and disseminate convincing messages via websites, social media, music, banners, speeches, and other innovative pathways. Much more empirical investigation is called for to understand how this creative framing work actually arrives and is absorbed by intended audiences. Protest music offers one encouraging avenue to understand the framing process in actual social movements. The explosion of web-based social media technologies provides a massive amount of real-time framing data that is in its infancy in the potential knowledge it can yield. The communication role of social media in conveying collective action frames across broad audiences is likely responsible for some of the largest mobilizations witnessed in the United States and across the world in recent decades.

SUGGESTED READINGS ON THE FRAMING PROCESS

Benford, Robert, and David Snow. 2000. "Framing Processes and Social Movements: An Overview and Assessment." *Annual Review of Sociology* 26: 611–39.
Jobin-Leeds, Greg, and AgitArte. 2016. *When We Fight We Win.* New York: New Press.

Johnston, Hank, and John Noakes. 2005. *Frames of Protest: Social Movements and the Framing Perspective.* Lanham, MD: Rowman & Littlefield.

Mansbridge, Jane, and Aldon Morris. 2001. *Oppositional Consciousness: The Subjective Roots of Social Protest.* Chicago: University of Chicago Press.

Snow, David A., Rens Vliegenthart, and Pauline Ketelaars. 2018. "The Framing Perspective on Social Movements: Its Conceptual Roots and Architecture." In *The Wiley-Blackwell Companion to Social Movements,* edited by D. Snow, S. Soule, H. Kriesi, and H. McCammon, 392–410. Oxford: Blackwell.

Snow, David A. 2004. "Framing Processes, Ideology, and Discursive Fields." In *The Blackwell Companion to Social Movements,* edited by D. Snow, S. Soule, and H. Kriesi, 1, 380–412. Malden, MA: Blackwell.

———, and Robert Benford. 1988. "Ideology, Frame Resonance, and Participant Mobilization." *International Social Movement Research* 1: 197–217.

———, and Robert Benford. 1992. "Master Frames and Cycles of Protest." In *Frontiers in Social Movement Theory,* edited by A. Morris and C. Mueller, 133–55. New Haven, CT: Yale University Press.

———, Robert Benford, Holly McCammon, Lyndi Hewitt, and Scott Fitzgerald. 2014. "The Emergence, Development, and Future of the Framing Perspective: 25+ Years Since 'Frame Alignment.'" *Mobilization* 19(1): 23–46.

———, and Catherine Corrigall-Brown. 2005. "Falling on Deaf Ears: Confronting the Prospect of Non-resonant Frames." In *Rhyming Hope and History: Activism and Social Movement Scholarship,* edited by David Croteau, Charlotte Ryan, and William Hoynes, 222–38. Minneapolis: University of Minnesota Press.

———, E. Rochford, S. Worden, and R. Benford. 1986. "Frame Alignment Processes, Micromobilization, and Movement Participation." *American Sociological Review* 51: 464–81.

———, Rens Vliegenthart, and Pauline Ketelaars. 2018. "The Framing Perspective on Social Movements: Its Conceptual Roots and Architecture." In *The Wiley-Blackwell Companion to Social Movements,* edited by D. Snow, S. Soule, H. Kriesi, and H. McCammon, 392–410. Oxford: Blackwell.

Tarrow, Sidney. 2013. *The Language of Contention: Revolutions in Words, 1688–2012.* Cambridge: Cambridge University Press.

SUGGESTED READING ON MUSIC AND SOCIAL MOVEMENTS

Blacking, John. 1995. *Music, Culture, and Experience: Selected Papers of John Blacking.* Chicago: University of Chicago Press.

Broyles-Gonzalez, Yolanda. 1994. *El Teatro Campesino: Theater in the Chicano Movement.* Austin: University of Texas Press.

Carawan, Guy, and Candie Carawan. 2007. *Sing for Freedom: The Story of the Civil Rights Movement through Its Songs.* Montgomery, AL: NewSouth Books.

Cruz, Jon. 1999. *Culture on the Margins: The Black Spiritual and the Rise of American Cultural Interpretation.* Princeton, NJ: Princeton University Press.

Eyerman, Ron, and Andrew Jamison. 1998. *Music and Social Movements: Mobilizing Traditions in the Twentieth Century.* Cambridge: Cambridge University Press.

Kirk, John M. 1984. "Revolutionary Music Salvadorean Style: Yolocamba I Ta." *Literature and Contemporary Revolutionary Culture* 1: 338–52.

Moore, William H. 1991. "Rebel Music: Appeals to Rebellion in Zimbabwe." *Political Communication and Persuasion* 8: 125–38.

Roscigno, Vincent, and William F. Danaher. 2004. *The Voice of Southern Labor: Radio, Music and Textile Strikes, 1929–1934.* Minneapolis: University of Minnesota Press.

Rosenthal, Rob, and Richard Flacks. 2012. *Playing for Change: Music and Musicians in the Service of Social Movements.* New York: Routledge.

Roy, William. 2010. *Reds, Whites, and Blues: Social Movements, Folk Music, and Race in the United States.* Princeton, NJ: Princeton University Press.

6   Individual Recruitment and Participation

Why do some individuals join social movements while many more stay at home and do not participate? This is the fundamental question of individual recruitment and participation in social movements. Chapter 4 focused on movement emergence and diffusion at the *group* or macrolevel of collective action. Movement participation addresses the *individual* level of social movements. Obviously, this is a critical level to explore. How is collective action even possible if individuals do not take the time and risk to join in social movement activities? Hence, this microlevel of political and social life is vital to the understanding of the origins of collective action and how movements build up into a critical mass with the participation of individuals (Oliver 2015). Only through the conscious volition of ordinary people deciding to join in a demonstration or other collective event can actions concatenate into a social movement.

The interest in social movement participation traces back to the classical social movement theories that originate from the collective behavior tradition. As repeatedly stated throughout this work, the classical theories emphasized the psychological strains pushing individuals to participate in emotionally charged collective action events such as mobs, riots, and authoritarian politics and mass parties, especially during periods of social disintegration (Useem 1998). The earliest theorizing focused on beliefs and values of the individual *exclusively*. Collective behavior scholars hypothesized that people harbored certain predispositions to join a protest movement. These could be psychological deficits, such as alienation, isolation, and low self-esteem (see Hoffer's *The True Believer* [1951]). Other belief attributes such as political ideology also became of interest along with various deprivation theories that focused on deep grievances (Gurr 1970; 2015).

Interest in explaining individual movement participation began methodically and empirically (i.e., beyond vague theories and impressions) in the 1960s. Advances in survey methods and automated computation that swept through the social sciences in general at this time made it easier to systematically assess and measure precipitants and levels of individual movement participation. Analysts could employ standardized questionnaires, random sampling techniques, and more precise measurements for quantitative studies of participation. In addition, the protest wave of the 1960s increased academic attention on nonroutine political participation. Scholars focused their participation studies on the civil rights movement as well as urban riots and uprisings (Paige 1971; Feagin and Hahn 1973). The federal government provided large grants for studies of riot participation in the late 1960s and early 1970s—providing a financial incentive to advance research (National Advisory Commission on Civil Disorders 2016 [1968]). These combined forces led to the modernization of recruitment and participation studies within social movement scholarship.

Currently there are several large studies that try to measure social movement participation nationally and cross-nationally, such as the World Values Survey (briefly discussed in chapter 2). Similar databases that incorporate questions about social movement participation and focus on specific world regions include the Latinobarometro, AmericasBarometer, Eurobarometer, African Barometer, and the Asian Barometer. These types of surveys allow us to compare protest involvement across countries and ask important questions about the national contexts of social movement participation, including comparisons along gender and class lines (Dodson 2015; 2016a). They also allow us to monitor the level of protest occurring around the world over time. Recent scholarship using the World Values Survey suggests that protest is increasing across the planet in the first quarter of the twenty-first century (Dodson 2011; Jakobsen and Listhaug 2014). More information about these data sets and how to access them is provided in table 5.

Notwithstanding the valuable information provided in large-scale and multicountry surveys that integrate questions about protest participation, these data sources have limitations for understanding individual involvement in collective action. Most important, large-scale population surveys are designed to measure dozens of social dimensions beyond protest participation (e.g., poverty, crime, trust, religiosity, discrimination, occupational status, education). The protest participation questions are asked in a very general manner such as, "Have you participated in a demonstration in the past year?" With this form of survey design we lack much of the specific

TABLE 5. Data Resources for Protest Participation

Data Source	Details	Location
Caught in the Act of Protest: Contextualizing Contestation (CCC)	Protest surveys in 110 actual protest demonstrations across 13 countries (including in Europe and Latin America). Data collected between 2009 and 2017. Issues include May Day, austerity, LGBT pride, antiracism, and environment among others.	http://www .protestsurvey.eu /index.php?page= index
World Values Survey	Comparative survey that covers over 65 nations across the world. Survey waves include 1981, 1990–91, 1995–97, 1999–2001, 2005–7, 2010–14, 2017–18.	http://www .worldvaluessurvey .org
European Values Survey	Comparative survey that covers up to 47 nations across Europe. Survey waves include 1981, 1990, 1999, 2008, 2017.	http://www.european valuesstudy.eu/
AmericasBarometer Survey	Comparative survey that covers 34 nations, including all of North, Central, and South America as well as a significant number of countries in the Caribbean (with stratified, nationally representative samples). Survey waves include 2004, 2006, 2008, 2010, 2012, 2014, 2016–17.	https://www .vanderbilt.edu /lapop/
Afrobarometer	Comparative survey that covers up to 35 nations across Africa. Survey waves include 1999–2001, 2002–3, 2005–6, 2008–9, 2011–13, 2014–15, 2016–17.	http://www .afrobarometer .org/
Asian Barometer	Comparative survey that covers up to 18 nations across East and Southeast Asia. Survey waves include 2001–3, 2005–8, 2010–12, 2014–16.	http://www .asianbarometer .org/
Latinobarómetro	An annual public opinion survey that involves some 20,000 interviews in 18 Latin American countries, representing more than 600 million inhabitants. First year of survey was 1995.	http://www .latinobarometro .org/lat.jsp
Arab Barometer	Comparative survey that covers up to 12 nations across the Arab world. Survey waves include 2006–8, 2010–11, 2012–14, 2016–17.	http://arabbarometer .org/
Global Barometer Survey	Combines Asian, Latino, Arabic, and Afrobarometers into one data set containing 55 countries (three continents, 48% of world population).	http:// globalbarometer .net
The Latino National Survey (LNS)	Contains 8,634 completed interviews of self-identified Latino/Hispanic residents of the United States. Interviewing began on November 17, 2005, and continued through August 4, 2006.	http://www.icpsr .umich.edu /icpsrweb/RCMD /studies/20862

context in which the decision to participate in a social movement actually occurs. Andretta and Della Porta (2014: 309) find that such national surveys have several weaknesses when analyzing protest behavior: "Declaring past participation in for instance, 'demonstrations,' does not say anything about what demonstration was attended, on what issues, organized by whom, and for what reasons. The resulting sub-sample of individuals who declare that they have protested is the aggregation of very heterogenous individuals, who mobilized for very different issues and for very different reasons." In short, we do not have information on the microcontext in the decision of an individual to participate in collective action.

To overcome the shortcomings of general population surveys, social movement scholars have used other archival materials and designed their own specific movement surveys. Some of the most influential individual participation research projects have been investigations that focus on a specific social movement or even protest campaign. These include McAdam's study (1988) of the Mississippi Freedom Summer campaign within the civil rights movement; Opp, Gern, et al.'s (1995) research on the demonstrations that brought down the East German government in 1989; Fisher et al.'s (2005) work on participation in global economic justice movements; Heaney and Rojas (2015) on anti-war demonstrations; Reese et al.'s (2015) surveys of World Social Forum participation; and Terriquez's (2017) study of Latinx youth activism. These studies benefited from the evolution of theoretical developments in participation research and used data that provided the microcontext shaping the individual's decision to take part in social movement activities.

EARLY BREAKTHROUGHS IN UNDERSTANDING INDIVIDUAL PARTICIPATION

The theoretical work of Anthony Orum (1974) helped push movement participation research into the modern era. Orum developed his multidimensional model of movement participation through empirical research on students in the civil rights movements. He retained psychological factors from collective behavior theory but placed them in a rational action perspective. In particular, he analyzed the role of subjective dissatisfaction and self-esteem in movement participation—high levels of either make one more likely to join in a protest (also see Paige's [1971] similar findings on urban riots). He also examined what current scholars refer to as "collective identity" in a dimension he called "subgroup identification." Finally, Orum developed a facilitating condition named "unstructured work routine."

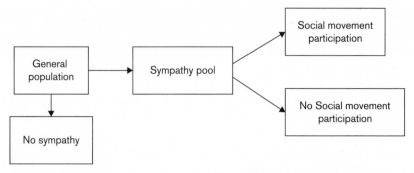

FIGURE 11.   Pathway to Participation. Construction based on Klandermans (1997).

In short, Orum presaged many of the core components that later analysts of movement participation would develop over the next four decades. His multidimensional model advanced scholarship to move beyond a single factor (such as ideology or psychological stress) driving individual engagement in protest. He demonstrated the importance of *multiple* correlates inducing people to collective action. The more these forces impinge on or characterize a person, the more likely the person feels motivated to contribute to mobilizing in his or her community. Factors such as self-esteem are now incorporated as personal efficacy: those with greater confidence that their individual efforts can make a difference are more likely to join a social movement. Orum also sensitized students of social movements to take collective identities and flexible work schedules into account when trying to understand the individual participation process.

By the 1980s, scholars began to consistently incorporate a series of ideological and structural features to predict protest behavior. One of the key breakthroughs in understanding participation involved explicitly acknowledging that only a small percentage of the population actually participates in demonstrations and social movements. Indeed, Marck Lichbach (1995) invokes the "5% rule" in stating that most revolutionary movements that threaten to overthrow national governments mobilize only 5 percent of the national population, or less. With this advancement in mind, scholars have developed better research designs in understanding the contours of political participation. Hence, contemporary scholarship outlines the steps toward participation from the general population, to a sympathy pool, to final participation (Klandermans 1997). En route to final participation, substantial portions of the population drop out. Figure 11 illustrates this process using a simplified version of Klandermans's (1997: 23) model of the steps toward participation.

CONTEMPORARY CONDITIONS PUSHING PARTICIPATION

Contemporary studies of movement participation usually begin by defining the sympathy pool and concentrating on what makes an individual move from positive attitudes toward the movement in question to actual participation. This is an essential distinction in order to understand the process of participation. It first acknowledges that individuals motivated and recruited to social movement activity come from a smaller subgroup of society than the general population (Andretta and Della Porta 2014; Munson 2010). The step model to participation presented in figure 11 also recognizes that sympathy with a social movement may not necessarily satisfy the conditions to actually participate in collective action. Therefore, much of the focus centers on explaining the differences between individuals in the sympathy pool who actually participate in a protest event and those who do not. Bert Klandermans (1997: 23) refers to the sympathy pool as the "mobilization potential" to collectively organize around a specific issue, and defines this subpopulation as "those members of a society, who in one way or another, may potentially be mobilized by a social movement. It includes everyone who has a positive attitude toward the movement; hence its boundaries need not coincide with those of the group whose interests it defends or represents."

A related issue involves the actual size of the sympathy pool. For new issues that have not reached the awareness of the general public, activists must work at creating a sympathy pool or expanding it. To move from the abstract to the concrete in this discussion of sympathy pools, let us introduce specific movements and campaigns. An example would be the problem of global warming when it became an emerging concern in the 1980s. At this stage, scientists and environmentalists worked on consciousness-raising strategies to influence public opinion. Mass mobilizations over climate change did not build momentum until the 2000s when the sympathy pool grew large enough to attract hundreds of thousands to participate in rallies and marches. The size of the population concerned with the issue in question thus informs the strategy for movement activists and leaders.[1] Is this the time for educational events, workshops, and teach-ins in order to create a sympathy pool for future actions, or do sufficient numbers of sympathetic people exist to recruit for protest events?

This issue can also be considered in geographic terms. In regions that lack support for a particular social movement, an educational awareness and community-building strategy may make more sense at first than trying to mobilize direct actions. The farmworker movement in California provides such a case of creating sympathy pools in new geographic regions. Cesar Chavez moved with his family from Los Angeles to the rural Central Valley town of Delano in 1962. The organizing team (including Dolores Huerta) conducted needs assessment surveys in their first years in the community to determine the most pressing issues of the region. With this information the team developed a credit union and insurance programs for farmworker families in several rural towns. This early community work helped build a sympathy pool of potential participants when the historic Delano farmworker grape strike erupted in late 1965 (Ganz 2009)—a strike that endured for five years.

In the fast-food worker campaigns that battle for a living wage, the sympathy pool would include most fast-food restaurant employees below manager. However, only a small portion of the 3.5 million fast-food industry workers actually participated in protests and strikes in the national days of action between 2013 and 2018 (recall the maps in chapter 4). What are the differences between the fast-food workers that decided to protest for higher wages and those workers that did not participate? In the historic Women's Marches in 2017 and 2018 against President Trump, the pool of sympathizers would include most of those that voted for Democratic candidate Hilary Clinton and others against the political platform and policies of the new president, such as youth under the voting age. Nearly sixty-six million citizens voted for former senator and secretary of state Clinton, but only four to five million people participated in the Women's Marches two months later. What conditions pushed less than 10 percent of citizens in the sympathy pool to join in the mass mobilizations against the newly installed Trump administration? How are these participants differentially situated from those in the sympathy pool that did not join in the record-breaking protests of January 2017 and January 2018?

Occupy Wall Street was one of the largest movements against economic inequality in the United States. During the Great Recession of 2008–9, millions of people lost their jobs and homes. Occupy activists framed their struggle as 99 percent of the population against an elite and greedy 1 percent. When the Occupy movement took off in late 2011, the actual number of participants in the protest encampments, strikes, and demonstrations was likely less than three hundred thousand people. Out of the millions of U.S. residents suffering the consequences of the economic recession, student debt, housing foreclosure/eviction, and the increasing concentration of wealth, only a small fraction actually joined an Occupy encampment or even a rally. Many sympathizers were also "conscience constituents" from the upper middle class (McCarthy and Zald 1977). What compelled people to move from being sympathizers to being actual Occupiers?

The above examples highlight how the understanding of participation in social movements has switched focus from what drives the general population into social movements to decisions of individuals within specific sympathy pools to join protest demonstrations. In recent years a number of dimensions have been documented that especially increase the likelihood of individual participation from the subpopulation of those generally concerned with the issue or cause in question. These dimensions include biographical availability, ideological/political beliefs, social networks, membership in organizations, collective identities, past participation experience, and new social media technologies.

Biographical Availability

Biographical availability involves one's life stage and amount of discretionary time or capacity to participate in social movement activities (McAdam 1988). Orum (1974) first focused scholarly attention on this dimension by emphasizing the importance of unstructured work routines in facilitating political participation. Life stages that are particularly conducive to movement participation include youth, young adults, and senior citizens. The related condition of unstructured work routines also includes the unemployed, the part-time employed, students, teachers (with summer breaks), and the retired. If an individual in the sympathy pool fits in one of these categories, we would expect her to be relatively more likely to participate in collective action.

We can observe many historical and contemporary examples of young people as the central participants in major movements and protest waves. Young adults dominated the protest wave of the 1960s and early 1970s in the United States. The civil rights, Chicano, and anti-war movements counted on a mass base of young people to participate in demonstrations and protests. A stereotypical mantra of the late 1960s to "not trust anyone over thirty years old" provides one piece of anecdotal evidence of youth dominance in the protest wave. One of the lasting legacies of the Chicano movement of the late 1960s and early 1970s can be found in the student-based organization MEChA—Movimiento Estudiantil Chicanx de Aztlán. MEChA chapters have proliferated across the United States in high schools, community colleges, and universities and encourage political participation for Latinx youth (Armbruster-Sandoval 2017).[2]

More recently, Milkman (2017) found that college-educated millennials facing employment precarity initiated four prominent movements in the contemporary United States: Black Lives Matter, the DREAMers, Occupy Wall Street, and university campaigns against sexual assault. Recent movements in Latin America against austerity measures and privatized education have been spearheaded by high school and college students (Somma 2012; Almeida 2014b; Von Bülow and Bidegain Ponte 2015). On a global scale, societies undergoing "youth bulges," where 25 percent or more of the adult population is between fifteen and twenty-four years of age, are more likely to experience popular rebellion (Goldstone 2015).

The density of young people in high schools and universities, along with flexible schedules, allows and encourages these individuals to participate more than others, especially those that are involved in youth organizations (Terriquez 2015b). The intensity of becoming aware of new issues in young adulthood also compels one to act on her beliefs. McAdam (1988), however, reminds us that teenagers are still largely under their parents' authority, making older teens and young adults more likely to participate in nonconventional politics than younger teens. This parental authority can be observed in the HBO film *Walkout* that portrayed the 1968 high school student protests in Los Angeles by Mexican American youth over discrimination in the public education system. The teenage protagonist in the movie comes under strong pressure from her father not to participate in the walkouts.[3] Yet despite parental authority, the United States witnessed an unprecedented upsurge in youth activism in 2018 with the movement for gun reform and against assault weapons motivating youth into thousands of marches and walkouts in high schools and middle schools (and even elementary schools) throughout the country (see chapter 4). Here we ask why some students joined the walkouts while others remained in the classroom.

Other movements have also benefited from people with flexible work schedules. One of the forces in the global justice movement in the Pacific Northwest and Canada is a group called the "Raging Grannies," composed of activist female senior citizens.[4] Guillemot and Price (2017) find that threats to social services act as a major catalyst for senior citizen protest participation, even in the face of mounting personal health difficulties. In a final example, of unemployment status, the unemployed workers' movement in Argentina acted as one of the largest social movements in Latin America in the late 1990s and early 2000s (Rossi 2017). In this case, unemployment was both a grievance and a force, which gave dismissed workers the time to organize.

In summary, biographical availability provides some individuals more time to engage in social movements than those with more daily constraints of work, family, and other obligations. At times, the groups that fall into the categories of biographical availability may be organized in blocs such as students, the unemployed, or senior citizens.

Beliefs and Ideology

Early movement participation theory focused on beliefs and values of the individual exclusively. People harbor certain predispositions to join a protest movement. As discussed at the opening of this chapter, these could be psychological deficits such as alienation, isolation, low self-esteem, or susceptibility to social pressures within crowds, according to the classical theories. More contemporary participation theories argue the opposite of classical theories in terms of more positive social psychological attributes of high self-esteem, personal efficacy, and social integration leading to individual engagement in social movements. Current participation perspectives focus on issues such as political ideologies, level of concern about an issue, perceptions of success, and level of experiencing a particular grievance (Klandermans 2018). Indeed, we can use these characteristics to define the boundaries of the sympathy pool of potential movement participants. Political ideology (a person's political beliefs and attitudes) is now usually one of several factors considered in multidimensional models of movement participation. For instance, scholars using the World Values Surveys across forty-seven countries in Europe found that those reporting more extreme political views (left-wing and right-wing) were more likely to participate in protest than those identifying with more moderate political beliefs (Jakobsen and Listhaug 2014). Similar findings have been found in national surveys in Peru and Israel (Opp, Finkel, et al. 1995) and participation in anti-austerity movements in Spain (Portos and Masullo 2017).

Social Networks

Beginning in the 1980s there was increasing interest in the role of social networks as important predictors of movement participation (Snow et al. 1980).[5] The connections individuals maintain with others shape protest participation. Indeed, one of the major advances of social movement research in the past three decades resides in the recognition that general values and beliefs alone are usually not sufficient to explain variation in individual-level participation (McAdam 1986). Mediating between movement-sympathetic beliefs and actual movement participation are social networks and organizations (Krinsky and Crossley 2014).

In this line of work, researchers want to identify the preexisting microsocial context of individuals immediately before they participate in social movement activities. This includes an individual's friendships, workplace, and neighborhood relationships (Gould 1995; Dixon and Roscigno 2003). Personal networks of family, friends, neighborhood, and workplace act as important reference groups in pulling receptive individuals from the sympathy pool into activism (Kitts 2000). Activists are especially successful in encouraging participation among people in groups with which they share a close social connection or bond (Lim 2008). Hence, both the number of ties to others sympathetic to a movement and the strength of those bonds play a major role in one's decision to participate. These types of everyday personal networks continue to be some of the best predictors of individual movement participation. In low income urban communities, at times, social networks may be used to pool resources into neighborhood economic survival more than collective action (Desmond and Travis 2018).

Several studies have shown that potential movement participants are more likely to join collective action campaigns when they interact with already participating activists (McAdam 1988; Gould 1995; Snow et al. 1980; Passy 2001). Being personally invited to take part in a street demonstration provides reinforcement and greater normative pressure for a person to attend such events (Schussman and Soule 2005; Walgrave and Wouters 2014). When the already-participating activist offering the invitation is a close friend or relative, the request is likely to be even more persuasive. Social networks can also pull in the opposite direction, away from participation. If one is connected to people that avoid social movement participation, the individual is also more likely *not to join* in collective action (McAdam 1988). As protest participation moves from low risk (e.g., a university rally) to high risk (e.g., the occupation of a building or public space, or protesting against a repressive government), deeper integration into activist social networks becomes an especially strong predictor of participation (McAdam 1988; Nepstad and Smith 1999; Almeida 2005; Viterna 2013).

Membership in Organizations

Membership in civic organizations and other social institutions provides incentives to participate in social movements similar to the incentives in personal networks (Gould 1995). Such organizational settings include student clubs, places of worship and churches, labor unions, and even recreational groups (such as a softball team or an exercise class). The core contribution of membership in organizations is that those more integrated in civic life are more likely to engage in social movement activities (Morris 1984; McAdam 1988). When people are already embedded in organizations, activists can generate rapid mobilization in times of crisis through bloc recruitment of many individuals in the same organization (Oberschall 1973; Morris 1984; McAdam 1999 [1982]).

Civic and political organizations offer individual participants a sense of personal efficacy (McAdam and Paulsen 1993; Gould 1995). Each organizational affiliation pulls people further away from countervailing pressures that may impinge on individual movement activity, such as relationships with persons outside the movement or opposed to movement participation (McAdam and Paulsen 1993; Kim and Bearman 1997; Gould 2003; McAdam 2003). Crosscutting pulls on individual activists would likely be even stronger in high-risk settings where activists face arrest or other harms. In addition, organizations provide important boundary-setting processes whereby the individual member's behavior increasingly converges with the normative obligations of their respective organization. This alignment process often takes place during internal organizational ceremonies and rituals (e.g., meetings, study groups, strategy sessions). Such ceremonies grant occasions for intense face-to-face interaction creating focused attention and shared definitions of the political situation where organizational in-group / out-group boundaries are constructed and reinforced (Collins 2001). Most important, these are locations where activists are most likely to have their interests reaffirmed and obliged by normative pressures to make individual contributions through active protest participation. For these reasons, and similar to social networks, affiliation with organizations that are even mildly sympathetic to a particular social movement is one of the most consistent predictors of individual protest participation (Somma 2010). In one recent example, Terriquez's (2017) study of Latinx youth in California showed that the strongest correlate of individual protest participation involved membership in organizations promoting civic engagement, including high school youth organizations and university enrollment.

Collective Identities

Personal networks and organizational affiliations do not emphasize the importance of these connections to an individual's sense of self, belonging, and personal identity (Viterna 2013). People whose self-identity is strongly tied to a political movement should be especially motivated to participate in collective actions related to the movement or issue (Van Stekelenburg and Klandermans 2017). Indeed, David Snow and Doug McAdam (2000: 47) find that "the existence of a movement provides an avenue for the individual to act in accordance with his or her personal identity." Individuals are energized by group attachments. The collective sense of solidarity and identification motivates future rounds of protest participation (Taylor et al. 2009; Van Stekelenburg and Klandermans 2017; Stryker 2000). In contrast, other individuals are often held back from joining social movements because they lack an identity and emotional attachment to the subgroups organizing and participating in the events (Jasper 2018). Analysts of social movements expect those individuals who identify with participants and organizations tied to specific demonstrations or movements to be more likely to participate, since the collective event itself reinforces the identity in question (Van Stekelenburg and Klandermans 2017).

In addition, as risk and uncertainty increase in the type of protest activity, the participant should experience a deepening of identification and solidarity with fellow activists. This activist identity is also reinforced as increasing political experience integrates the individual with other like-minded activists over time (McAdam and Paulsen 1993; Viterna 2013).

Previous Participation Experience

Another primary dimension increasing the probability of individual participation in social movements is past protest experience. Past participation in social movement activities often provides a sense of personal efficacy, making future opportunities to join in protest mobilizations much more appealing than for those without such experiences, especially if the earlier movement was successful in achieving goals. This is a consistent finding across a wide variety of individual recruitment studies, including the recent Indignados movement against economic austerity in Spain (Portos and Masullo 2017). Such participation may also reinforce a person's identity with the protesting collectivity and provide additional benefits of emotional energy and positive feelings (Collins 2004). Every additional round of individual activism may also offer a sense of building one's overall civic engagement skills (Schussman and Soule 2005; Van Dyke et al. 2007; Schlozman et al. 2018). Individuals lacking in past social movement participation would be relatively more likely to view political protest as an ineffective means to express political opinions and influence social change. They must overcome elite stereotypes dominating mass media coverage that protest and social movements are ineffectual and irrational (Sobieraj 2011; Cable 2019).

Social Media

In addition to political ideology, biographical availability, everyday networks, membership in organizations, collective identities, and previous protest experience, becoming aware of forthcoming demonstrations and rallies from different forms of mass and online social media may also motivate individuals to participate in demonstrations in the digital era (Earl and Kimport 2011; Odabas and Reynolds-Stenson 2017). Television and newspapers rarely provide information for potential participants about upcoming protest events. However, increasingly scholars have recognized the role of new social media technologies in providing information about upcoming protest events and motivating participation in demonstrations (Carty 2015; Bennett and Segerberg 2013). Indeed, the new social media technologies arguably provide the most important communication resource generating the massive protest campaigns of the new millennium, including immigrant rights, the Women's Marches, gun control, climate justice, and many others. The new internet communication technologies provide a tremendous expansion in scale and mobilization potential by instantaneously reaching large portions of the sympathy pool that are connected online or via mobile networks.

Those in the sympathy pool that are not exposed to social media messages about upcoming demonstrations would be less likely to participate. This lack of awareness and information about an upcoming protest event would greatly inhibit participation. The instantaneous diffusion capacity of social media has revolutionized protest participation around the world over the past two decades. Already by 2006 the social networking site myspace. com played a major role in the immigrant rights movement by mobilizing high school students in Dallas for a record-breaking march of some five hundred thousand participants. Since that time, social media platforms such as Facebook, Twitter, and WhatsApp have played an integral role in mobilizing individuals in likely every major social movement in the United States and around the world, including the Arab Spring, Indignados of Spain, climate justice, Black Lives Matter, and the Umbrella movement in Hong Kong. This pattern follows in tandem with the global spread of information and communications technologies and their accessibility by ordinary people, especially via cell phones in the global South. A major question for movement participation in the twenty-first century focuses on the level of digital solidarity produced by social media-induced mobilization. In other words, how thick are the relationships and bonds in social media-driven protest campaigns compared to face-to-face organizing? Under what conditions are social media-directed recruitments and mobilizations sustained over time? What makes such actions different from "flash activism" that countermovements and elite critics use to label and stigmatize contemporary movements seeking progressive social change (Earl and Kimport 2011; Carty 2015)?

To summarize, we began this section on the core components motivating individual participation in a variety of social movements by defining and highlighting the importance of the sympathy pool. From here the question focused on what moves a person from having mobilization potential or support to actually joining in social movement activities. Contemporary understandings of movement participation view it as a multidimensional process, with several conditions pulling individuals from the sympathy pool to actual protest engagement. These factors include ideological beliefs, availability of time, everyday social networks, organizational affiliations in civic associations, past movement experience, and exposure to social media activism. These conditions often overlap for a single individual, providing especially strong inducements to participate in movements. An example would be when a young adult with deeply held political convictions enjoys a friendship circle that largely communicates with social media while the members of the circle belong to the same set of progressive civic organizations.

FIGHT FOR $15, WOMEN'S MARCH, AND OCCUPY WALL STREET

Three major movements in the contemporary United States can now be understood from the microlevel of individual participation: the Fight for $15, the Women's March, and Occupy Wall Street. Earlier in the chapter, general questions were posed about defining the sympathy pool for these large movements and campaigns. With knowledge of the key conditions driving people from the sympathy pool to actual participation, a closer look at individual involvement in these three major US movement campaigns is in order. In the Fight for $15 fast-food worker movement, the decision for the individual employee is largely whether to participate in a strike or protest action. Movement participation frameworks would predict that those workers with biographical availability, network ties to activists and organizers, past protest experience, and exposure to upcoming national days of action via social media networks would be much more likely to participate than fast-food workers lacking these conditions. Collective identities along race, class, and gender lines (i.e., intersectionality) also likely draw workers into the struggle. In addition, because the protest was based at the workplace in most instances, participation was relatively high risk for fast-food employees, with the real possibility of facing dismissal for involvement.

Similar participation decision dynamics would have been in play for the 2017 and 2018 Women's Marches. The events were held on a Saturday, making it easier for many to take the time to join in a local demonstration. Since these marches were quite festive and peaceful (i.e., low risk), invitations from family and friends would likely have been quite persuasive. Indeed, in a survey implemented during the 2017 Washington, DC, Women's March, 60 percent reported going to the march with family members and nearly

70 percent attended the march with a friend. One third of those sampled in the same study reported being first-time protest participants (Fisher et al. 2017). Strong political ideology and convictions also played a major role in the choice to join the Women's March, as the polarizing and perceived demagogic campaign speeches of the president-elect created a backlash of determined citizens diametrically opposed to racism, sexism, and homophobia.[6] The leading feminist coordinators of the march also organized the campaign online from day one with a centralized website (https://www.womensmarch .com/) and hundreds of Facebook pages set up in participating cities. Collective identities by gender, race, and sexuality also provided a strong pull to participate in this colossal event (Fisher et al. 2017).

Participation in the Occupy Wall Street protests in the fall of 2011 also was largely conditioned by the core dimensions outlined above. Facebook and Twitter played important roles in conveying information in real time, and Facebook pages were set up in almost every city with an encampment (Gaby and Caren 2012). Since Occupy was a protest that took over public spaces in hundreds of cities, the *level of participation* is also important to document in this case. If one participated at the level of camping out at a protest site, it would be an enormous time commitment versus just attending one Occupy rally or demonstration. Those with high biographical availability would be more likely candidates for a prolonged encampment (which at times lasted several weeks). Gould-Wartofsky (2015) reports up to seven thousand arrests during the period that Occupy was most active, making participation a higher risk than in less disruptive protests. Hence, for prolonged participation, deeper social ties to other activists and past protest participation experience likely increased the likelihood of joining (similar to participation in the Fight for $15 campaign). Social movement scholarship still awaits systematic participation studies of these three major movements, but the above sketches indicate where attention would likely focus. The same tools could be used to study the new youth movement for gun control and against access to military-style assault weapons.

STATE OF THE ART IN PARTICIPATION STUDIES

The latest in the participation studies literature is the project Caught in the Act of Protest: Contextualizing Contestation (CCC).[7] Beginning in the 1990s, European scholars began to survey demonstrators during real-time protest events. By 2003 a major multinational project was launched to survey ten demonstrations against the impending war in Iraq in ten countries on the same day—February 15, 2003—one of the largest days of protest in world history (Walgrave and Rucht 2010; Heaney and Rojas 2015). Later in the decade, Stefaan Walgrave and Bert Klandermans put together a team of scholars to initiate the CCC project. As of 2017, CCC has counted protest surveys in 110 actual protest demonstrations across fourteen countries (Netherlands, Belgium, United Kingdom, Sweden, Spain, Czech Republic, Switzerland, Denmark, Mexico, El Salvador, Costa Rica, Honduras, Chile, and Argentina). Data were collected in demonstrations between 2009 and 2017. Issues of the surveyed demonstrations include May Day, austerity, LGBTQ pride, antiracism, and climate justice among others.

In these studies teams of researchers (often made up of university students) enter into an actual protest and survey the demonstration using random sampling techniques within the event (Klandermans 2012). In some countries a survey is handed out for some participants to take home and mail back to the university where the research is headquartered (as well as filled out during the demonstration by other participants). In other cases, as in Latin America, the survey is implemented in the demonstration (Inclán and Almeida 2017). In the CCC project, protest participants are compared across different types of demonstrations (such as gay pride parades versus anti-austerity marches) and across countries to see if people are mobilized and motivated to participate for different reasons. The project compares protest participants across countries in similar demonstrations and within and between countries on different types of protest events. Because the surveys are carried out in real time, researchers have a better understanding of the motivations for participation compared to a survey conducted several months or years after an event has occurred.

In Mexico, María Inclán implemented the CCC survey in six large urban demonstrations in Mexico City between 2011 and 2012 (Nolan-García and Inclán 2017). In one study she found that those who participated in ritual demonstrations were mobilized by their social networks, while those participating in more spontaneous protests related to elections were more likely mobilized by their past protest experience (Inclán and Almeida 2017). In another study related to the CCC project, Almeida enlisted the support of colleagues at the University of El Salvador, the University of Costa Rica, and the National Autonomous University of Honduras to implement a modified version of the CCC survey in May Day marches in San Salvador, San José, and Tegucigalpa. Teams of thirty university students descended on the streets of their respective nation's capital at 7 A.M. on May 1, 2014, to implement the survey (see photos in figures 12, 13, and 14 of the research teams). Nearly five hundred surveys were completed in each country for a total sample size of 1,500 May Day participants in Central America.

FIGURE 12 (Top).   Honduran Team Training, April 2014.

FIGURE 13 (Bottom).   Costa Rican Research Team, May Day 2014.

FIGURE 14.   El Salvador Team, May Day 2014. Photo by author.

The first preliminary study from the Central America CCC project ana-lyzes the relationship between social movement participation and electoral participation. In this study, the May Day marchers were used as a sympathy pool for participation in electoral campaigning for left-wing political parties. All three countries had presidential, parliamentary, and local elections within the past eight months before the May Day march. This first study found that socialist political ideology, anti–free trade beliefs, civic organizational membership, and past social movement participation made one much more likely to volunteer and campaign for a left-wing political party (Almeida and Sosa 2015). Hence, the CCC project provided a valuable study design to empirically test and demonstrate the relationship between social movement participation and participation in electoral politics. And more concretely, the CCC research design in this case establishes that subaltern forces in poor countries must use their human capital within social movements to mobilize for electoral gains in the face of overwhelming economic resources and material wealth held by traditional, elite-led political parties and social classes, which tend to finance their campaigns via the control of the major mass media outlets and by their use of paid campaigners.

SUMMARY

This chapter covered the process of individual-level participation in social movements. The discussion addressed a foundational question of collective action: why do some people participate in movement activities (demonstra-tions, strikes, rallies, marches, walkouts) while many more do not? Several studies draw on large national and cross-national data sets with survey items about civic and political engagement (examples are provided in table 5). Other studies focus on participation and nonparticipation within specific social movements and protest campaigns. These studies of particular movements draw from the framework that participants originate from distinct sympathy pools (subpopulations with an interest in the movement in question). From this vantage point the key issues involve what moves an individual from the sympathy pool to actual participation. Students of social movements find that some of the most important factors pushing people from sympathy to activism include ideological beliefs, organizational affiliations, social network ties, collective identities, previous protest experience, and new social media technologies. These tools assist us in understanding participation in historic movements of the past as well as contemporary movements, such as the Women's Marches, campaigns against police violence and abuse, and the ongoing battle for a living wage by excluded social groups.

The next chapter moves back to the macrolevel of social movements. It provides an overview of the outcomes or the impacts of social movement mobilization in creating social change. Understanding social movement outcomes and their relationship to mobilization is a critical area of investigation to show that popular collective action offers a pathway to the transformation of modern societies.

7 Movement Outcomes

Up to this point, this text has largely focused on social movement mobilization, not on outcomes. We have covered basic terms, methods, theories, and components of the emergence and spread of collective action. Even the discussions of framing and movement participation (chapters 5 and 6) centered on the mobilizing process and how individuals become recruited to protest campaigns. This chapter addresses potentially the most important questions overall in relation to social movements. How do we observe and document social movements creating social change? What are the conditions associated with successful movements that achieve some of their demands and goals? Activists and scholars alike must confront such issues to establish the significance of the social movement form of mobilization as a rational collective response to social exclusion in contemporary societies. The arena of social movement outcomes provides the analytical tools for such an exercise.

Social movements produce enduring changes in society and in the lives of the people that participate in the struggles for those changes. Understanding the long-term consequences of social movements is one of the most critical arenas of collective action scholarship. Activists, community organizers, labor union leaders, and academic researchers all seek to identify the conditions that more likely produce movement success. In other words, how do movements win? This crucial subfield of social movements is referred to as *movement outcomes*. Outcomes range from total failure and movement collapse to movement victories in the form of new favorable policies, such as the legalization of gay marriage or the popular ousting of an authoritarian government. At the same time, adversaries of social movements work arduously to prevent collective actors from achieving goals by placing several obstacles in their path (Cable 2019).

Students of collective action examine movement outcomes at the micro-, meso-, and macrolevels of political and social life. Within these levels scholars and activists seek to understand such questions as the lasting impacts of movements on participants' life trajectories, on government, institutions, culture, and the broader society. In order to better comprehend how much success a movement achieves, it is essential to develop working definitions of movement outcomes in terms of how to measure and identify them. One of the most common ways to examine movement success is to determine if movements accomplish their stated goals. Such an approach analyzes "the formally stated objectives of political movement organizations: the goals publicly presented in speech or writing to non-movement actors such as movement targets, the media, or bystander publics" (Burstein et al. 1995: 282).

Movement goals are most often found in movement documents/propaganda, websites, speeches of leaders, chants and banners of rank-and-file participants, and in negotiations with elites. The specificity of goals varies by movement. The fast-food workers' slogan "Fight for $15" offers an example of a very precise goal: raising the local minimum wage to fifteen dollars per hour. Other national social movements that are large and enduring often issue multiple goals, several of which appearing as quite abstract, such as persuasive calls for "economic justice" or "animal rights." Maintaining multiple goals also likely results in activists experiencing both triumphs and failures within the same national social movement as some objectives are achieved while others are not. These contradictory outcomes make it difficult at times to assess the overall success of a national movement.

Given that national-level social movements often adopt multiple and abstract goals, it is easier to analyze particular campaigns that have more specified and singular goals in order to determine the level of success. For the environmental movement, this may mean observing a bounded campaign of targeting a local or state government to commit to a precise percentage of renewable energy used by a region's power distribution grid, as opposed to evaluating the success of the environmental movement in general. Local grassroots movements are especially useful for observing movement outcomes because of some of their core properties (discussed in chapter 2). These characteristics include their shorter life spans and espousing very specific goals, such as preventing the impending arrival of a garbage incinerator in the community or demanding street lighting in a neighborhood. Hence, these local, shorter-term movements with specified goals provide tractable cases to identify causal processes shaping movement success or failure (Almeida and Stearns 1998; Halebsky 2009; Biggs and Andrews 2015). Specified goals also enhance prospects for success by providing power holders and movement targets concrete information by which to negotiate and bargain.

Another major strategy for determining movement success centers on observing the benefits received by the population the movement claims to represent (Amenta 2006). These may be cases in which a movement fails to achieve its stated goals but the constituents of the movement still receive substantial benefits. In a popular historical example, Amenta (2006) shows that the movement for a fixed income for the aged and retired in the 1930s—known as the Townsend movement—failed to convince the United States Congress to authorize such a policy. In its place, Congress passed the Social Security Act in 1935, which provided a supplemental payment system for the retired based on contributions throughout one's employment career. The Social Security Act legislation would likely not have passed without the Townsend movement's mobilization. The movement failed to achieve its stated goals but its constituents (senior citizens) benefited in the long term from the new social security legislation. In a more recent example, fast-food workers demanding a fifteen-dollar hourly wage may not succeed, but a city or county could pass other ordinances in response to the struggle, such as subsidized healthcare or free public transportation for low-income workers. Even another industry outside of the fast-food sector may be influenced by such a campaign, as in the case of Amazon agreeing to a fifteen dollar hourly minimum wage for its employees as well as several city and state governments.

It should also be noted when examining outcomes and success that the movement may be driven by the bad-news model of *threats*, elaborated in chapter 3. In these types of mobilizations, movements determine success by preventing "collective bads" or worsening conditions, such as an erosion of economic welfare, environmental quality, rights, or safety. One common varying outcome associated with struggles over threats involves the ability of social movements to prevent economic austerity measures and privatization policies that would take social citizenship benefits away from working-class, lower-income, and vulnerable groups (Almeida 2008a; Della Porta 2015). In the twenty-first century, turning back worsening conditions (xenophobia, economic and environmental decline) serves as a major goal for social movement campaigns on continents around the world. In short, a positive outcome in "bad news" type mobilizations centers on blocking unwanted changes.

GAMSON'S EARLY MODEL OF SOCIAL MOVEMENT OUTCOMES

William Gamson (1990 [1975]) pioneered the study of movement outcomes. He sampled a registry of over five hundred social movement organizations (SMOs) between 1800 and 1945. His final sample contained fifty-three SMOs ranging from the Tobacco Night Riders to the Young People's Socialist League. He measured success by (1) whether the movement was accepted by elites as a legitimate challenger, and (2) whether the challenging movement received new advantages and benefits it was explicitly seeking. Gamson refocused attention on the use of *disruptive tactics,* one of the main contributions from this early study of movement outcomes. He found that the majority of challenging groups that used disruptive protest strategies more likely gained acceptance (62%) and more likely won new advantages (75%). He referred to this major discovery as "the success of the unruly." The effectiveness of assertive protest tactics is qualified by the need for public opinion support, and in the modern era for positive mass media exposure (Gamson 1989). The findings provided a direct challenge to the pluralist model of power (chapter 3) which maintained that institutionalized participation in politics is sufficient for citizens to exercise their rights and resolve grievances. Gamson found the opposite: only through mass disruptive actions will social change be likely to occur for excluded social groups.

Gamson (1990 [1975]) provided several other insights in his foundational study of movement outcomes. Besides the use of disruptive protest to produce positive movement outcomes, Gamson found that groups with specified goals and organized along more bureaucratic lines (using formal organizations) were more successful than groups that lacked these characteristics. He also showed that challenging groups suffering from state and elite violence were much less successful than other social movements— highlighting how repression of mobilization and the actions of adversaries contribute to movement failure. In summary, Gamson's research laid the groundwork for the study of movement outcomes in the following decades.

CURRENT UNDERSTANDINGS OF MOVEMENT OUTCOMES

The study of movement outcomes has grown immensely in recent years (Bosi et al. 2016). One of the most common areas in which to explore movement success focuses on policy changes. With so many movements directing their demands to different levels of government (local, state, national, and international bodies), examining policy outcomes provides one measure of understanding the level of success. Political thinkers such as Schumaker (1975) and Burstein et al. (1995) have directed attention to a scale of escalating levels of policy success related to social movement actions. Table 6 presents the policy scale of Schumaker and Burstein and his colleagues along with a few modifications. Such classification systems allow a precise means to determine how successful a particular movement is over time, across political/geographical units, or in comparison to other movements.

Importantly, social movement struggles are often not successful. This is consistent with movements representing excluded and marginalized populations in the context of the unequal distribution of power. Elites and those with power have structured the political system in a way that privileges groups with wealth, routine institutional access, and abundant resources.[1] Power holders most commonly resist or act indifferently to attempts to change the balance of power by excluded and subordinated groups. Hence, initial attempts to mobilize for social change will find elite groups and adversaries ignoring the claims of a movement. When social movements persuade government representatives to meet with them and listen to demands, they are beginning to make some progress, namely with *access responsiveness* (table 6). When demands are pushed even further, a promising accomplishment is to convince policy makers to place specific demands on the agenda of a legislative body or to receive a hearing in the courts (which is referred to as *agenda responsiveness*).

At minimum, agenda responsiveness acts as a symbolic victory for social movements—it legitimates the claims of a movement as worthy of political and legal debate. If a government body approves the policy item (*policy responsiveness*), it counts as an even higher level of success, especially if the state or institution in question immediately implements and enforces the policy by the law (*output responsiveness*). When the new legislation reduces the grievances that drove the original mobilization into existence, movement leaders may characterize the struggle as a high level of success (*impact responsiveness*). In historically rare cases, a transformative movement, such as the African American civil rights movement, can create such major policy change that it has *structural impacts* (Burstein et al. 1995). Indeed, the 1964 Civil Rights Act included legislation that banned employment discrimination based on race, religion, sex, or national origin. The environmental justice movement also invokes the Civil Rights Act to protect vulnerable groups from public health hazards (Bullard 2005). In this situation, the policy success of the African American civil rights movement created legislation *benefiting several other groups* beyond the focal struggle.

TABLE 6. Level of Movement-Generated Policy Success

Level of Success	Policy Change	Examples
No success	Ignored by political and economic elites	City council refuses to meet with local living-wage movement
Level one	Access responsiveness	City council agrees to meet and hear demands of local living-wage movement
Level two	Agenda responsiveness	City council places living-wage ordinance on the agenda to be discussed at upcoming city council meeting
Level three	Policy responsiveness	City council approves living-wage ordinance in the form that the movement originally requested
Level four	Output responsiveness	The city implements the new living-wage ordinance and local employers effectively abide by it.
Level five	Impact responsiveness	The higher wages make it easier for low-income workers in the city to meet the basic needs of their families
Level six	Structural impacts	The living-wage ordinance improves health and well-being indicators for the entire city and makes it easier for other marginalized populations to take their grievances to the city council

SOURCE: Adapted and modified from Burstein et al. (1995: 284, table 1).

Table 6 details the deepening of policy success of social movements with the illustrative example of the living-wage movement. The living-wage movement took off in the 1990s with the goal of inducing local governments to enact ordinances requiring employers to offer salaries high enough to meet a family's basic needs (health, nutrition, housing, clothing, etc.) (Luce 2017). In the hundreds of living-wage campaigns there is considerable variation in the level of success (Swarts and Vasi 2011). Table 6 provides a rubric to determine the relative success of these local struggles. This "policy success table" can be viewed with multiple frameworks in mind. First, it can be used to determine the success of a single movement after the struggle terminates, by deciphering how far into the policy process the movement penetrated. Second, movement leaders and analysts can use the table in real time to observe how to move from one stage to the next and which tactics and pressure points to employ to keep pushing the policy process to higher levels of success. Finally, the table can be utilized to compare local campaigns of the same movement (such as the living-wage movement) across cities and counties to determine which regions succeeded and which ones failed. With such knowledge, analysts could trace back to decipher if activists experienced common conditions in the successful campaigns versus the less successful ones. Such vital information could serve future campaign strategies in where to invest scarce movement resources.

Beyond policy changes at different levels of government, social movements also direct their attention to other institutions to achieve social change and positive outcomes (Van Dyke at al. 2004; Armstrong and Bernstein 2008; Bell 2014). These targets include a wide range of societal institutions, such as public education, universities, hospitals, mental health establishments, private business and corporations, the military, religious organizations, and many others (Walker et al. 2008). Labor strikes and conflicts in private industry represent one of the classic social movement battles outside of the state (although the government may intervene to arbitrate or suppress the movement). Lesbian, gay, and bisexual employees have successfully mobilized in large corporations to reduce workplace discrimination (Raeburn 2004). African American, Asian American, Latinx, and Native American students have also effectively organized social movement campaigns to establish ethnic studies majors and courses in universities (Rojas 2007; Armbruster-Sandoval 2017). This struggle continues in the public school system: the state of California has now instituted an ethnic studies curriculum in the high schools (chapter 4). In another example, Bell (2014) shows how the Black Power movement influenced the profession of social work in the United States with black case workers organizing within national bodies and implementing new racial norms and other practices in the social welfare system.

CORRELATES OF MOVEMENT SUCCESS

Social movement studies now offer a plethora of cases on social movement outcomes whereby students of collective action have repeatedly identified several conditions associated with success (and failure) in a variety of struggles (Amenta, Andrews, and Caren 2018). Table 7 enumerates these factors associated with positive movement outcomes as well as the mechanisms that contribute to increasing the chances of success. These dimensions contributing to the bargaining and negotiating power of social movements

TABLE 7. Common Factors Related to Movement Success

SUCCESS FACTORS	MECHANISMS INCREASING LIKELIHOOD OF SUCCESS
Movement strategy factors	
Framing strategies	Inclusive framing strategies bring multiple groups into the struggle as allies. Also effective are framing strategies that resonate with cultural beliefs, or that effectively connect the problem/grievance to the cause.
Disruptive/novel tactics	Disruptive tactics create bargaining leverage by interrupting established routines of power holders. Effectiveness depends on public opinion support.
Size	Large mobilizations demonstrate the level of support to power holders and the potential costs of not negotiating with the movement.
Enduring infrastructure	Sustained local resources keep up pressure on authorities to implement positive policy changes over the long term.
External allies/coalitions	
Youth/students	Youth enjoy free time to volunteer for a movement, and provide large contingents to demonstrations. They maintain a high density of energy to sustain short-term campaigns.
Experts/ professionals	Scientists, lawyers, and other professionals become especially useful at the negotiations stage, when movements engage with legislatures or courts. Scientists can provide expertise in health and environmental movements. Lawyers help movements navigate the legal and political system.
Religious organizations	Religious groups bring in large numbers of parishioners and give moral authority and legitimacy to the cause of the movement.
Other social movements	Other social movements can instantly bring many more people into the struggle who are already mobilized, and can help spread the movement to more geographical regions. The labor movement and labor unions can play this role.
Oppositional political parties	Oppositional parties can contribute by mobilizing their members and sympathizers and negotiating with legislative and parliamentary bodies on behalf of the movement.

Mass media	Mass media can reach a broad audience and legitimate the movement within public opinion (via radio, television, newspapers, internet platforms). It also helps diffuse the movement to new regions, strengthening overall mobilization.
State actors	Sympathetic state agencies and their employees may also boost themselves vis-à-vis other state offices by assisting a movement in their sphere of competence. They also may share or leak valuable information to movements.

Political environment factors

Elite conflict	When elite groups are in conflict with one another, the political system is more vulnerable. Elites cannot ignore, stigmatize, or repress social movements with a unified voice during crises. Renegade elites may align with a social movement.
Public opinion	When a majority of the population supports the goals of a social movement, policy makers are more likely to negotiate—or face being removed from elected office. Favorable public opinion provides a promising environment to use more noninstitutional protests.
Elite blunders	Publicly observed blunders by elites during a social movement conflict bring more support to a social movement and harm the legitimacy of elite targets.
Countermovements	Countermovements put a focal movement on the defensive by challenging goals and framing and by influencing public opinion.

group into the following categories: movement strategy factors; external allies/coalitions; and political environment factors.

Movement Strategy

Unlike the other conditions associated with positive outcomes in table 7, social movements maintain control of their strategies to influence chances of success. Hence, the choices movements make about which frames, numbers of people to attempt to mobilize, and tactics to employ are critical for efficacious mobilization. Movement strategy also occurs in the context of available allies, past experiences, and the larger political environment.

Framing Strategies   Chapter 5 offers a detailed description of the framing process. Activists must frame their movement in compelling ways not only for effective recruitment and mobilization, but also to increase the likelihood of a final victory. In a comparative study of fifteen homeless group SMOs in eight US cities, Cress and Snow (2000) highlighted the critical role of articulate movement framing strategies in winning more rights, resources, and relief than those with less coherent frames. In particular, they examined the ability of homeless social movements to define problems, attribute blame, and develop solid mobilizing campaigns (i.e., diagnostic, prognostic, and motivational framing). The study shows that even the poorest sectors in US society (the homeless) may be able to improve their social conditions by creating clearly intelligible and convincing frames that properly outline grievances, their causes, and specific plans of action for their resolution.

In the immigrant rights movement in the United States, Bloemraad et al. (2011) found that the movement was much more effective when using framing strategies that highlighted the US flag and working families than when referring to national origin, human rights, or immigration history. In more recent work, immigrant movement framing strategies that focused on family integrity were found to be much more resonant than framing citizenship struggles around civil rights or economic conditions (Bloemraad, Silva, and Voss 2016). The inclusiveness of framing strategies has also been associated with successful movement outcomes. When movements can go beyond narrow interests in their ideological appeals, it brings more groups potentially into the struggle. In Halebsky's (2009) comparative study of six Walmart store siting controversies, he showed that one of the conditions for local movement success in preventing Walmart from establishing a store in a small town centered on broad framing strategies that discussed several of the community-wide problems a superstore may bring. These problems included more traffic, the loss of a special sense of community place, and the decline of local retail establishments. Others have simply highlighted the complexity of the framing process as a warning not to take the social construction of grievances for granted. For example, Snow and Corrigall-Brown (2005) showed that activists often fail to convincingly connect their core grievance with the agents culpable for creating the social problem, eventuating in the dissolution of the movement.

Disruptive Protest and Novel Tactics   As Gamson (1990 [1975]) and Piven and Cloward (1979) emphasized several decades ago, disruptive protest strategies tend to be more effective than relying solely on conventional tactics. Several qualifications are necessary to contextualize this proposition. First, most social movement campaigns seeking to achieve specific goals deploy a *repertoire* of tactics, including conventional and noninstitutional protest (Tilly 1978; Taylor and Van Dyke 2004). This may include petitions, rallies, letter-writing campaigns, teach-ins, as well as more assertive tactics such as sit-ins, roadblocks, and occupations. Second, nonconventional protests usually need the support of public opinion and other facilitating conditions in order to be successful (Marti Puig 2012). This means groups employing disruptive tactics such as a sit-in or obstructing traffic would benefit from a majority of the public sympathizing with the movement or the issue in question. Without public opinion support, elites can more easily call on the forces of public order (such as the police) to repress disruptive protest with little outcry beyond the immediate movement. A final qualification is that defining a tactic as "disruptive" or "noninstitutional" may be culturally determined. For example, environmental movements using a lawsuit as a tactic would be viewed as an institutional strategy in the United States but part of a noninstitutional repertoire in Japan, where social movements traditionally seek conflict resolution with other branches of government or informal agreements with elites (Broadbent 1998).

The key force of disruptive protest is that it brings leverage to subordinated groups to bargain with elites (Piven and Cloward 1979; McAdam 1999 [1982]; Tarrow 2011).[2] With public opinion support, noninstitutional protests create increased costs for elite groups that do not concede to demands (Luders 2016). These costs may be financial, through lost investments and sales (in the case of boycotts), or they may be political in the loss of electoral support. Disruptive protest also interrupts the daily routines of more privileged target groups (Kolb 2007). Targets such as state officials and company executives depend on their constituencies (e.g., the electorate, stockholders, customers) and on routine operations to function effectively from day to day. Political and economic elites also need to be perceived as conducting business consistent with social mores of "right" and "wrong," so as to be recognized as legitimate in their own organizational fields, as well as socially responsible in the broader society (Armbuster-Sandoval 2005; Soule 2009). If a social movement can convincingly threaten or activate disruptive tactics that convey its plight to the targets' constituencies, the targets will begin to feel pressure to negotiate with movement representatives (Almeida and Stearns 1998).

A growing and rich literature emphasizes the efficacy of *nonviolent* disruptive protest versus more violent actions, even against repressive governments (Schock 2015a; Kadivar 2018). Social movements fill the historical record with dramatic mobilizations of civil disobedience leading to positive outcomes. From the civil rights movement using sit-ins and other mass actions in order to break down the Jim Crow system of racial segregation and electoral exclusion (Morris 1993), to Latinx student walkouts in 2006 in California and other states to successfully prevent the passage of national anti-immigrant legislation, mass disruptive actions have changed the course of history. Biggs and Andrews (2015) offer empirical evidence of the power of disruptive protest through a local-level analysis of 334 cities in southern states between 1960 and 1961. They found that not only cities experiencing the disruptive tactic of a sit-in were more likely to desegregate along racial lines, but also even cities nearby mass action events. Of course, caution is in order. Most movements struggle simply to achieve sustained mobilization, as discussed in chapter 4. It usually takes a combination of favorable conditions, including noninstitutional tactics, for movements to experience triumphs (McCammon 2012).

The novelty of protest tactics by subordinated groups can be equally disruptive. In the early twentieth century, the women's movement used suffrage parades (McCammon et al. 2001) as a creative tactic to bring women into the public sphere and win the right to vote (Taylor and Van Dyke 2004). Activists groups such as ACT UP pushing for federal policy and scientific research to address the HIV/AIDS crisis in the late 1980s and early 1990s also effectively used a range of novel tactics creating spectacles such as the "die-in," where hundreds of people lie in a public place or occupied building feigning to be dead (Gould 2009). The die-in tactic has become so successful that even the anti-tobacco television commercial campaign "Truth" (www.thetruth.com) used it in its advertisements to help bring down the rate of teenage cigarette smoking over the past two decades. In another study on the power of "spectacular" actions, Armbruster-Sandoval (2017) demonstrated the success of student hunger strikes on three California university campuses in expanding Chicano studies programs in a hostile and inopportune political environment of budget cuts and anti-immigrant legislation.

Size One of the simplest explanations of movement success centers on examining the size of the protest movement. Movements that generate large mass mobilizations of thousands or even tens of thousands of people would seem to be able to place more pressure on elected officials and those in power (Tilly 1999). For the reasons discussed in chapter 4 on movement emergence, however, producing large-scale mobilizations is not an easy task. Placing massive numbers of people on the streets in dozens of US cities certainly helped put the brakes on the anti-immigrant House Bill 4437 in 2006 (Zepeda-Millán 2017). At other times, enormous protests fail to achieve their goals. In one of the largest protests in world history, on

February 15, 2003, over eight hundred cities and thirty million people around the globe participated in demonstrations and attempted to stop the imminent United States invasion of Iraq (Heaney and Rojas 2015). The movement failed to prevent the war and the US began a bombing campaign and invasion in March. The transnational movement against global warming, called "climate justice," has also produced unprecedented mobilizations across the planet involving millions of participants in over one thousand cities, with mixed results. Nonetheless, even if large-scale mobilizations fail to achieve their immediate goals, they likely build lasting networks among activists and organizations and affect the lives of the participants as secondary outcomes.

Enduring Infrastructure A movement can create a lasting organizational infrastructure to sustain pressure on authorities for concessions over the long term. Andrews (2004: 5) defines such infrastructures as a "combination of leaders, indigenous resources, and local organizations." Andrews examined this infrastructure at the local level in Mississippi in the context of the African American civil rights movement. He showed that counties with a stronger infrastructure in the mid-1960s received many more long-term benefits in terms of Black political representation, voting rights, and poverty relief programs than counties that lacked this infrastructure. In California's impoverished Central Valley, Mora (2016) showed that local-level immigrant rights struggles in 2006 had much more long-term success in cities with more elaborate movement infrastructures. In major social movements that use community organizing strategies over several years, such as in the case of the civil rights movement and the California farmworker movement, the long-term activism deposits a legacy of experienced organizers that go on to lead successful campaigns in other struggles. Key participants in the United Farm Workers from the 1960s to the 1980s went on to leadership positions in urban labor movement campaigns and other community-based struggles as an outcome of the original organizing (Shaw 2008).

In authoritarian countries, civil society groups often take advantage of periods of political liberalization when the regime allows some space for organizing. During these crucial periods of "thaw" in the repressive context, activists can build a durable infrastructure of organizations, labor unions, and civic associations as an *outcome* of the opening of the regime. This newly available, sustainable organizational infrastructure then may be used to resist the dictatorship once the regime closes back down and returns to repressing civilians. This was the pattern of some of the Arab Spring countries in 2011–12 as well as several cases in Latin America, including resistance to the military coup in Honduras in 2009 (Sosa 2015).

External Allies and Coalitions

Movements may try to coordinate broad coalitions to enhance their probability of success (Van Dyke and Amos 2017). This means bringing several sectors of society into the struggle. Broad and diverse coalitions demonstrate that multiple sectors of society are concerned about the issue. Broad coalitions signify to power holders that they may suffer costs in public and economic support if they fail to negotiate. The ability to form large coalitions is not completely under the core movement's control. The outside groups that align with the focal movement must be available and willing to join in the struggle. During waves of protests (discussed in chapter 2), many more allies would be available and already mobilized to form broad and strong coalitions. While broad coalitions may be most desirable, they are difficult to achieve in most times and places (McCammon and Van Dyke 2010). More common are cases where a core social movement campaign joins in an alliance with one or two outside groups, which are referred to as *external allies* (Tarrow 2011). Some of the types of external allies most frequently joining a movement are enumerated below along with the benefits they bring to increasing the likelihood of success.

Youth and Students   While youth often form the core participants of a wide variety of social movements, such as Occupy Wall Street, the DREAMers, MEChA, gun control, and even Antifa, teenagers and young adults can also be a resourceful *ally* to a social movement campaign. The flexible schedules and life stages of youth allow them a greater propensity to join in solidarity with other social movements (Vommaro 2015). The concept of "bloc recruitment" again helps explain youth participation, with entire student associations from high schools or nearby colleges joining in to assist a movement campaign (as witnessed in the immigrant rights movement). University enrollment growth in the United States and around the world since the mid-twentieth century provides a special external ally with enormous mobilization potential for movements (Goldstone and McAdam 2001; Schofer and Meyer 2005). Students and young people may be more likely to engage in disruptive tactics and risk arrest. Some students have experience in disruptive protest, while others' lifestyles and precarious employment status make them available for action even on short notice. Students play a pivotal role by providing bodies to occupy the front line in public demonstrations and confrontations with authorities. Students and youth continue to be active in local and national movements as key allies, from the Black Lives Matter campaign and environmental justice struggles in the US to the anti–government corruption and fraud protests in Honduras, Nicaragua, and Guatemala (Sosa 2016; Velasquez Nimatuj 2016). Indeed, the power of youth mobilization manifested in March 2018 when over three thousand schools (including high schools, middle schools, and elementary schools) across the United States participated in student walk-outs for gun reform (see map in figure 8, chapter 4).

Experts and Professionals Depending on the type of movement and struggle, different kinds of expert knowledge may be extraordinarily useful to achieving movement goals, negotiating with elites, winning new bene-fits, or avoiding damages. Experts can donate their talents to social move-ments via published works or through other creative tasks that capture the attention of the larger public. Medical, life, and chemical scientists can assist health- and environmental-based movements by gathering scientific evi-dence or demonstrating the link between the source of pollution and a con-taminated region. Other specialists such as lawyers can aid movements in court and the legislative process with their expertise. These kinds of skills would be especially beneficial in moving further down the policy success scale presented in table 7.

Other Social Movements Other social movements already mobilized often come to the aid of a particular social movement campaign. The labor movement and labor unions offer one particularly beneficial active social movement (Voss and Sherman 2000). The involvement of labor unions in social movements that are not strictly labor struggles has resulted in a new term, "social movement unionism" (Clawson 2003; Schock 2005). This may include a labor union assisting in an immigrant rights campaign to block deportations and police raids, or a labor union joining an environmental movement struggle. The women's movement and the civil rights move-ment also commonly come to the assistance of other movements (Brown and Jones 2016). As noted above for coalitions, during a protest wave mul-tiple social movements are active and able to assist a particular campaign.

Religious Organizations Religious organization also make for passionate external allies. At times, religious allies provide a sense of moral authority and bestow legitimacy to a social movement cause. Similar to schools and other institutions, entire groups (congregations) can come to align with a social movement, such as the Fight for $15 fast-food worker strikes and rallies, and the struggles of immigrants and other low-income communities (McCarthy and Walker 2004; Wood and Fulton 2015). Indeed, one of the largest networks of community-based activism in the contemporary United States is the "People Improving Communities through Organizing" (PICO) network founded by a Jesuit priest in the early 1970s (Whitman 2006; 2018). Now called Faith in Action, PICO engages as a multidenominational faith- and church-based ally in dozens of local struggles (Flores 2018), from living-wage campaigns to establishing community healthcare clinics, and it is currently active in 150 cities in seventeen states.[3] Moreover, a revitalization of Martin Luther King Jr.'s Poor People's campaign for economic and racial justice has emerged to align with marginalized communities, with leadership from church officials such as Pastor William Barber II.[4]

Oppositional Political Parties   By taking up a social movement issue, an oppositional political party may be able to strengthen its position vis-à-vis the dominant party, especially under conditions of public opinion support for the movement in question. The oppositional party also builds a constituency in the near term by adopting issues with widespread appeal (Hutter et al. 2018). In order to sustain a nationwide campaign, social movements need allies with organizational resources across a wide geographical space. The symbiotic relationship between political parties and social movements has been termed "social movement partyism" (Almeida 2006; 2010b). In the neoliberal age, few civil society associations maintain a national-level organizational reach. Trade unions are weakened by labor flexibility laws and global competition for reduced manufacturing costs. In the global South, rural peasant and farmer associations have also lost organizational power. While these debilitated traditional actors predominated in the social movement sector during the previous period of state-led development/Fordism, in the neoliberal era the political party remains one of the only nationally organized entities in many societies. Political parties can use their organizational structure to mobilize in the streets by calling on their supporters in multiple locales to participate in collective action campaigns (Somma 2018). Political parties may also act inside the polity to push for new favorable policies or the retraction of unfavorable measures. These insider activities provide social movements with an incentive to join with political parties, which can work on their behalf inside of parliament. Inside the government, political parties also assist movements in achieving the kinds of policy success described in table 7. Having an advocate inside the polity also raises success expectations for activists, encouraging wider mobilizations.

The use of political parties to obtain movement demands has occurred on multiple continents in the twenty-first century. These episodes include the Movement Toward Socialism Party in Bolivia, mobilizing with indigenous peoples collectives to overturn the privatization of natural gas. Other prime examples come from Europe, where the newly created Podemos Party in Spain and the Syriza Party in Greece mobilize hundreds of thousands of people on the streets to turn back harsh economic austerity policies (Della Porta et al. 2017). Even on the political right, parties mobilize social movements, such as elite factions of the Republican Party serving as a key sponsor of Tea Party protests in the United States (Almeida and Van Dyke 2014).

Mass Media and Social Media   The mass media are a powerful force for resource-poor social movements. Extensive media coverage acknowledges and gives testimony to a social problem (Szasz 1994). It transmits the plight of a social movement to a vast public, eliciting the attention of both potential supporters and the state. The presence of the mass media also encourages disruptive tactics, because they dramatize the situation and thus are more "newsworthy" (Kielbowicz and Scherer 1986). Moreover, "spectacle" has been theorized as a defining feature of the neoliberal era (Harvey 2005). Social movements that strategically halt traffic, disrupt government and corporate meetings, or keep polluting industries from routine operations through sit-ins or sympathetic labor strikes will be more likely to draw the media's attention (Almeida and Stearns 1998), but not always to the level of depiction which activists desire (Sobieraj 2011).

In the twenty-first century, movements and individual activists have a much greater capacity to reach general and targeted audiences through new social media built from the internet communication technology infrastructure. Castells (2013: xxiv) interprets this new development as a "counterpower" in that "the expansion of mass self-communication has supported an unexpected, extraordinary broadening of the ability of individual and social actors to challenge the power of the state." The accessibility of instant messaging, Facebook, Twitter, and WhatsApp for excluded collective actors is a major advantage in overcoming the obstacles of corporate-controlled mass media outlets that have evolved into oligopolistic conglomerates. Information about local movement victories can diffuse instantly and be emulated by others through the contagion of success.

State Actors   Actors inside the government may also provide valuable resources to a social movement campaign (Banaszak 2010; Verhoeven and

Duyvendak 2017). Actors inside the state include government agencies, city councils, the courts, and individual bureaucrats (Stearns and Almeida 2004). State actors participate in state-movement coalitions for a variety of reasons. Some state actors are institutional activists, defined as "social movement participants who occupy formal statuses within the government and who pursue social movement goals through conventional bureaucratic channels" (Santoro and McGuire 1997: 503). These institutional activists are committed to the social movement's objectives and motivated by intrinsic rewards (Ganz 2009). While such alliances have the potential to be ongoing, they generally endure for short time periods. Some state actors also enter an alliance with a social movement because they are ideologically predisposed to the movement's objectives; for example, a local EPA officer assisted the victims of the Flint, Michigan, water and lead poisoning crisis by forcing government officials to finally take action (Rosner and Markowitz 2016).

Other state actors participate with social movements as a means of promoting their own agendas. They enter the alliance primarily to pursue their own extrinsic rewards (further their careers, increase their status). Still other state actors, because of the location and function of their unit, take up the claims of a social movement to increase their unit's vitality and legitimacy within the state apparatus (Stearns and Almeida 2004). External assistance from within the state, regardless of the state actors' motivations, increases the probability of positive outcomes for social movements. In the context of this symbiotic relationship, social movements are granted a level of legitimacy and, perhaps more important, indirect access to the state's decision-making structures.[5]

Political Environment

Public Opinion Public opinion provides a political environment that either facilitates or hampers a movement's struggle in achieving its demands. Challenging groups must be able to properly read and interpret the public mood in order to devise an appropriate strategy that corresponds to the general sentiments of society for the issue in question. Movement success is much more likely when a majority of public opinion is sympathetic to the demands of the movement. For the women's movement in the USA, states more likely ratified the Equal Rights Amendment (ERA) where a greater level of public opinion supported women's equality and the ERA (Soule and Olzak 2004). When public opinion is less than favorable (below 50 percent support), activists and leaders need to focus on public education campaigns. The women's movement in the United States took up this strategy in the early twentieth century in order to earn the right to participate in court juries within the justice system. Women's groups traveled to state fairs, farmer associations, and churches to raise consciousness on the importance of women's rights to serve on juries. This continued mobilization targeting public opinion led to more states passing laws allowing jury service for women (McCammon 2012).

Elite Conflict   Recall from chapter 3 that elite conflict is a core dimension in the good-news political opportunity model of social movements (McAdam and Tarrow 2018). When elite groups are conflicting with one another the political system is more vulnerable to challenges from below. Elites cannot ignore, stigmatize, or repress social movements with a unified voice during periods of infighting. Under such circumstances the political system may concede to social movement demands. The susceptibility of the political system during elite conflicts encourages groups to mobilize with the incentive of a greater chance of success. For instance, in the 1930s during the Great Depression, unemployed workers, striking industrial labor unions, and middle-class reform movements (such as the Townsend movement) took advantage of the rivalry between banking and industrial elites to win the passage of the Social Security Act and several other progressive laws (Jenkins and Brents 1989). Renegade elites may even align with a social movement during such periods of conflict, providing the types of political, economic, and legal resources that enhance winning new advantages or favorable policies for marginalized groups.

Elite Blunders   Mistakes by elites and authorities may strengthen a social movement campaign and the prospects to win more concessions (Halebsky 2009). These may include leaked documents from government offices or corporations that emphasize plans of action the general public would find appalling. Elite blunders also include outlandish acts of state repression that are far out of proportion to a movement's demands (Goldstone 1998; Francisco 2005). Such acts bring in much more support from inside and outside the community, which may contribute to a movement's success.

Countermovements   Because social movements mobilize subordinated and excluded groups, elites and other more privileged sectors vehemently resist these efforts. Sometimes this resistance surfaces in the form of countermovements. McCarthy and Zald (1977: 1218) provide a general definition: "A countermovement is a set of opinions and beliefs in a population opposed to a social movement." Countermovements usually create an uphill struggle for the core movement. Not only do movements need to mobilize people and convince bystanders and the public of the worthiness of the cause; they must also attempt to negotiate with elites and authorities to achieve their goals. Countermovements opposed to the core movement add an additional obstacle in this process. Countermovements may attack a movement's frame as well as question the merit and value of the movement's grievances, goals, and strategies (Luna 2017). In short, the appearance of countermovements may make movement success less likely (Soule 2004; Halebsky 2009). Indeed, in the battle over the Equal Rights Amendment for women in the United States mentioned above, states that maintained active anti-ERA organizations were much less likely to ratify the amendment (Soule and Olzak 2004).

Countermovements most likely arise after a movement has gained some policy success but not a decisive triumph (Meyer and Staggenborg 1996). María Inclán (2012) found such dynamics in play in the Zapatista movement in Chiapas, Mexico, in the late 1990s and 2000s. When pro-Zapatista groups (e.g., EZLN) won concessions from the government or even the population in general, anti-Zapatista mobilization would increase. Cultural cleavage issues over abortion, religion, and gun ownership are especially likely to produce strong countermovements. Large corporate enterprises (e.g., Walmart) often organize and fund countermovements to influence public opinion (Walker 2014). Because of the artificial nature of corporate-funded countermovements, opponents disparage such mobilizations with the term "astro-turf" movements.

In some historical cases, countermovements have used intimidating violence, such as white supremacy movements in the United States countering movements for racial equality and citizenship rights (Blee 2017). The Ku Klux Klan and related hate groups employ countermovement violence as a core tactic. Andrews (2004) found that segregationist violence at the local level in Mississippi between the late 1960s and 1980s resulted in less favorable civil rights movement outcomes, including less Black political representation and antipoverty funding, versus regions that did not suffer from these organized repressive actions. In El Salvador in the late 1970s and early 1980s, extreme "death squad" violence took place, where military and paramilitary units dressed in plain clothes killed civilians and suspected opposition movement members and their families, preventing an escalating wave of protest from overthrowing a military government (Stanley 1996; Almeida 2008a). Similar dynamics also occurred in Guatemala (Figueroa Ibarra 1991; Brockett 2005).

COMBINED CONDITIONS: CASE STUDIES OF MOVEMENTS AGAINST NEOLIBERALISM

As stated from the beginning, movement success occurs infrequently. Positive outcomes usually require a combination of the conditions detailed in table 7 to be present. Powerful, well-entrenched elites have little reason to oblige or accommodate a social movement representing excluded social groups; they find it easier to apply repression to the group, channel the protest into routine conflict resolution procedures, or simply ignore the group. The presence of innovative strategies, indigenous organizational structures, external allies, and a favorable political environment provides a social movement with resources (human, financial, and tactical) to conduct and sustain its actions, as well as the means (vocal public support and mass media exposure) to protect it from state apathy or repression. Thus, resource infrastructures, supporters, and an encouraging political environment expand a social movement's bargaining resources. Therefore, social movements that exercise disruptive tactics in a context of multiple favorable conditions are more likely to sustain protest and receive concessions from their adversaries and the state than social movements that find themselves in circumstances with few facilitating conditions.

These combined conditions producing favorable movement outcomes can be observed in the dramatic cases of antineoliberal social movement campaigns in Latin America. As the first quarter of the twenty-first century rapidly unfolds, the world appears to be run more by free trade and free market principles, leaving vulnerable populations unprotected (Almeida and Chase-Dunn 2018). Nonetheless, in specific times and places social movement struggles have slowed down or turned back the relentless march toward full neoliberalism. For example, two major battles took place in the early 2000s over privatization in the countries of El Salvador and Costa Rica. In El Salvador between 1999 and 2003 the government attempted to privatize part of the public healthcare system. In Costa Rica in 2000 the government attempted to privatize telecommunications and electrical power distribution. Social movement campaigns involving tens of thousands of ordinary citizens rose up to defeat both of these efforts in the two countries, resulting in relatively successful outcomes.

The campaign in El Salvador to defend public healthcare from privatization represented one of the largest and most enduring national mobilizations against privatization in Latin America with up to two hundred thousand participants in coordinated demonstrations (3 to 4 percent of the entire national population). The campaign against privatization in Costa Rica was equally impressive with street marches reaching up to one hundred thousand people and protest events coordinated across the national territory. How did both campaigns accomplish this success in a world that is increasingly privatized?

The largest campaign in El Salvador surfaced between September 2002 and June 2003 against the privatization of part of the public healthcare system—the Instituto Salvadoreño del Seguro Social (ISSS). The government created the ISSS in 1949 as a health insurance and medical program for workers in the formal sector during the period of state-led development in the global South (see chapter 8). Campaigners, health workers, and doctors framed the government's attempts to begin outsourcing the ISSS hospital system and medical services to the private sector as a threat that would dismantle the entire public healthcare system, in which 80 to 90 percent of the population depends (González and Alvarenga 2002). They even used a few evocative *framing* slogans to encapsulate the struggle succinctly. One slogan stated, "Healthcare is a right, not a commodity." Another common chant in street protests and on banners was the morbid phrase "Either pay or die," emphasizing the for-profit consequences of a privatized medical care system. Opponents of healthcare privatization also highlighted the role of international financial institutions such as the World Bank and Inter-American Development Bank in financing the reforms as part of the larger process of globalization. Nationally representative public opinion polls taken before the campaign also showed a majority of the public to be against the privatization (Almeida and Delgado 2008). Hence, the campaign enjoyed large numbers of participants, compelling frames, and public opinion support.

The campaign in Costa Rica took place in March and April of 2000 against the privatization of the state-controlled telecommunications and electrical power system—the Instituto Costarricense de Electricidad (ICE). The Costa Rican state established the ICE in 1949 and added telecommunications to the institute in 1963 at the height of state-supported economic development in Latin America. The ICE stands as one of the public's most favored state institutions with its low-cost utility services (electrical power and telecommunications) to consumers and breadth of coverage (recall the reference to the ICE in the anti-CAFTA protest song in chapter 5). By the late 1980s, scholars report that Costa Ricans possessed telephones in their homes nearly three times higher than the average in Latin America (Trejos 1988). ICE labor associations and allied activists made frequent framing references to the ICE as an integral component of the "national patrimony" that "is not for sale," during rallies and street marches. The Costa Rican campaign to impede the ICE privatization legislation involved tens of thousands of participants (likely 4 percent of the national population) and major mass actions in all seven of the nation's provinces.

In El Salvador protest events against healthcare privatization occurred in 26 percent of municipalities, and in Costa Rica 63 percent of municipalities (*cantones*) experienced at least one protest event. The El Salvador antiprivatization campaign produced 550 reported protest events, and the Costa Rica campaign generated 473 distinct protests. Similar to other Latin American campaigns responding to economic globalization that use barricades as a core feature of the repertoire of assertive actions, 32 percent of protest events in El Salvador and 51 percent in Costa Rica involved obstructing traffic (roadblocks). In both countries, nearly two-thirds of protest events included the participation of allies external to the ISSS and ICE institutions, generating broad coalitions (Almeida 2014b). These external allies included many of the types mentioned in table 7, including labor unions, students (university and high school), religious organizations, oppositional political parties, women's associations, and NGOs. In El Salvador, besides the use of highway roadblocks, the activists held massive *marchas blancas* (white marches) in multiple cities, where all participating sectors (including external allies) would dress in white to demonstrate their solidarity with the public healthcare profession.

Both antiprivatization campaigns ended in negotiations with the central government. The governments agreed to halt the privatization process, and the labor unions in charge of the campaigns agreed to desist using disruptive protests such as roadblocks and return to work. In stark contrast, a few years later both countries experienced similar protest campaigns that attempted massive mobilizations to halt the Central American Free Trade Agreement (CAFTA) from being ratified (Raventós Vorst 2018). The general public in both countries was much less aware and more divided about the meaning of CAFTA compared to public sector privatization; this combined with strong US pressure for the respective governments to approve the treaty (Spalding 2014). In the end, CAFTA was approved in both countries despite large-scale resistance, especially in Costa Rica. These exemplary cases demonstrate the special combination of conditions that need to be in place to increase the likelihood of movement success.

CULTURAL OUTCOMES

Movements not only change policies and institutional practices. They also generate impacts in the larger culture. At times, they change the dominant values, beliefs, and norms of a society (Taylor and Van Dyke 2004). We know much less about cultural outcomes, but they deserve much more attention since they are more likely to leave lasting impacts than attempts at policy reform (Van Dyke and Taylor 2018). The protest wave of the 1960s generated a corresponding countercultural movement composed of an alternative lifestyle and several other cultural impacts. Large and successful ethnic-, gender-, and sexuality-based movements expanded collective identities beyond their initial base of support (Earl 2004). In the United States, the LGBTQ movement over the past forty years has dramatically changed beliefs about gay marriage (Van Dyke and Taylor 2018). Schnabel and Sevell (2017) demonstrate that as recently as 1988, only 12 percent of Americans supported the legalization of gay marriage, but by 2014 over 57 percent of Americans were in favor. These shifts in societal beliefs over gay marriage are the result of both social movement mobilization and education campaigns by the LGBTQ movement. The process also followed a similar path in Europe through active national and transnational LGBTQ mobilizations (Ayoub 2016). Often the battle over changing a society's values and beliefs involves movements and countermovements.

In the United States in recent decades movements and countermovements have battled in the so-called cultural wars over abortion rights, legalization of marijuana, and the impact of climate change and global warming. Positive movement outcomes in the cultural arena are often associated with the quality of the messaging of the collective actors and the modularity of the performance. Scholars thus examine if new belief systems and cultural practices become adopted by groups beyond the core movement (Van Dyke and Taylor 2018).

INDIVIDUAL-LEVEL OUTCOMES

Movements also influence the microlevel in transforming the lives of participants. Because one participated actively in a social movement, it may have altered his or her life trajectory. Often these are unintended consequences of activism (Giugni 2004). Participation in social movements has been found to influence people's employment histories, marital status, and subsequent political ideology and political participation. The most examined period of individual-level participation outcomes is in the wave of protest of the 1960s. In the following decades of the participants' lives, they reported to be more likely to continue participating in social movements than those who did not previously participate. Participation in social movements provides positive incentives, such as feelings of camaraderie, collective identity, and personal efficacy (Taylor et al. 2009). Social movement participation has also been found to lead some to work in the service or public sector (McAdam 1988). Social movement activists are also more likely to marry later in life or be divorced. Other studies examining gender differences also have shown that activism by women in progressive movements led to higher salaries than for nonparticipating women, suggesting activism may be a factor in breaking down traditional gender roles with respect to employment (Van Dyke et al. 2000). Others have shown that women's participation in the New Left, Chicano, and civil rights movements of the 1960s directed many of those participants into distinct branches of second wave feminism in the 1970s, namely white, Chicana, and Black feminism (Roth 2004).

FRONTIERS OF SOCIAL MOVEMENT OUTCOMES

Understanding social movement success and failure continues as a vibrant arena for social movement activists and scholars. A focus on more than the policy aspects of movement outcomes increasingly captures the attention of current work. As dynamic and interactive collective performances, movements are much more than the dyadic relationship between excluded groups and their adversaries. The struggles themselves deposit lasting legacies on the social landscape. These legacies include strategies and tactics that failed but may be altered by others in future rounds of contestation, showing that learning has occurred and improving the prospects for success (McCammon 2012). They also include explaining how one protest campaign may "spill over" into the next (Meyer and Whittier 1994; Whittier 2004), such as global economic justice campaigns spilling into the anti-war and climate justice movements via the participation of the same individuals, networks, and organizations. Other enduring remnants include the personal memories, songs, and social ties established during the months and years of mobilizing. How these cultural deposits of social movement struggles persist to influence the larger society and value system remains a fertile ground for scholarship. Finally, knowledge of the combined conditions that lead to more favorable outcomes for collective action should be in urgent demand as we face mounting threats in the twenty-first century over economic inequality, xenophobia, environmental decline, and many other daunting problems.

ADDITIONAL READINGS AND RESOURCES ON MOVEMENT OUTCOMES

Amenta, Edwin, Kenneth Andrews, and Neal Caren. 2018. "The Political Institutions, Processes, and Outcomes Movements Seek to Influence." In

The Wiley-Blackwell Companion to Social Movements, edited by D. Snow, S. Soule, H. Kriesi, and H. McCammon, 449–65. Oxford: Blackwell.

———, Neal Caren, Elizabeth Chiarello, and Yang Su. 2010. "The Political Consequences of Social Movements." *Annual Review of Sociology* 36: 287–307.

Bosi, Lorenzo, Marco Giugni, and Katrin Uba, eds. 2016. *The Consequences of Social Movements*. Cambridge: Cambridge University Press.

Gamson, William. 1990. *The Strategy of Social Protest*, 2nd ed. Belmont, CA: Wadsworth.

Giugni, Marco, Doug McAdam, and Charles Tilly, eds. 1999. *How Social Movements Matter*. Minneapolis: University of Minnesota Press.

Kolb, Felix. 2007. *Protest and Opportunities: The Political Outcomes of Social Movements*. New York: Campus Verlag.

The Youth Outcomes Database. http://yapdatabase-yppnetwork.net/?page_id=2

8   Pushing the Limits

Social Movements in the Global South

This chapter provides focused attention on social movement mobilization in the global South. Previous chapters generally examined social movement dynamics in the global North with some notable exceptions. The "global South" refers to countries in the developing world outside of the industrialized democracies of North America, western Europe, Japan, and Australia. The label "South" is used as the majority of developing countries are geographically located in the southern hemisphere.[1] Making sweeping statements about social movement dynamics in the global South presents several dangers given the diversity of countries in this wide categorical grouping. Indeed, the global South includes countries ranging from the relatively industrialized nations of Mexico, South Korea, South Africa, and Brazil to the lesser developed countries of Honduras, Burma, Mozambique, and Jamaica.

With this heterogeneity in culture, population size and density, degree of economic and technological development (including communications infrastructure), history of colonial conquest, ethnic diversity, natural resource endowments, system of political governance, and ties to world society (A. Baker 2014), there is a corresponding variation in the capacity for excluded groups to mobilize and the form mobilization takes once collective action materializes (Fadaee 2016). The study of social movements largely evolved from an overemphasis on countries in the global North, especially the experience of western Europe and North America (Boudreau 2004). This body of work viewed social movements developing in a relatively linear pattern with the expansion of nation-states, parliamentary democracies, urbanization, and industrialization (Tilly and Wood 2012).[2] In the global South, would-be challengers and subaltern groups confront several different political and economic contexts (as well as obstacles) driving collective action to a variety of trajectories—from revolution to complete demobilization and, in extreme cases, even genocide (Almeida 2008a). The present chapter focuses on these formidable challenges for social movements in the global South with an emphasis on (1) state repression, (2) globalization, and (3) transnational movements.

STATE REPRESSION

Large portions of the territories of Asia, Africa, and the Americas came under colonial domination between the sixteenth and twentieth centuries. European colonial conquest was often accompanied by ideologies of racial hierarchy in order to dehumanize native populations (Williams 1944; Fanon 1963; Rodney 1981; Smedley and Smedley 2012).[3] Collective resistance by colonized people faced extraordinary barriers of imprisonment, torture, enslavement, and death. Many anticolonial acts of noncompliance came in the form of everyday types of resistance, discussed in chapter 2. Beginning in the sixteenth century in the colonized Caribbean and Latin America, Black slaves escaped forced labor and plantation agricultural systems and formed Maroonist communities, in some cases staging larger rebellions (Robinson 2000). From the initial Iberian and later British conquest of the Americas through the twentieth century, indigenous peoples of North, Central, and South America launched major uprisings against foreign occupiers, often ending in brutal campaigns of ethnocide perpetrated by the colonial and neocolonial forces (Galeano 1997; Go 2011). The indigenous resistance to colonialism in Latin America leaves a long list of rebellion leaders and legends (e.g., Cuauhtémoc, Bartolina Sisa, Túpac Katari, Túpac Amaru, Anastasio Aquino, Victoriano Lorenzo, Tecún Umán) that inspired cultures of opposition in subsequent centuries. Beginning with the Haitian Revolution at the dawn of the nineteenth century, regions throughout the global South erupted in national-level rebellions for independence and national sovereignty, continuing into the twentieth century as national liberation struggles.

In contemporary sociological studies, scholars largely focus on governmental repression in authoritarian countries that are at least nominally independent or neocolonial states—nations under the economic influence or dependence of more powerful nations (Go 2011). They ask the perplexing question of how excluded social groups mobilize in the context of a military government or some other form of dictatorship. This obviously serves as an important line of inquiry in terms of the human rights implications for populations living under nondemocratic regimes. Repressive governments intentionally craft systems of social control to deter collective opposition (Johnston 2011). Approximately 30 percent of countries in the world today are classified as authoritarian or nondemocratic, while another 24 percent are "semi-authoritarian," mixing state repression with some democratic elements such as partially competitive elections.[4] About 45 percent of the global population resides in semiauthoritarian or authoritarian states.

Repressive regimes employ a variety of strategies to suppress social movement activity from emerging (Menjívar and Rodriguez 2009). These strategies include restrictions on basic civil rights such as freedom to assemble and form civic organizations, associations, and labor unions. Authoritarian governments are usually not represented by elected officials and do not hold competitive elections between political parties having different interests and political ideologies and perspectives. Some authoritarian states also employ elaborate infrastructures of surveillance, including spy networks, paramilitary bodies dispatched in rural regions, and tight control over the communication channels of average citizens (including information and communication technologies, ICTs). Colombia, for example, established an elaborate paramilitary network between the 1980s and the 2010s to suppress leftist insurgents, narco-trafficking, and even rural social movements (Archila Neira et al. 2012). Table 8 lists some of the primary characteristics of authoritarian and semiauthoritarian governments.

Despite these central obstacles for collective action under repressive regimes, there are circumstances in which oppressed populations can overcome the impediments and initiate and even sustain movement campaigns. Chapter 3 briefly outlined some of these facilitating conditions under the discussion of "repressive threats" and "erosion of rights" within the threat-based theoretical model of collective action. Over the past few decades many cases of social movement resistance have emerged in repressive contexts in the global South that enhance our understanding of collective action under unlikely circumstances. Some of the most common factors pushing collective action in authoritarian and semiauthoritarian regimes include (1) organizational infrastructures, (2) erosion of rights, and (3) state repressive actions.

Organizational Infrastructures

In order to establish resistance to a repressive government, the opposition requires some form of organizational basis. Just as routine social movements in democratic contexts are more likely to arise from established institutions and organizations (McAdam 2003), so too are movements in authoritarian regimes. In the global South a variety of potential organiza-

TABLE 8. Characteristics of Authoritarian Governments

Authoritarian Characteristic	Role in Suppressing Collective Action
Restrictions on freedom of assembly	Creates obstacles for excluded groups to work together and publicly express grievances
Restrictions on freedom of association	Limits ability of civil society groups to form autonomous organizations to advocate on behalf of marginalized populations
Special states of emergency (martial law, curfews, restrictions on movement)	Difficult to mobilize public actions without incurring severe repression
Restrictions on freedom of the press and social media	Hampers attempts to keep the public informed and to investigate government actions. State restrictions on social media and ICT access impede civil society's ability to communicate, share critical political information, and coordinate actions
Heavy police and military presence in public places, state spy networks, paramilitary infrastructure	Intimidates and instills fear in the general population, making collective action much costlier. Surveillance structures also generate sentiments of distrust between individuals (deterring joint action)
No elections, fraudulent, or noncompetitive elections	Government is more likely to act with impunity against attempts at collective opposition (there is no electoral accountability or risk of removal from office). Collective movements have no ally in a political party to advocate for legislation

tions and institutions may play a role in uniting and protecting individuals and groups attempting to collectively resist a violent government.

The religious sector provides one grouping of institutions that at times offers space, moral authority, and resources to mobilize against dictatorships. Temples, churches, and mosques provide locations to coordinate actions without attracting attention from the state security forces. In many societies in the global South, major religious institutions act as the largest organizational force beyond the government. Parishes and other places of worship are distributed throughout the national territory, even in rural regions with smaller populations. This geographical dispersion allows for the expansion of collective action on a national scale—a process Tarrow and McAdam (2005) refer to as "scale shift."

The role of religious organizations as an oppositional force promoting collective resistance is usually an exceptional situation. In most times and places, dominant religions and religious institutions may legitimate the status quo and the ruling authoritarian regime. Indeed, an authoritarian government would likely not permit an oppositional religion or church to thrive that criticized its existence. One historically exceptional situation occurred in Latin America in the 1960s and 1970s. The Catholic Church elaborated a series of social reforms as part of its official doctrine in the early 1960s called Vatican II. Later in the decade, at the 1968 Latin American Bishops' Conference in Medellín, Colombia, these reforms were pushed further when the church called on the "preferential option for the poor." At this time, many regimes in the region were authoritarian or semiauthoritarian. The change in church policy launched a number of social movements throughout Latin America led by parish priests, nuns, and empowered laypersons (Smith 1991; Mackin 2015). In Central America in the 1960s, backed by Vatican II reforms, the Catholic Church initiated a number of modest campaigns, including organizing rural cooperatives, literacy projects, and more informal Christian Base Communities. When authoritarian governments in El Salvador, Guatemala, Honduras, and Nicaragua began to repress these Catholic initiatives, larger, more militant social movements emerged from these Catholic organizations, including revolutionary organizations in the 1970s (Vela Castañeda 2012; Wood 2003; Marti Puig 2012; Chávez 2017).

The enormous impact of Vatican II and liberation theology in mobilizing the poor against state repression cannot be discounted. Catholic Church-based organizations of the 1960s and 1970s that struggled against authoritarian regimes endured into the 1980s and 1990s. This early organizational work is largely responsible for some of the largest social movements in Latin America, including the Landless Workers movements in Brazil (Wolford 2010), the Zapatista rebellion in Chiapas, Mexico (Harvey 1998), and human rights movements in Argentina, Chile, and Uruguay (Loveman 1998). Mosque networks played a similar role in the 1979 Iranian Revolution (Kurzman 2005).

Another major organizational force challenging repressive regimes is found in the educational sector. High school and university students as well as public school teachers have served to organize social movement campaigns against authoritarian states. This sector already begins with an awareness of basic civil and human rights, and would likely question authoritarian forms of governance. Similar to religious institutions, public schools are located throughout the national territory. Since the 1950s, there has been a tremendous growth in public education throughout the global South (D. Baker 2014). This includes enrollments in primary and secondary education and the physical building of schools and universities (part of the historic process of state-led development discussed below). Public universities not only provide opposition via the student body; they provide "safe spaces" for civic groups to meet, build coalitions, and strategize campaigns of resistance to the regime (Polletta 1999). Examples abound of the role of universities in major movements against authoritarian rule, from Latin American revolutionary movements (Wickham-Crowley 1992) to the 1989 Tiananmen Square movement in Beijing (Zhao 2001). University students acted as the vanguard in opposing the Korean dictatorship from the 1960s to the early 1980s (Chang 2015). During the Arab Spring in Yemen, "college campuses played a central role in political mobilization and activism" (Gasim 2014: 123). After a military coup in Honduras in 2009, the "backbone" of the resistance movement in the immediate aftermath was the public school teachers' associations—one of the largest organized forces in the country (Sosa 2013). School teachers' labor unions also took on the one-party system in Mexico prior to democratization in 2000 (Cook 1994).

Other types of civil society organizations also resist authoritarian regimes. Labor unions act as a prodemocracy movement in relatively more industrialized repressive states in the global South. In Argentina, Brazil, Chile, South Africa, and Uruguay the labor movement served as the most organized sector to confront nondemocratic governments in the 1970s and 1980s (Drake 1996; Seidman 1994). A number of other social organizations, such as nongovernmental organizations (NGOs), women's associations, human rights groups, indigenous communities, agricultural cooperatives, and peasant associations, also have mobilized against dictatorships. These groups are especially threatening to governments when they come together in large coalitions. This is precisely what took place in Honduras in 2009 following the military coup, when a variety of groups united in a large coalition called the Frente Nacional de Resistencia Popular, including NGOs, universities, public school teachers, LGBTQ communities, Garifuna, indigenous peoples' alliances, feminist organizations, rural cooperatives, and organized labor. Other everyday organizations and groups may also emerge as an oppositional force. These include routine organizations such as recreational clubs and sports teams, neighborhood committees, and youth groups, discussed in chapter 4. Such common groups can better escape the attention of repressive authorities than more overtly political groups. Oppositional forces may also appropriate everyday organizations as a way to expand the struggle.

A remaining puzzling question, however, centers on explaining how organizations emerge under a repressive government in the first place. Historical timing matters. Often the organizations resisting dictatorship materialize during a less authoritarian phase of the regime—a period of relatively less repression. At times, repressive governments may go through a stage of political liberalization (a "thaw") whereby power holders allow some civil liberties and restricted electoral competition. During such brief openings, activists and civil society may be able to establish organizations such as student associations, labor unions, and teachers' unions. They can use this newly created organizational infrastructure to mobilize in the present as well as draw on these social ties to sustain resistance when the regime closes the opening. In short, using a glacial analogy, periods of political liberalization "deposit" organizations in civil society that may endure and be used to resist dictatorships in future, less hospitable conditions, when the landscape has changed (Almeida 2008a).

Erosion of Rights

The organizational infrastructure only provides part of the story on resistance under a repressive government. Organizations explain "the how" of opposition. Erosion of rights and state repressive actions provide the core threat incentives to challenge despotic governments—or "the why" of collective resistance.[5] Authoritarian regimes by their nature take away fundamental rights. They deny basic international human rights enshrined by the United Nations Universal Declaration of Human Rights and likely fail to deliver on rights, protections, and freedoms formally stated in their own national constitutions. Given these ongoing circumstances, when do people finally decide that a lack of basic rights is intolerable and rebel? One of the most dramatic signals of a loss of rights comes with tampering in the electoral process.

In long-standing authoritarian regimes, conducting fraudulent elections intensifies already-existing grievances against the state. Fraudulent elections act as one of the most fundamental violations of the relationship between citizens and government that motivate mobilization. Such governmental actions instantly place a large segment of the national population under similar circumstances, while the prior election campaign season gives oppositional groups a short period to organize (Kadivar 2017). Elections that are perceived to be fraudulent or the canceling of elections frequently set off movements of mass defiance (McAdam and Tarrow 2010; Norris et al. 2015). For example, Kalandadze and Orenstein (2009) documented seventeen major electoral fraud mobilizations between 1991 and 2005 in Eurasia,

Africa, and Latin America. In a separate study between 1989 and 2011, Brancati (2016: 3–5) identified 310 major protests to "adopt or uphold democratic elections" in ninety-two countries. Since 2011, electoral mobilizations over perceived fraud have continued throughout the world, as in Cambodia in 2013. The 2009 general elections in Iran unleashed the largest postrevolution mobilization, witnessed in the country as the "Green Movement," launching weeks of street marches contesting the election results as illegitimate (Kurzman 2011; Parsa 2016). Even the extremely narrow electoral victory in the 2006 Mexican presidential elections generated a month of mass street demonstrations and disruptions with claims of fraud by the defeated candidate of the left, Andrés Manuel López Obrador (later elected in a landslide in 2018). In late 2017 and 2018, perceived fraud and systematic irregularities in the Honduran presidential elections resulted in multiple street marches of over one hundred thousand people, general strikes, and hundreds of roadblocks erected by citizens across the country (Sosa 2018).

Ongoing electoral fraud in multiple and sequential electoral cycles may even alter the *character* of collective action to take on more radical forms with the focus of overthrowing the prevailing regime (especially when the fraud is combined with the threat of state repression). This follows the pattern of El Salvador in the 1970s. After a period of political liberalization in the 1960s, the military regime held four consecutive fraudulent national elections between 1972 and 1978. After several rounds of massive nonviolent demonstrations against the unfair elections, many sympathizers of the center-left opposition parties radicalized their position and eventually threw their support behind insurgent revolutionaries, eventuating in El Salvador's long decade of civil war and violence (Almeida 2003; 2008a). Finally, military coups that interrupt the constitutional order and overthrow popularly elected governments may also generate large-scale collective action. This was the case following the 2009 military coup in Honduras that ousted the democratically elected government of Manuel Zelaya. Immediately following Zelaya's expulsion, an anticoup mass movement erupted that sustained the largest mobilizations in Honduran history until Zelaya's return in 2011, with street demonstrations reaching up to a reported four hundred thousand participants (Sosa 2012). A similar but much more concise dynamic of an anticoup mass movement took place following the short-lived military coup in Venezuela in 2002 that attempted to drive out President Hugo Chávez Frías.

State Repressive Actions

Acts of state repression provide another factor driving collective resistance in authoritarian regimes. Repression occurs when states coerce, harass, detain, torture, and kill residents under their jurisdiction. The state repression literature offers a vast and complex accounting of the dynamics between governmental violence and popular response (Chang 2015; Davenport 2010; Earl 2011; Earl and Soule 2010). At times, state repression quells attempts at collective action because of the heavy risks incurred in the mobilization process (Johnston 2011). This aspect of state repression is more consistent with the political opportunity strand of political process theory discussed in chapter 3. At other times, state and police repression encourages heightened attempts at protest (Brockett 2005).

In authoritarian states, continued repressive action against nonviolent social movements may change the nature of collective action itself and switch the trajectory of protest onto a much more radical path (Alimi, Demetriou, and Bosi 2015; Almeida 2007a). This was clearly the case in the Arab Spring with Libya, Yemen, and Syria and, to a lesser extent, Egypt (Khatib and Lust 2014). These protests began as campaigns of mass nonviolence in 2011 and 2012, what Schock (2005; 2015b) refers to as "unarmed insurrections." When the states of Libya, Syria, Yemen, and later Egypt violently repressed these nonviolent challenges, after they had been sustained for several weeks and months, the movements radicalized and began using violent and more military-style tactics (Alimi 2016). In contrast, in countries implementing softer forms of repression, states may "contain escalation" from converting into radicalized mobilization, as in the case of Jordan during the Arab Spring (Moss 2014). Scholars of revolutionary movements find that radicalization appears much more likely under exclusionary types of authoritarian regimes that fail to incorporate the middle and working classes into structures of political participation or to distribute the benefits of economic growth (Foran 2005; Goodwin 2001). At the microlevel, outrageous acts of state repression also push individuals to take on new roles and identities as revolutionary activists and participants (Viterna 2013).

This unique property of repressive actions, with the potential to radicalize collective action, explains why protest escalates into revolutionary movements. Promising areas for advancing studies of the impacts of state repression by way of predicting the likelihood of protest escalation, or of demobilization, include the severity and probability of the repressive action being carried out (Einwohner and Maher 2011; Maher 2010); the cataloging of repressive tactics used by the state (Boudreau 2004; Moss 2014); and the precise type and level of organizational infrastructure necessary to sustain mobilization under high-risk conditions (Loveman 1998; Pilati 2016). Equally important for understanding whether collective resistance will surface against a repressive regime is the ability of movement leaders and cultural activists to construct compelling collective action frames and tap into political cultures of opposition and resistance (Foran 2005; Selbin 2010), as elaborated in chapter 5.

GLOBALIZATION: THE DEEPENING OF NEOLIBERALISM

While combatting state repression and authoritarianism in the global South remains one of the most vital areas of social movements to comprehend, especially in the protection of human rights, another transformative process induces perhaps even greater levels of mass mobilization in more countries: economic globalization. With a new wave of worldwide democratization taking off in the 1970s, today fewer countries are classified as authoritarian (Huntington 1991; Markoff and Burridge 2018). The most powerful trend in the global South over the past four decades is found in the shift toward economic liberalization. Academics and activists alike use the popular term "neoliberalism" to describe the dynamics of free market-driven globalization.

Classical economic liberalism covered the period of the late nineteenth century until the Great Depression in the 1930s (Polanyi 1944). This era was largely dominated by unregulated business activities and markets, creating vast amounts of wealth along with a number of social problems, including intensive labor exploitation, public health crises, and a worldwide economic depression. From the 1930s to the 1970s, the pendulum swung in the other direction with governments around the world regulating economic activities and investing heavily in basic economic and public infrastructures to stimulate demand; this is referred to as "state-led development." With the rise of greater global economic competition in the 1970s and an economic slowdown, a new doctrine of neoliberalism was ascendant by the 1980s.

Neoliberalism is both an ideology and a set of economic development practices whereby state intervention in the economy is scaled back to basic functions of social order, governance, defense, the protection of property rights, and the attraction of private investment (Bockman 2011). Neoliberal practitioners in international financial institutions, think tanks, transnational corporations, and economic ministries are turning once again to a more liberalized economy via global integration, free trade, privatization, and deregulation of economic activities (Spalding 2014). In the global South, neoliberalism represents a distinct economic context in which subaltern groups struggle for survival. In many respects, neoliberalism represents a homogenizing force in that across Asia, Africa, Latin America, and eastern Europe, countries face similar external pressures to liberalize their economies—what sociologists refer to as "structural equivalence" (see chapter 4). Most of the global South faces similar circumstances in terms of economic policies, and social movements have erupted in several world regions mobilizing over similar economic measures (Walton and Seddon 1994). In order to place neoliberalism in a proper historical context, an excursion into earlier epochs of economic development and social movement struggles is necessary.[6]

Each major epoch of economic development in the global South in the twentieth and twenty-first centuries produced a dominant form of oppositional collective action. The economic development templates include, in sequential and historical order, (1) agro-export of a few basic agricultural/resource commodities, (2) state-led development, and (3) neoliberalism. While these broad forms of development stretching across the globe are well known as distinctive strategies for capitalist accumulation, they also correspond to types of social movement activity within a historical and comparative framework. Each development strategy generated conflicts in specific economic sectors between particular groups. Under monoculture production (1900–1940s), peasant cultivators and rural wage earners confronted agro-industrialists, landlords, state agents, and transnational agricultural companies. During the period of the expansion of the development state (1940s–1980s), urban workers battled industrial capitalists and the state while rural sectors demanded that modernizing governments implement agrarian reform. In the current era dominated by neoliberal development strategies, we see NGOs, new social movements, and sectors surviving from state-led development enter into conflicts with the shrinking welfare state and with transnational capital. Table 9 summarizes these historical periods and the most prevalent forms of collective action.

As table 9 summarizes, in the first half of the twentieth century nations and colonized territories of the global South were characterized by agro-export production and mineral extraction. Some of the largest revolts occurred in these sectors, especially when laboring groups were threatened by subsistence survival in the form of mass unemployment, wage cuts, and new forms of taxation. In the aftermath of World War II and decolonization in Africa and Asia, governments in the developing world engaged in a variety of state modernization and industrialization projects (Cohn 2012). From the 1950s to the 1980s, urbanization, industrialization, and state infrastructural expansion accelerated at an impressive pace. The process produced a greater variety of groups and civil society actors with a number of demands. Organized groups viewed the expanding state and economy as "good news," as a *political opportunity* to expand existing benefits and gain new advantages by legalizing their labor associations, extending welfare

TABLE 9. Development Strategies and Forms of Collective Action in the Global South

Economic Development Strategy	Core Economic Activities	Core Oppositional Actors in Movement Activities	Forms of Collective Resistance
Agro-export, monoculture, and raw material exports (1900–1940s)	Export limited number of agricultural commodities to global North	Peasants and rural wage earners (sometimes aligned with urban craft and artisanal labor)	Everyday forms of resistance, rural strikes, insurrections
State-led development (1940s–1980s)	Diversify agricultural activities, initiate manufacturing on a larger scale, massive expansion of the state social and economic infrastructure	Rural cooperatives, urban labor unions in state and manufacturing sectors, educational sectors	Urban and rural strikes, urban street mobilizations
Neoliberal development (1980s–2010s)	Diversify agricultural sector into nontraditional export crops, privatize state-run manufacturing and public infrastructure, open to greater foreign investment and free trade	Public sector unions, NGOs, new social movements, oppositional political parties (often in broad multisectoral coalitions)	National-level campaigns against neoliberal policies, demonstrations, road blocks on major highways, civic strikes

SOURCE: Almeida (2016).

and social security benefits, and securing new urban services and resources such as education, basic healthcare, land titles, electricity, and potable water (Castells 1983). Urban labor unions, students, educators, and other professional associations often served as the vanguard in these struggles as the rural sector organized in cooperatives and peasant organizations demanding that the modernizing state enact agrarian reform.

The neoliberal era of the 1980s to the present scaled back on state intervention in the economy and opened nation-states to greater foreign investment and integration into new global markets (Robinson 2014; Spalding 2014). The foreign debt crisis of the 1980s inaugurated the period and provided sustained external pressure to enact economic liberalization and privatization. Such practices were viewed by the working and middle classes as a direct threat to the economic and social gains achieved in the previous period of state-led economic development (Walton and Seddon 1994; Silva 2009).

By the early 1980s, the development state entered into stagnation with the onset of the third-world debt crisis. Unprecedented levels of borrowing from banks in the global North in the 1970s rapidly deteriorated the terms of trade with a rise in interest rates and decline in third-world commodity prices (Walton and Seddon 1994). Between 1980 and 1982, third-world commodity prices dropped by one third to their lowest levels in thirty years (Walton in Schaeffer 2009: 87), making debt payments even more difficult. Countries as diverse as Romania, Poland, Mexico, and Costa Rica defaulted on their loans early in the decade, and with the threat of dozens of other countries also defaulting, the World Bank and International Monetary Fund (IMF) stepped in to manage the crisis. These international financial institutions renegotiated the schedule of the original foreign loans and provided new lines of credit in exchange for the economic liberalization of third-world governments. These conditionality agreements became known as "structural adjustment loans" (Vreeland 2007). Between 1982 and 1986, thirty-seven structural adjustment agreements were signed between the international financial institutions and states in the global South (Walton and Seddon 1994). The result was a slow dismantling of already feeble welfare states in the developing world.

The erosion of the development state occurred in two sequential phases. Between the early 1980s and the 1990s, governments reached multiple structural adjustment agreements with the IMF and the World Bank. In this first phase, nations in the global South implemented a variety of austerity policies, including currency devaluation, wage freezes, mass layoffs in the public sector, labor flexibility laws, privatization of state-run enterprises and factories, and subsidy cuts to dozens of areas, including food, housing, transportation, education, healthcare, and agricultural credit and inputs. Structural adjustment agreements often explicitly stipulated a series of such conditions or policy changes.[7] By the 1990s, a second phase of neoliberal policy making occurred. These policies included privatization of the state infrastructure and free trade (Almeida 2010a). The privatization programs of the late 1990s and early 2000s were fundamentally different from the selling off of government-run factories in the 1980s. The more recent round of privatization centered on the basic economic and social infrastructure of electrical power production and distribution, telecommunications, ports, mail, pensions, healthcare, education, and even water and sewage. Such processes were already accelerating in Africa in the 1980s. Young (1991: 51) reports in 1985 that only fourteen African states had a privatization policy on the public agenda, but by 1990 forty African nations (90 percent of countries on the continent) were preparing a major program of privatization. By 2008 most countries in the global South had been under an IMF or World Bank structural adjustment agreement for several years (see Almeida [2015] for a global map of structural adjustment duration by country).

A second related strategy to dismantling the import substitution industrialization model of development focused on the signing of regional free trade agreements. This neoliberal pathway broke down earlier protectionist policies that characterized state-led development to shield domestic industries from international competition. In the western hemisphere, free trade commenced with the North American Free Trade Agreement (NAFTA), which was first implemented in Canada, the United States, and Mexico in 1994. In 1996 the World Trade Organization was established from several rounds of GATT negotiations in order to liberalize trade on a global scale.[8] In the 2000s, the United States negotiated several free trade agreements with Central America (CAFTA), Panama, Peru, Colombia, Chile, and South Korea (Spalding 2014). The Bush administration in the United States faced stiff social movement opposition in attempting a Latin American-wide free trade agreement—the Free Trade Area of the Americas (Von Bülow 2011)— and a treaty with Ecuador in 2006 that ultimately ended in defeat.

These free trade agreements occurred in the context of a new international division of labor taking shape in the late twentieth century (Nash and Fernandez-Kelly 1984). Transnational corporations in the global North took advantage of the new communications and transportation (e.g., containerization) technologies to expand and accelerate manufacturing operations in the global South (Gereffi 1994; Bonacich and Wilson 2008). Export processing zones of textile and light industrial manufacturing in the Caribbean and Latin America represented the prototype of this new mode of economic development (Dicken 2011). Such manufacturing enterprises have surpassed the production value of agricultural exports in many traditional agrarian economies (Robinson 2008; Anner 2011). Export processing zones usually avoid labor organizing and unions, but the largely female labor forces in these industries have successfully mobilized on occasion (Armbruster-Sandoval 2005; Bickham Mendez 2005; Mckay 2006) and at times escalated to full-scale strike waves (Anner and Liu 2016). The new international division of labor has evolved in the twenty-first century into a global production process via a series of commodity chains linking resource extraction and raw material processing to manufacturing, retailing, and research and development (Bair 2009).

Given the strict limits of social movement organizing in the newer export processing industries, some of the most prominent social movement activity over the past three decades has occurred over the implementation of government austerity and privatization policies (Almeida 2010a). First occurring through coercive isomorphism (DiMaggio and Powell 1983) associated with debt dependency, these neoliberal policies became legitimated by executive branches of government around the world (Markoff and Montecinos 1993; Babb 2013). In Asia, Africa, eastern Europe, and Latin America, privatization conflicts have arisen exceedingly in the late 1990s and 2000s. In China hundreds of thousands of workers have participated in strikes and petitions against the closure and privatization of thousands of state-owned firms between the 1990s and the 2010s (Cai 2010; Chen 2011). Massive strikes have taken place by public employees in India in the late 1990s and 2000s (Uba 2008), including the largest strike in human history with 180 million Indian workers protesting privatization in September 2016.[9] Similar mass actions throughout the developing world demonstrate that the transition to a neoliberal economic development strategy is not uncontested.

Since neoliberal reforms act as a direct reversal of the state-led development policies of the previous five decades, the sectors driving the opposition to privatization, austerity, and free trade often derive from the institutions that were established or expanded rapidly under state-led development (Walton 1998; Almeida 2012; 2015). These sectors include universities, public schools, public hospitals, as well as the energy and telecommunication sectors. In larger, newly industrializing countries characterized by mixed economies, such as Brazil, India, Mexico, South Africa, and South Korea, opposition also comes from workers and labor unions in state-run factories and banks (Sandoval 2001).

Not only have organized opponents used strikes, road blockades, and street actions in an attempt to redirect the neoliberal state, but oppositional groups have also turned to electoral mobilization. Indeed, the "pink tide" governments of the left and center-left in Latin America have largely triumphed in electoral contests via grievances over neoliberal development strategies (Silva 2009; Levitsky and Roberts 2011). Between 1998 and the 2010s, this pathway included elections in Argentina, Bolivia, Brazil, Chile, Ecuador, El Salvador, Mexico, Nicaragua, Paraguay, Uruguay, and Venezuela.

Foran (2005) even states that we may now be viewing an innovative route to revolution through the ballot box, if the newly installed governments enact the same far-reaching structural changes as an insurrectionary movement that attains power via extraconstitutional means.

While neoliberal development strategies benefit particular domestic class-fractions, such as transnational elites in the financial sector, new middle classes in the service sector (Cordero Ulate 2005), export sector capitalists, and agribusinesses in nontraditional export crops, the variety of economic policies and structural adjustment austerity measures creates the potential to drive collective action in multiple sectors of civil society. For example, labor flexibility laws that eroded collective bargaining rights secured in the previous period of state-led development resulted in some of the most intensive protests by labor unions in Korea (Koo 2001), Panama (Almeida 2014b), and Brazil. Privatization policies that affect multiple social sectors such as healthcare, water, and electricity distribution have encouraged broad coalitions of multiple groups to organize antiprivatization protest campaigns. As illustrated in chapter 7, these multisectoral coalitions may include public sector labor unions, opposition political parties, women's groups, students, NGOs, and environmental associations (Almeida 2014b).

Earlier histories of state-led development often determine the particular composition of the oppositional coalition. For example, states with a strong corporatist history of incorporating popular sectors into state structures and state-sponsored associations often maintain relatively strong labor unions into the neoliberal period (Anner and Liu 2016). Hence, in Argentina, Brazil, India, Mexico, and Panama, labor unions are well represented in oppositional coalitions against privatization. In nations with an extremely repressive past, excluded social sectors had to form their own civil society associations to meet everyday needs and agitate for social change. This legacy continues in the present with grassroots NGOs participating with high frequency in antineoliberal campaigns in El Salvador, Guatemala, Nicaragua, and Bolivia (Almeida 2014b; Boulding 2014). NGOs in the global South are also increasingly connecting to transnational social movements (Silva 2013; Smith and Wiest 2012).

Because the neoliberal period of development has coincided with the democratization of substantial portions of the global South, the participation of political parties in antineoliberal protest episodes occurs with greater frequency. Opposition political parties can use unpopular economic liberalization measures to mobilize new constituencies in future electoral rounds while at the same time using their membership base to actively participate in street demonstrations (Almeida 2010b). Democratization also allows more political space for emerging new social movements and NGOs to coordinate activities without facing the extreme forms of suppression that less democratic regimes employ (Almeida and Johnston 2006; Tilly and Wood 2012). This particular combination of democratization and orthodox free market reforms provided both the political opportunities and the economic threats driving massive waves of antineoliberal protest in the late 1990s and 2000s in Argentina, Bolivia, and Ecuador (Silva 2009), as well as several record-breaking protest campaigns in Central America over free trade, privatization, and neoliberal restructuring (Almeida 2014b). In the 2010s, Brazil and India have experienced record-breaking strikes over similar neoliberal reforms. Comparable campaigns over water privatization have occurred in Indonesia and Uruguay, while Bulgaria exploded in nationwide protests in 2013 over electricity price hikes connected to privatization by European energy companies in the preceding years. Costa Rica endured its largest general strike in modern history in 2018 over an austerity policy (*reforma fiscal*) that would increase the costs of basic consumption items on the working and middle classes.

The organizers of these campaigns often are most concerned with the loss of access to state-subsidized services and resources, such as electricity, health, education, sanitation, basic foods, and transportation, which were more readily available under state-led development (Walton and Seddon 1994; Auyero 2002; Eckstein and Wickham-Crowley 2015). More sustained resistance is expected in nations where past economic liberalization policies failed to lower costs and increase access to vital services and resources (Spronk and Terhorst 2012). In sum, much of the organizational basis of the opposition in the neoliberal period of development is rooted in the state sectors that were built up in the previous state-led development period. Social movements draw on their identities of social citizenship rights to mobilize campaigns against austerity and the weakening of the welfare state. Much work still needs to be undertaken by students of collective action on the particular neoliberal measures that tend to create the highest levels of mobilization and on which social groups are most likely to participate in the resistance movements.

Glocalization: Local Resistance to Neoliberalism and the Case of Mexico

Our preceding discussion centered on how globalization produces national-level resistance in the global South against the policies associated with neoliberalism (e.g., privatization, free trade, subsidy cuts, labor flexibility, wage freezes, mass layoffs). On closer inspection, mobilization tends to be a local process that may scale up into national-level campaigns. Just as in our previous cases in the global North with the maps of the Women's Marches, Fight for $15, and Occupy Wall Street, there is variation in the global South across local units within nations in terms of which communities rise up against neoliberalism. By moving the analysis to the local level, we can capture a more fine-grained analysis of the forces actually mobilizing people. Scholars refer to the interaction between global forces and local communities as "glocalization" or "glocal mobilization" (Auyero 2001).

The local-level conditions associated with community resistance to economic globalization include (1) state structures such as highways, administrative offices, universities, and public schools, (2) community infrastructures such as local organizations, local chapters of political parties, and NGOs, and (3) community experience in collective action (Almeida 2012; 2014b). We would predict more resistance to neoliberalism in towns and villages with these attributes than in localities that lack such conditions. Administrative offices offer places for movements to bring their demands to state officials. These state offices are usually concentrated in provincial capitals and in the capital cities of the developing world. Highways and transportation corridors provide locations for collective actors to exercise leverage by blocking roads. Universities and public schools also allow for students and public educators to join in protest campaigns. Community organizations and local chapters of political parties are also unevenly distributed across national territories, creating inequities in mobilization potential between geographic regions. Communities that have successfully mobilized in the recent past would also be more likely to mobilize in the present.

We can see these local mobilization processes with the case of the "Gasolinazo" that occurred in Mexico in 2017. The Gasolinazo was a major protest campaign against Mexico's economic liberalization policy to deregulate the price of petroleum and gas for consumers. It is a neoliberal policy in that it turns the price of gasoline to free market forces in place of protecting citizens via state-sponsored subsidies. The change in policy also runs counter to one of the major achievements of the Mexican Revolution—the nationalization of petroleum and the creation of PEMEX, the Mexican state petroleum institution.

The dominant political parties voted to take away the subsidization of gasoline costs for consumers in late 2016. The new neoliberal policy went into effect in January 2017. Protests erupted immediately in many locations throughout the country when citizens saw the rise in gas prices. In

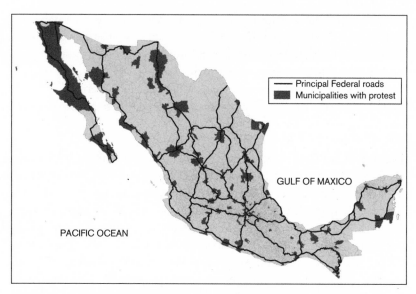

FIGURE 15.   Mexican Gas Protests, 2017. Constructed from data at www
.eluniversal.com.mx and https://www.animalpolitico.com.

January 2017 alone, there were thousands of individual protest events over
the new gas prices (Mexico City alone reported 405 protest events).[10] It is
one of the largest sustained protest campaigns in Mexico in decades—
evidence once again that neoliberalism creates some of the most extensive
and dramatic mobilizations in the contemporary era. Figure 15 illustrates
the distribution of the municipalities in Mexico that held at least one
protest event.

  Figure 15 shows the local-level actions against the gas price hikes in
Mexico. Over 139 municipalities reported at least one protest event against
the subsidy cut. The local protests clearly targeted administrative offices
with twenty-nine out of thirty-one (94%) state capitals reporting mobilizations (protest events were reported in Aguas Calientes, Guanajuato,
Guadalajara, Colima, Toluca, Morelia, Mexicali, Cuernavaca, Xalapa,
Oaxaca, etc.). In addition, many of the individual protest events involved
roadblocks on highways as a means to place pressure on the government
(often led by transportation workers). As the map illustrates, a major
national highway intersects 99 of the 139 municipalities (71%) participating in the protest campaign. Protest campaigns against neoliberal economic
policies in Argentina, Bolivia, Costa Rica, Colombia, Ecuador, El Salvador,

Guatemala, Honduras, Nicaragua, Panama, Paraguay, and Peru have also used highway barricades and roadblocks as a core protest tactic (Auyero 2002; Almeida 2014b; Rossi 2017). As the protests continued in mid-January, local chapters of opposition political parties (such as MORENA) also began to organize mobilizations. Similar fuel subsidy cuts in Nigeria in 2012 and Haiti in 2018 created massive protest campaigns similar to Mexico's.

Ecological Crises and Globalization

The global South may be entering a new period or a new phase within neo-liberalism whereby the axis of conflict is moving away from the battle over welfare state institutions to environmental and ecological battles (Almeida and Pérez Martin 2019). In the past ten years in Central America, for example, environmental conflicts have been beginning to replace the mobilizations of the earlier neoliberal period over public sector privatization, austerity, and free trade. Most of the battles are local, and they are occurring with greater frequency over mining, hydroelectric projects, deforestation, pesticide poisoning, and biofuels (Cordero Ulate 2009). In 2018 the trends of ecological crisis and neoliberalism combined to produce an explosive national uprising in Nicaragua. Early in the year, protests took place over the environmental threats of mining, the construction of an interoceanic canal, and the failure of the state to impede a major fire in a protected tropical forest. By mid-April the environmental protests converted into a national uprising when the government announced it was changing the structure of the national social security system (INSS) based on suggestions from the IMF—raising the age of retirement and demanding higher individual contributions with fewer benefits. Students and INSS beneficiaries began a series of protests in dozens of towns and cities against the neoliberal reforms and were met with brutal repression in which government security forces killed up to four hundred people.

A new global round of intensive resource extraction (Bunker and Ciccantell 2005; Bebbington and Bury 2013) may be the economic development strategy that drives the newer forms of collective action throughout the global South (Arce 2014). Many of these resource conflicts are merging with peasant movements in rural Africa, Asia, and Latin America that have struggled against cheap foreign agricultural imports and the adoption of new agribusiness models that threaten their livelihoods (McMichael 2008). These new collective struggles over natural resources, climate change, and sustainable environments may become the dominant form of social movement activity in the global South before the mid-twenty-first century.

TRANSNATIONAL MOVEMENTS

The rise of transnational movements serves as another trend shaping collective action in the global South in the twenty-first century. Chapter 2 defined transnational movements as social movements operating in at least two countries (Tarrow 2005). The more countries in which the movement is active, the more extensive its "transnationalness." Hence, there exists wide variation in the global reach of transnational movements, from two countries to nearly all nations on the planet (in the case of climate justice). Even though rudimentary transnational movements have existed for centuries, deepening globalization in the late twentieth century has produced a steep rise in the number of transnational movement campaigns. The past three decades alone have witnessed a near tripling in the number of transnational social movement organizations, with 25 percent installing their headquarters in the global South (Smith and Wiest 2012). Transnational collective action also represents a diversity of types of movements, from international terrorist networks to nonviolent campaigns to end child labor exploitation, human sex trafficking, and sweatshop labor in export processing zones. The infrastructure undergirding the new transnational activism centers on the expansion of ICT networks and international organizational connections.[11]

Students of transnational movements recognize that the predecessors of contemporary transnational movements emerged in the nineteenth century, namely the international labor movement, the women's suffrage movement, and the slavery abolition struggles (Markoff 2015a; Keck and Sikkink 1998). The transnational diffusion of clusters of successful social movements (achieving desired outcomes) has also been associated with the emergence of large civil society organizations over the past two hundred years, such as mass political parties and labor associations (Weyland 2014), which provided the organizational infrastructure for earlier transnational movements and which offer insights into the informational channels of current global movements. In the present era, large international organizations such as the United Nations and the International Labor Organization help cement ties between movements in the global South via international conferences and forums (Anner 2011; Smith and Wiest 2012; Caniglia et al. 2015).

Many scholars of transnational social movements in the global South have focused on the global economic justice movement, the climate change movement, the World Social Forum, and international feminism. These studies address how the movements have sought to overcome the problems of coordinating activities across multiple national territories and languages.

Transnational movement research addresses how the network ties made possible by global communications have greatly expanded the potential reach for movement mobilization beyond national borders. Key activist websites assembled by the Independent Media Center, People's Global Action, ATTAC, Avaaz, and 350.org (as well as movement-specific Facebook pages and free international messaging applications such as Skype, WhatsApp, Twitter, and Telegram) serve a broker role for global civil society by connecting organizations and individuals that would otherwise not be linked. These websites and digital messaging applications offer logistical information in multiple languages for coordinating local events as essential components of larger transnational campaigns (Almeida and Lichbach 2003; Howard 2010). Web-initiated activism has been found to be most successful (in producing large-scale and ongoing mobilization) when coordinated with preexisting NGOs and civil society associations in the global South as opposed to exclusively recruiting and targeting unaffiliated individuals or the general public (Van Laer 2010; Lewis et al. 2014).

While large numbers of sustained transnational movements emerged in the 1980s over issues such as nuclear disarmament, ending South African apartheid, and achieving peace in Central America, they were largely concentrated in the global North. A notable uptick in transnational movement activity took place in the 1990s in the global South. Transnational activists innovated by using the communications technologies emerging in the late 1990s—e-mail, mobile phones, websites, and rapid language translation—to coordinate simultaneous protest events across cities on multiple continents. Castells (2013) views the new social media and digital resources as a major turning point in power relations in the twenty-first century, with subaltern groups attaining an unprecedented capacity to employ "self communication" for the purposes of mass mobilization. For the global South, Howard (2010) has documented a tremendous growth in access to ICTs as well as a substantial reduction in costs for average citizens in the first decade of the new millennium. Indeed, in the first decade of the twenty-first century, the populations residing in the megacities of the developing world (e.g., Jakarta, Delhi, Mumbai, Tehran, Lagos) experienced a remarkable reduction in costs for internet use. In the year 2000, the average person had to spend over 60 percent of their daily income to pay for one hour of internet use! By 2010 the cost per hour was down to 7 percent of daily income (Howard 2010: 141), and continues to decline. This increasing ICT access for ordinary people in the global South partially explains the rapid transnational diffusion of protest in the Arab Spring countries in 2011.

The reduction in costs and increasing access of ICTs in the global South also likely accounts for increased representation in transnational movement networks that were traditionally dominated by movements in the global North. Figure 4 in chapter 2 mapped the global participation in the 1999 World Trade Organization protests. There was minimal global South participation beyond the most industrialized nations of Argentina, Brazil, Mexico, South Africa, and India. Already by 2003, countries in the global South were well represented in the transnational movement against the US military invasion of Iraq.

By the 2010s, perhaps half of the cities participating in the global climate justice movement were located in the global South and 22 percent of all Southern transnational social movement organizations (TSMOs) focused on environmental issues (Smith et al. 2018). Indeed, progressive governments in the global South have taken up leadership positions within the larger climate justice movement (the international movement against global warming). After the failure of the UN Climate Change Conference (COP 15) to reach substantial international accords to reduce global warming in Copenhagen in 2009, the government of Bolivia facilitated a more radical climate justice summit in 2010 entitled the "World People's Summit on Climate Change and the Rights of Mother Earth." The summit called for more immediate global actions by civil society groups to pressure governments and industries to reduce carbon emissions. Bolivia conference activists also demanded that wealthy nations in the global North acknowledge their ecological debts owed to countries in the global South in the process of industrial development (Smith 2014). Figure 16 illustrates the countries participating in at least one protest event for climate justice (against global warming) in November and December 2015 immediately prior to COP 21 and the Paris Climate Accords. Notice the representation of nations from the global South compared to the World Trade Organization protests map (figure 4 in chapter 2).[12] The global South will continue to play an indispensable role in planetary mobilization and transnational movements in the twenty-first century.

One of the strongest networks of transnational movements in the global South is found in the World Social Forum (WSF). The WSF emerged as a counter to the World Economic Forum (WEF) held in Davos, Switzerland, every year since the late 1980s. The WEF is an elite economic conference of finance ministers and business leaders to advance the policies of economic globalization and neoliberalism outlined above. Labor unions in Brazil and other activist groups in the global South began to coordinate by early 2000 to plan the WSF in order to strategize alternatives to neoliberalism. Between 2001 and 2013 an annual WSF gathering was held. In each forum between

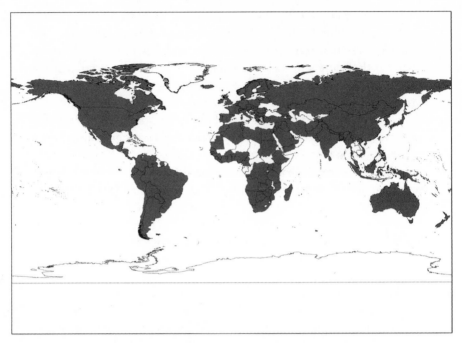

FIGURE 16.   Protests for Climate Justice, December 2015.

110 and 150 countries were represented with tens of thousands of activist participants from NGOs, labor movements, political parties, and a variety of other sectors (Breckenridge-Jackson et al. 2015). The first WSF annual meetings were held in Brazil, but the annual conference was soon moved to other global South cities, such as Nairobi, Mumbai, Karachi, Caracas, Tunis, and Dakar. The WSF also organizes several smaller regional forums throughout the developing world. The most recent WSF took place in Salvador, Brazil, in March 2018.[13]

The WSF gatherings discuss and share experiences of national- and local-level struggles against neoliberal policies, ethnic discrimination, immigration, ecological crisis, and patriarchy. The most enduring outcome from the WSF process centers on building lasting ties between activist groups across borders. The WSF represents one of the high points in the coordination of transnational movements for progressive social change on a global scale in the new millennium. Building these types of solidarity networks across the world may provide the best hope in confronting the mounting challenges of the current century—the topic of this book's Conclusion.

CONCLUSION

This chapter opened with a caution about generalizing mobilization processes in the global South. The wide variety of countries within this grouping makes sweeping theories difficult to justify. Instead, we focused on processes driving large-scale mobilization and the potential to establish ties of solidarity across countries in the form of transnational movements. These processes included movements resisting nondemocratic governments, acts of state repression, and eroding rights. The organizational basis of the resistance is found in civil society organizations and everyday institutions such as religious bodies and public schools. In the twenty-first century, the deepening of free market globalization continues to present new challenges and harms, which in turn initiate campaigns of resistance.

Civil society groups resist economic globalization at the national and local levels of political life. Neoliberal policies such as privatization, free trade, labor flexibility, and subsidy cuts generate some of the largest mobilizations of the past two decades. Climate change acts as a more recent ecological threat, bringing nations of the global South together in transnational movement campaigns. The World Social Forum provides another promising international infrastructure for progressive sectors in the developing world to coordinate actions and place demands on wealthier countries in the global North.

Conclusion

Mounting Crises and the Pathway Forward

This book has introduced readers to the basic features of social movements and the specialized subfields within the discipline. The Conclusion offers suggestions on future directions of social movements and the mounting crises excluded groups face in the twenty-first century. While the new social media communication technologies continue to produce record-breaking national and transnational protests in the scale of mobilizations and provide evidence of the power in numbers, other challenges remain. The dark side of the new millennium includes rising inequality, a resurgence of authoritarian populism, and a deepening ecological crisis. Before turning briefly to these issues, we will look at promising new lines of inquiry in the major areas of movement research and the connections between these areas.

NEW LINES OF INQUIRY

Defining Social Movements

This text began by defining social movements as excluded social groups that mobilize using noninstitutional tactics to target political and economic elites. While this is a somewhat standard definition of social movements (Snow and Soule 2009; Tarrow 2011), much more work is required on the "exclusion" part of the classification (Burawoy 2017). Beyond economic, racial, and gender inequality and discrimination, social exclusion appears in a variety of forms (Mora et al. 2017). This includes exclusion based on religion, national origin, sexuality, citizenship status, disabilities, and many others. Activists and students alike need to better conceptualize the intersectionality of exclusions, as critical race scholars have carried out with race, gender, and class (Nakano Glenn 2004; Valdez 2011; Collins 2015; Terriquez et al. 2018). The focus may be to understand how to piece together movement coalitions across multiple forms of exclusion, and more important, how to sustain those coalitions.

Methods

In the arena of social movement methods, several advances are underway in analyzing collective action by excluded groups. One fascinating specialty continues to be in the field of social network analysis. The ties between individuals, organizations, and geographical regions offer several insights on where collective action likely emerges and then multiplies via diffusion mechanisms. The existence and strength of ties between individuals and organizations along with the network configuration of the entire social movement field allow students of movements to explore many scenarios and potential outcomes. New geographic information system software is just beginning to be utilized to demonstrate the significance of spatial ties in promoting popular mobilization. Another major opening for social movement methods resides in the vast amount of information (and its accessibility) available from information and communication technologies and social media. The possibilities of future contributions of internet and social media-based data in promoting and understanding movement emergence, protest event distribution, recruitment, framing, and coordinating transnational mobilization are truly astonishing.

Theory

Social movement theory continues in a vibrant state. The synergy of theoretical contributions over the past four decades is largely responsible for advances in explaining the timing and outcomes of social movements. More specifically, the conceptual contributions come from scholars in different specialty areas in the social sciences who have not permitted disciplinary boundaries to block theoretical collaboration in order to build better frameworks and models of collective action. These include social psychologists and scholars of religion; political scientists from the comparative politics tradition; historians of earlier rebellions; social anthropologists who highlight the role of culture in mobilization; and sociologists with advanced training in organizations, social network analysis, and comparative-historical methods. Indeed, the political process framework evolved by combining insights from resource mobilization approaches and the social psychological advances of framing theory. Continuing on this trajectory of combining complementary perspectives in theory building appears to be the best path forward.

The renewed emphases on collective identities and emotions provide additional perspectives for a multidimensional view of social movements to endure. Given the shrinkage of the state in the neoliberal period, scholars are also pushing theoretical frameworks to investigate movements targeting institutions beyond the political state, such as corporations, medical systems, and educational and religious bodies, showing the power of movements in multiple spheres of social life. Finally, this book has focused on many of the threats, or the "bad news," that communities confront; with so many of the major mass mobilizations of the past two decades driven by threats (e.g., war, climate change, economic austerity/inequality, and the erosion of immigrant and women's rights), we need to continue elaborating more precise understandings of how threats mobilize (such as magnitude, proximity, and scope of threat) and which conditions are associated with successfully preventing unwanted changes.

Emergence

Social movement emergence has been given more attention by analysts and activists than any other dimension of collective action. One fascinating area to explore with greater depth resides in the nonobvious institutions, organizations, communities, and networks that may contribute to the initial rise of a movement. We know that preexisting SMOs and labor unions often contribute to movement emergence. We know much less about why organizations, institutions, and networks not explicitly established for social movement mobilization, such as NGOs, neighborhood associations, public schools, or recreational clubs, become converted or annexed by activists to launch a protest campaign. Equally interesting, for both right-wing and left-wing movement emergence, is the role of elite groups in sponsoring mobilization, such as financial elites, political parties, bosses in patron-client relationships, and even criminal networks of narco-trafficking.

Framing

The framing perspective will largely advance through the accumulation of more empirical studies illustrating the social construction and interpretation of grievances in action. Chapter 5 gave substantial attention to protest music as one of the avenues used to construct collective action frames. Framing work would benefit from exploring more real-world examples from the actual propaganda documents and cultural artifacts used by or left over from previous mobilizations. The tripartite task of diagnostic, prognostic, and motivational framing remains a useful categorical scheme to apply to the empirical evidence. Also, studying how various audiences absorb and react to framing strategies would provide greater comprehension of these processes and strike a better balance between the signalers (activists engaged in framing) and the receivers (targeted groups for mobilization) than currently exists.

Individual Participation

The last section of chapter 6 introduced a new research design for capturing individual participation in real-time demonstrations—the project Caught in the Act of Protest: Contextualizing Contestation (Klandermans 2012). Such designs provide high response validity because researchers implement the protocol while the participation is occurring. The standardization of the survey also allows for comparisons across types of demonstrations (e.g., climate change versus LGBTQ pride). The next phase for these kinds of designs centers on incorporating a comparison group of nonparticipants, those who came close to participating in the sympathy pool but failed in the end to attend a demonstration. In the twenty-first century, ordinary people are increasingly recruited online to participate in social movement activities. Knowing more about the mechanisms of receiving an invitation to participate via different social media platforms and about the origins of the invitation (from a friend or family member versus a stranger or SMO) will be a useful line of research for students and community organizations.

Outcomes

The study of social movement outcomes is essential for understanding how social change occurs. Chapter 7 focused on policy outcomes and many of the complex sets of conditions determining the likelihood of success. More work is needed on analyzing cultural outcomes and the outcomes of transnational movements in an increasingly globalizing world. Just as with the study of movement emergence, nonobvious aspects of movement outcomes also require further attention. In particular, movements that seem not to achieve their stated goals (or even appear to have failed) may have "hidden outcomes." Think about the 2017 and 2018 Women's Marches; they have not turned back many of the administration's policies, but they may influence future elections and the larger culture about sexual harassment and gender discrimination, and the increasing participation of women as electoral candidates. One of the world's largest mobilizations, the anti-war demonstrations in February 2003, did not stop the US invasion of Iraq, but the mass actions may have partially spilled over into the transnational climate justice movement and other campaigns coordinated on an international scale. Finally, more studies are required on the combination of conditions that result in favorable outcomes.

Global South

Social movements in the global South face so many obstacles. Finding the time and the resources to mobilize presents daunting challenges for ordinary people in poorer countries. One of the most pressing issues for movements in authoritarian states is to democratize the government. The heroic citizens in the Arab Spring mobilizations of 2011 largely focused on overthrowing nondemocratic regimes. Another major battle centers on the loss of social citizenship rights (access to social welfare, potable water, basic utilities, education, and healthcare). Even in the world's poorest countries, governments made efforts to expand the welfare state between the 1950s and 1980s. With the rise of the third-world debt crisis and the ideological dominance of economic liberalization, mobilizations are occurring across Africa, Asia, eastern and southern Europe, and Latin America to protect access to food and fuel subsidies, healthcare, education, and other benefits created in the period of state-led development. New transnational initiatives such as the World Social Forum and climate justice may be embryonic forms of generating more collective power and negotiating leverage for the global South.

Final Connections

All of the major themes and subareas of social movements considered above and throughout this text connect to one another. Defining movements, developing methods of inquiry, and constructing theoretical explanations begin the journey of understanding collective action. We use these fundamental tools to examine movement emergence, framing, individual participation, and outcomes. The framing perspective alone has stretched its analytical utility to applications ranging from movement emergence and recruitment to movement success. Students of collective action currently employ all of the social movement subareas to comprehend rebellions and collective resistance campaigns in the global South, including transnational movements. At the same time, struggles in the global South shape and inform current social movement frameworks by forcing scholars to account for the wide variety of political and economic contexts faced by protest campaigns in difficult circumstances.

ECONOMIC INEQUALITY, INCREASING AUTHORITARIANISM, AND ECOLOGICAL CRISES

As the twenty-first century advances, excluded social groups face a number of major threats. Three substantial issues include the threats of economic inequality, increasing authoritarianism, and ecological crises. Social movement mobilization offers one pathway to attempt to slow these encroaching negative conditions. Globalization processes are creating new winners and losers in the world economy. In the global North, the globalized economy has launched new social movements against inequality and austerity, such as Occupy Wall Street in the United States and anti-austerity movements throughout Europe, as well as the ongoing global justice movement. Indeed, government-commissioned reports already predict that by 2030 the wealthiest 1 percent of individuals will own two-thirds of the world's wealth.[1] In the global South, free trade, privatization, austerity, land grabs, and labor flexibility have generated some of the largest demonstrations in the past three decades. Most of these struggles are carried out at the local and national levels. Stronger transnational ties are a minimum requisite to place pressure on international institutions and the most powerful nation-states to ensure a basic livelihood in a world with a growing population that must scrape out a precarious existence.

In the 2018 Rule of Law Index, 70 of the 113 countries sampled report an erosion in human rights, including the United States.[2] Scholars relate the findings to backlash mobilizations associated with economic globalization. Over the past two decades, right-wing political parties have used economic globalization, free trade, and international immigration in their framing appeals during election campaigns. Since the global recession of 2008–9, the appeals are gaining traction. As mentioned in chapter 5, such framings have been associated with empowering right-wing movements and extremist extraparliamentary groups to become more assertive and public, resulting in upsurges in hate crimes and anti-immigrant violence. Much more research has been undertaken on progressive movements than on right-wing mobilizations. The reality of this academic imbalance has been manifested in scholars' inability to predict the resurgence of authoritarian populism in the new millennium. Equally important is for citizens to remain vigilant of eroding rights and prepared to defend constitutional protections and vulnerable groups via social movement mobilization.

Perhaps the biggest threat of all is ecological crisis, more specifically global warming and climate change. With the ten warmest years on record occurring since 1997 (with data going back to 1880), there is a scientific consensus that the planet is warming at an alarming rate. As the world already experiences monster storms and weather events, major droughts, massive wildfires and rising sea levels, the mounting ecological threats are pushing more collective action. Indeed, as of 2018 the transnational movement to turn back global warming (known as "climate justice") represents the largest social movement in human history. The movement is now coordinated in nearly every country on the planet and has successfully mobilized simultaneous actions across the globe since at least 2006. These transnational mobilizations occurred concurrently or just before major conferences and global summits on climate change, including the Paris Climate Agreement of 2015, which committed the nations of the world to reduce carbon emissions to the point of slowing global warming to less than two degrees Celsius in the present century. Even with the US withdrawal from the treaty, this incipient worldwide movement offers another glimpse of optimism for the future. If this emergent movement continues to grow, we can hope for many of the benefits provided by social movements, as discussed throughout these pages, on a global scale.

Notes

CHAPTER 1. SOCIAL MOVEMENTS: THE STRUCTURE
OF COLLECTIVE ACTION

1. www.womensmarch.com/mission/

2. Conservative movements in the USA would be another major collective mobilization over the past decade. The Tea Party movement emerged rapidly on the political scene in the first of months of 2009 immediately following the historical inauguration of Barack Obama to the presidency. The first coordinated actions on a national scale occurred on April 15, 2009 (tax day), and were followed up by aggressive protests in the summer of 2009 during town hall discussions of Obama's new national health insurance program (Van Dyke and Meyer 2014). By late 2010 the Tea Party had shifted emphasis to electoral politics, winning major contests at the local and national levels. The trend would continue in national and local elections in 2012 and 2014, respectively (Vasi et al. 2014). By 2016 several Tea Party candidates competed in the Republican primary for president of the United States. As the Tea Party moved into electoral politics, it transformed the US two-party system by polarizing the Republican Party into an establishment branch and a libertarian branch (Skocpol and Williamson 2012), prior to the rise of Trumpism.

Even though the base of the movement includes white working-class groups, it has large funders and does not represent the most excluded social groups in the United States.

CHAPTER 2. HOW TO STUDY SOCIAL MOVEMENTS:
CLASSIFICATION AND METHODS

1. For these examples, see Alonso-Fradejas (2015); Fu (2016); Jenkins (2017); Lapegna (2016); McAllister (2015); Touch and Neef (2015); and Kenney-Lazar et al. (2018).

2. Communities for a New California (CNC). 2018. "You Can Change Your Neighborhood." Special Advertising Supplement. January. CNC Education Fund.

3. For succinct reviews of protest waves, see Tarrow (1989); Koopmans (2004); Della Porta (2013); and Almeida (2014a).

4. Movement infiltration commonly occurs in movement campaigns around the world that seek to alter the distribution of economic and political power (Cunningham 2004).

5. The General Social Survey (GSS) can be accessed at http://gss.norc.org/.

6. American Citizen Participation Study can be accessed at www.icpsr .umich.edu/icpsrweb/ICPSR/studies/6635.

7. The newsletter is currently archived at the University of California, San Diego, at the Farmworker Movement Documentation Project.

8. *LexisNexis* and *NewsBank* are newspaper data storage companies that digitally house hundreds of newspapers, cable reports, and other news outlets. Many universities have a paid subscription to this service for the use of students, staff, and faculty. See also Hutter (2014: 340) for a list of nine publicly available protest event databases. Other protest event databases include Arthur Banks' Cross National Time Series Data (www.cntsdata.com/); Erica Chenoweth's Nonviolent and Violent Campaigns and Outcomes (NAVCO) Data Project (www.du.edu /korbel/sie/research/chenow_navco_data.html); and J. Craig Jenkins's *The World Handbook of Political Indicators* (https://mershoncenter.osu.edu/research /2010–2011/world-handbook-of-political-indicators-iv.html).

9. This protocol is a modified version used by Almeida (2008a) for research on protest waves in El Salvador. It was modeled on Tarrow's (1989) coding scheme of protest waves in Italy.

10. https://web.stanford.edu/group/collectiveaction/cgi-bin/drupal/. For a brief poster description of the project, see www.unc.edu/~fbaum/papers /August_2007_Conference/dynamics_of_collective_protest.ppt.

11. For a list of publications from the Dynamics of Collective Protest project, see https://web.stanford.edu/group/collectiveaction/cgi-bin/drupal/node/5.

12. See Erica Chenoweth and Jeremy Pressman. 2018. "January's Women's March Brought Out More Than a Million People—And Many More Protested during the Month." *Washington Post*, February 26.

13. Data for Occupy Wall Street protests mapped in figure 5 were collected from www.theguardian.com/news/datablog/interactive/2012/sep/17/occupy-map-of-the-world and http://directory.occupy.net/search?f[0]=field_ occupation_address%253Acountry%3AUS.

CHAPTER 3. THEORIES OF SOCIAL MOVEMENT MOBILIZATION

1. I distinguish classical social movement theories in this section from the general sociological theorists at the beginning of the chapter as to avoid erroneously conflating "classical sociological theory" with "classical social movement theory." Nonetheless, the early classical social movement theories were probably influenced by Durkheim more than other early theorists.

2. Senator Kennedy's advocacy for farmworkers comes alive in the Public Broadcasting Corporation documentary, *Chicano! The History of the Mexican*

American Civil Rights Movement (1996). The part 2 segment, "Struggle in the Fields," with Senator Kennedy in Delano, California, can be seen at www.youtube.com/watch?v=iUkb3rCfvvQ.

3. I use the phrase *"relatively* more favorable" because mass deportations of undocumented immigrants actually increased under the Obama administration (Golash-Boza 2015).

4. Even the high school movement for gun reform in the United States is calling the legalization of military grade assault rifles a public health issue in the wake of continued mass shooting incidents at schools.

CHAPTER 4. SOCIAL MOVEMENT EMERGENCE: INTERESTS, RESOURCE INFRASTRUCTURES, AND IDENTITIES

1. From chapter 2's discussion of everyday forms of resistance, recall James Scott's (1985) observation that oppressed people constantly undermine oppressive authority via small acts of dissent and sabotage. Hence, everyday forms of resistance offer an alternative perspective to Piven and Cloward's.

2. Zepeda-Millán (2017), for example, found that a regional soccer league played a major role in mobilizing immigrant rights protests in south Florida in 2006.

3. These dates do not exhaust the national days of mobilization between 2013 and 2017; protests occurred on several other days as well.

4. See Dave Jamieson. 2018. "Union behind Fight for $15 Cuts Funding for Fast-Food Campaign." *Huffington Post,* March 31.

CHAPTER 5. THE FRAMING PROCESS

1. Chapter 8 discusses the organizational contributions of liberation theology to social movements in the global South.

2. The song was found in a Catholic church bookstore on cassette tape in El Salvador in the late 1990s by the author.

3. Lyrics and music by Marité Valenzuela; the rhythm is Calypso.

CHAPTER 6. INDIVIDUAL RECRUITMENT AND PARTICIPATION

1. The size of the sympathy pools parallels the discussion of frame centrality in chapter 5.

2. See MEChA website for more information: www.chicanxdeaztlan.org/.

3. See www.democracynow.org/2006/3/29/walkout_the_true_story_of_the.

4. For more information, see http://raginggrannies.org/.

5. In the following sections on networks, organizations, collective identity, and new social media, see Inclán and Almeida (2017) for an application on how these dimensions shaped protest participation in large demonstrations in Mexico City.

6. See Julia Llinas Goodman. 2018. "2018 Women's March: How the Movement Is Growing, by the Numbers." *50 States of Blue*, January 24. www.50statesofblue.com/2018/01/womens-march-2018-dana-fisher-protest/

7. www.protestsurvey.eu/index.php?page=index

CHAPTER 7. MOVEMENT OUTCOMES

1. See McAdam et al. (2001: 10–13), and Tilly (1978: 52–55), for a detailed description of the concentration of power in modern societies and its relationship to collective mobilization by insider and outsider groups.

2. For a longer discussion of the power of disruptive protest, see Almeida and Stearns (1998).

3. See www.piconetwork.org.

4. See www.poorpeoplescampaign.org/.

5. This discussion draws partially from a larger study by Stearns and Almeida (2004). For more lengthy examinations of the relationship between actors inside the state and social movements, see Santoro and McGuire (1997); Banaszak (2005; 2010); and Verhoeven and Duyvendak (2017).

CHAPTER 8. PUSHING THE LIMITS: SOCIAL MOVEMENTS IN THE GLOBAL SOUTH

1. Nonetheless, dozens of developing countries are also located in the northern hemisphere—such as India, Afghanistan, and many former Soviet republics—but they are still classified in the "global South." At the same time, the wealthier countries of New Zealand and Australia are positioned in the southern hemisphere but are included as part of the global North.

2. There are important historical caveats to this linear interpretation of the study of social movements in the global North with its democratic reversals and antidemocratic waves, especially following World War I (Markoff 2015a).

3. For a classical account of the plundering of Africa by Western colonial powers, see Rodney (1981). For a depiction of the extraction of mineral wealth in Latin America by colonial powers, and the indigenous resistance to it, see Galeano (1997).

4. See the 2016 Democracy Index of the Economist Intelligence Unit (2017), www.eiu.com/public/topical_report.aspx?campaignid=DemocracyIndex2016.

5. See Almeida (2018) for a longer discussion of the role of repressive threats and the erosion of rights in generating collective action.

6. The following discussion is based on Almeida (2016).

7. Negotiations between the IMF and individual countries in the global South regarding austerity policies can be viewed on the fund's website, www.imf.org/en/countries.

8. GATT stands for the General Agreement on Tariffs and Trade. GATT is a United Nations-based framework developed in the aftermath of World War II to promote international trade among nations.

9. See www.theguardian.com/world/2016/sep/02/indian-workers-strike-in-fight-for-higher-wages.

10. See "9 marchas al día por 3 años." *El Universal,* February 7, 2018.

11. For a longer discussion of globalization and social movements, see Almeida and Chase-Dunn (2018).

12. The author participated in one of these actions in San Pedro, Costa Rica.

13. See wsf2018.org.

CONCLUSION: MOUNTING CRISES AND
THE PATHWAY FORWARD

1. See www.theguardian.com/business/2018/apr/07/global-inequality-tipping-point-2030.

2. See Will Bordell and Jon Robins. 2018. "'A Crisis for Human Rights': New Index Reveals Global Fall in Basic Justice." *Guardian* (US edition), January 31. www.theguardian.com/inequality/2018/jan/31/human-rights-new-rule-of-law-index-reveals-global-fall-basic-justice.

References

Abul-Fottouh, Deena, and Tina Fetner. 2018. "Solidarity or Schism: Ideological Congruence and the Twitter Networks of Egyptian Activists." *Mobilization* 23(1): 23–44.

Aguirre, Benigno E., Dennis Wenger, and Gabriela Rico. 1998. "A Test of the Emergent Norm Theory of Collective Behavior." *Sociological Forum* 13: 301–20.

Alimi, Eitan Y. 2016. "Introduction: Popular Contention, Regime, and Transition: A Comparative Perspective." In *Popular Contention, Regime, and Transition: The Arab Revolts in Comparative Global Perspective*, edited by Eitan Alimi, Avraham Sela, and Mario Sznajder, 1–24. Oxford: Oxford University Press.

———, Lorenzo Bosi, and Chares Demetriou. 2015. *The Dynamics of Radicalization: A Relational And Comparative Perspective*. Oxford: Oxford University Press.

Almeida, Paul D. 2003. "Opportunity Organizations and Threat Induced Contention: Protest Waves in Authoritarian Settings." *American Journal of Sociology* 109(2): 345–400.

———. 2005. "Multi-sectoral Coalitions and Popular Movement Participation." *Research in Social Movements, Conflicts and Change* 26: 67–102.

———. 2006. "Social Movement Unionism, Social Movement Partyism, and Policy Outcomes." In *Latin American Social Movements: Globalization, Democratization, and Transnational Networks*, edited by H. Johnston and P. Almeida, 57–73. Lanham, MD: Rowman & Littlefield.

———. 2007a. "Organizational Expansion, Liberalization Reversals and Radicalized Collective Action." *Research in Political Sociology* 15: 57–99.

———. 2007b. "Defensive Mobilization: Popular Movements against Economic Adjustment Policies in Latin America." *Latin American Perspectives* 34(3): 123–39.

———. 2008a. *Waves of Protest: Popular Struggle in El Salvador, 1925–2005*. Minneapolis: University of Minnesota Press.

———. 2008b. "The Sequencing of Success: Organizing Templates and Neoliberal Policy Outcomes." *Mobilization* 13(2): 1655–87.

———. 2010a. "Globalization and Collective Action." In *Handbook of Politics: State and Society in Global Perspective*, edited by Kevin Leicht and J. Craig Jenkins, 305–26. New York: Springer.

———. 2010b. "Social Movement Partyism: Collective Action and Political Parties." In *Strategic Alliances: New Studies of Social Movement Coalitions*, edited by N. Van Dyke and H. McCammon, 170–96. Minneapolis: University of Minnesota Press.

———. 2012. "Subnational Opposition to Globalization." *Social Forces* 90(4): 1051–72.

———. 2014a. "Cycles of Protest." In *Oxford Bibliographies in Political Science* Oxford: Oxford University Press.

———. 2014b. *Mobilizing Democracy: Globalization and Citizen Protest.* Baltimore: Johns Hopkins University Press.

———. 2015. "Unintended Consequences of State-Led Development: A Theory of Mobilized Opposition to Neoliberalism." *Sociology of Development* 1(2): 259–76.

———. 2016. "Social Movements and Economic Development." In *Sociology of Development Handbook*, edited by Greg Hooks, Paul Almeida, David Brown, Sam Cohn, Sara Curran, Rebecca Emigh, Ho-fung Hung, Andrew K. Jorgenson, Richard Lachmann, Linda Lobao, and Valentine Moghadam, 528–50. Berkeley: University of California Press.

———. 2018. "The Role of Threat in Collective Action." In *The Wiley-Blackwell Companion to Social Movements*, edited by D. Snow, S. Soule, H. Kriesi, and H. McCammon, 43–62. Oxford: Blackwell.

———, and Christopher Chase-Dunn. 2018. "Globalization and Social Movements." *Annual Review of Sociology* 44: 189–211.

———, and Roxana Delgado. 2008. "Gendered Networks and Health Care Privatization." *Advances in Medical Sociology* 10: 273–99.

———, and Hank Johnston. 2006. "Neoliberal Globalization and Popular Movements in Latin America." In *Latin American Social Movements: Globalization, Democratization, and Transnational Networks*, edited by Hank Johnston and Paul Almeida, 3–18. Lanham, MD: Rowman & Littlefield.

———, and Mark I. Lichbach. 2003. "To the Internet, from the Internet: Comparative Media Coverage of Transnational Protest." *Mobilization* 8(3): 249–72.

———, and Amalia Pérez Martín. 2019. "Economic Globalization and Social Movements in Latin America." In *Oxford Handbook of Latin American Sociology*, edited by Xóchitl Bada and Liliana Rivera. Oxford: Oxford University Press.

———, and Eugenio Sosa. 2015. "May Day Demonstrations in Central America: The Case of Honduras." Con las Manos en la Protesta Conference-Sondeo de Protestas Alrededor del Mundo: Motivaciones, Dinámicas, y Contextos de Movilización. CIDE, Mexico City, November 19.

————, and Linda Brewster Stearns. 1998. "Political Opportunities and Local Grassroots Environmental Movements." *Social Problems* 45(1): 37–60.

————, and Nella Van Dyke. 2014. "Social Movement Partyism and the Rapid Mobilization of the Tea Party." In *Understanding the Tea Party Movement,* edited by David Meyer and Nella Van Dyke, 55–72. London: Ashgate.

Alonso-Fradejas, A. 2015. "Anything but a Story Foretold: Multiple Politics of Resistance to the Agrarian Extractivist Project in Guatemala." *Journal of Peasant Studies* 42(3–4): 489–515.

Amenta, Edwin. 2006. *When Movements Matter: The Townsend Plan and the Rise of Social Security.* Princeton, NJ: Princeton University Press.

Amenta, Edwin, Kenneth Andrews, and Neal Caren. 2018. "The Political Institutions, Processes, and Outcomes Movements Seek to Influence." In *The Wiley-Blackwell Companion to Social Movements,* edited by D. Snow, S. Soule, H. Kriesi, and H. McCammon, 449–65. Oxford: Blackwell.

————, Neal Caren, Elizabeth Chiarello, and Yang Su. 2010. "The Political Consequences of Social Movements." *Annual Review of Sociology* 36: 287–307.

Andersen, Kurt. 2011. "2011 Person of the Year: The Protester." *Time* 178(25): 52–89.

Andretta, Massimiliano, and Donatella Della Porta. 2014. "Surveying Protestors: Why and How." In *Methodological Practices in Social Movement Research,* edited by D. Della Porta, 308–34. Oxford: Oxford University Press.

Andrews, Kenneth. 2004. *Freedom Is a Constant Struggle: The Mississippi Civil Rights Movement and Its Legacy.* Chicago: University of Chicago Press.

————, Marshall Ganz, Matthew Baggetta, Hahrie Han, and Chaeyoon Lim. 2010. "Leadership, Membership, and Voice: Civic Associations That Work." *American Journal of Sociology* 115(4): 1191–1242.

Anner, Mark. 2011. *Solidarity Transformed: Labor Responses to Globalization and Crisis in Latin America.* Ithaca, NY: Cornell University Press.

————, and Helen Liu. 2016. "Harmonious Unions and Rebellious Workers: A Study of Wildcat Strikes in Vietnam." *Industrial and Labor Relations Review* 69(1): 3–28.

Arce, Moises. 2014. *Resource Extraction and Protest in Peru.* Pittsburgh: University of Pittsburgh Press.

Archila Neira, Mauricio, et al. 2012. *Violencia contra el sindicalismo, 1984–2010.* Bogota: CINEP.

Armbruster-Sandoval, Ralph. 2005. *Globalization and Cross-Border Labor Solidarity in the Americas: The Anti-Sweatshop Movement and the Struggle for Social Justice.* New York: Routledge.

————. 2017. *Starving for Justice: Hunger Strikes, Spectacular Speech, and the Struggle for Dignity.* Tucson: University of Arizona Press.

Armstrong, Elizabeth A. 2002. *Forging gay identities: Organizing sexuality in San Francisco, 1950-1994.* Chicago: University of Chicago.

———, and Mary Bernstein. 2008. "Culture, Power, and Institutions: A Multi-Institutional Politics Approach to Social Movements." *Sociological Theory* 26(1): 74–99.

Autor, D., D. Dorn, G. Hanson, and K. Majlesi. 2016. "A Note on the Effect of Rising Trade Exposure on the 2016 Presidential Election." Working paper, MIT.

Auyero, Javier. 2001. "Glocal Riots." *International Sociology* 16(1): 33–53.

———. 2002. "Los Cambios en el Repertorio de la Protesta Social en la Argentina." *Desarrollo Económico* 42: 187–210.

———. 2006. "The Moral Politics of Argentine Crowds." In *Latin American Social Movements: Globalization, Democratization, and Transnational Networks*, edited by H. Johnston and P. Almeida, 147–62. Lanham, MD: Rowman & Littlefield.

———, Maricarmen Hernandez, and Mary Ellen Stitt. 2018. "Grassroots Activism in the Belly of the Beast: A Relational Account of the Campaign against Urban Fracking in Texas." *Social Problems* 65. https://doi.org/10.1093/socpro/spx035

———, and Debora Alejandra Swistun. 2009. *Flammable: Environmental Suffering in an Argentine Shantytown*. Oxford: Oxford University Press.

Ayoub, Phillip. 2016. *When States Come Out: Europe's Sexual Minorities and the Politics of Visibility*. New York: Cambridge University Press.

———, Chris Zepeda Millán, and Sophia Wallace. 2014. "Triangulation in Social Movement Research." In *Methodological Practices in Social Movement Research*, edited by D. Della Porta, 67–96. Oxford: Oxford University Press.

Babb, Sarah. 2013. "The Washington Consensus as Transnational Policy Paradigm: Its Origins, Trajectory, and Likely Successor." *Review of International Political Economy* 20(2): 268–97.

Bair, Jennifer. 2009. "Global Commodity Chains: Genealogy and Review." In *Frontiers of Commodity Chain Research*, edited by Jennifer Bair, 1–34. Stanford, CA: Stanford University Press.

Balsiger, Philip, and Alexandre Lambelet. 2014. "Participant Observation." In *Methodological Practices in Social Movement Research*, edited by D. Della Porta, 144–72. Oxford: Oxford University Press.

Baker, Andy. 2014. *Shaping the Developing World: The West, the South, and the Natural World*. Los Angeles: Sage.

Baker, David. 2014. *The Schooled Society: The Educational Transformation of Global Culture*. Stanford, CA: Stanford University Press.

Banaszak, Lee Ann. 2005. "Inside and Outside the State: Movement Insider Status, Tactics, and Public Policy Achievements." In *Routing the Opposition: Social Movements, Public Policy, and Democracy*, edited by D. Meyer, V. Jenness, and H. Ingram, 149–76. Minneapolis: University of Minnesota Press.

———. 2010. *The Women's Movement Inside and Outside the State*. Cambridge: Cambridge University Press.

Bardacke, Frank. 2012. *Trampling Out the Vintage: Cesar Chavez and the Two Souls of the United Farm Workers*. London: Verso.

Bartley, Tim. 2018. *Rules without Rights: Land, Labor, and Private Authority in the Global Economy.* Oxford: Oxford University Press.

Bebbington, Anthony, and Jeffrey Bury, eds. 2013. *Subterranean Struggles: New Dynamics of Mining, Oil, and Gas in Latin America.* Austin: University of Texas Press.

Beissinger, Mark. 2001. *Nationalist Mobilization and the Collapse of the Soviet State: A Tidal Approach to the Study of Nationalism.* Cambridge: Cambridge University Press.

Bell, Joyce. 2014. *The Black Power Movement and American Social Work.* New York: Columbia University Press.

Benford, Robert D., and Scott A. Hunt. 2003. "Interactional Dynamics in Public Problems Marketplaces: Movements and the Counterframing and Reframing of Public Problems." In *Challenges and Choices: Constructionist Perspectives on Social Problems,* edited by James A. Holstein and Gale Miller, 153–86. New York: Aldine de Gruyter.

———, and David Snow. 2000. "Framing Processes and Social Movements: An Overview and Assessment." *Annual Review of Sociology* 26: 611–39.

Bennett, W. Lance, and Alexandra Segerberg. 2013. *The Logic of Connective Action: Digital Media and the Personalization of Contentious Politics.* Cambridge: Cambridge University Press.

Berezin, Mabel. 2009. *Illiberal Politics in Neoliberal Times: Cultures, Security, and Populism in a New Europe.* Cambridge: Cambridge University Press.

Berry, Marie, and Erica Chenoweth. 2018. "Who Made the Women's March?" In *The Resistance: The Dawn of the Anti-Trump Opposition Movement,* edited by David Meyer and Sidney Tarrow, 75–89. Oxford: Oxford University Press.

Bickham Mendez, Jennifer. 2005. *From the Revolution to the Maquiladoras: Gender, Labor, and Globalization in Nicaragua.* Durham, NC: Duke University Press.

Biggs, Michael, and Kenneth Andrews. 2015. "Protest Campaigns and Movement Success Desegregating the U.S. South in the Early 1960s." *American Sociological Review* 80(2): 416–43.

Blee, Kathleen M. 2017. *Understanding Racist Activism: Theory, Methods, and Research.* New York: Routledge.

———, and Verta Taylor. 2002. "The Uses of Semi-Structured Interviews in Social Movement Research." In *Methods in Social Movement Research,* edited by Bert Klandermans and Suzanne Staggenborg, 92–117. Minneapolis: University of Minnesota Press.

Bloemraad, Irene, F. Silva, and K. Voss. 2016. "Rights, Economics, or Family? Frame Resonance, Political Ideology, and the Immigrant Rights Movement." *Social Forces* 94(4): 1647–74.

———, Kim Voss, and Taeku Lee. 2011. "The Protests of 2006: What Were They, How Do We Understand Them, Where Do We Go?" In *Rallying for Immigrant Rights: The Fight for Inclusion in 21st Century America.* Berkeley: University of California Press.

Bob, Clifford. 2005. *The Marketing of Rebellion: Insurgents, Media, and International Activism*. New York: Cambridge University Press.

Bobo, Lawrence. 2017. "Racism in Trump's America: Reflections on Culture, Sociology, and the 2016 US Presidential Election." *British Journal of Sociology* 68(Suppl. 1): S86–104.

Bockman, Johanna. 2011. *Markets in the Name of Socialism: The Left-Wing Origins of Neoliberalism*. Stanford, CA: Stanford University Press.

Bonacich, Edna, and Jake Wilson. 2008. *Getting the Goods: Ports, Labor, and the Logistics Revolution*. Ithaca, NY: Cornell University Press.

Bosi, Lorenzo, Marco Giugni, and Katrin Uba, eds. 2016. *The Consequences of Social Movements*. Cambridge: Cambridge University Press.

Boudreau, Vincent. 2004. *Resisting Dictatorship: Repression and Protest in Southeast Asia*. Cambridge: Cambridge University Press.

Boulding, Carew. 2014. *NGOs, Political Protest, and Civil Society*. Cambridge: Cambridge University Press.

Bourdieu, Pierre. 1986. "The Forms of Capital." In *Handbook of Theory and Research for the Sociology of Education*, edited by John G. Richardson, 241–58. New York: Greenwood.

Bracey, Glenn E. 2016. "Black Movements Need Black Theorizing: Exposing Implicit Whiteness in Political Process Theory." *Sociological Focus* 49(1): 11–27.

Brancati, Dawn. 2016. *Democracy Protests: Origins, Features, and Significance*. Cambridge: Cambridge University Press.

Bratton, M. 2008. "Poor People and Democratic Citizenship in Africa." In *Poverty, Participation, and Democracy*, edited by Anirudh Krishna, 28–65. Cambridge: Cambridge University Press.

Breckenridge-Jackson, I., N. Radojcic, E. Reese, E. Schwarz, and C. Vito. 2015. "Latin American Social Movements and the Social Forum Process." In *Handbook of Social Movements across Latin America*, edited by P. Almeida and A. Cordero, 89–100. New York: Springer.

Broadbent, Jeffrey. 1998. *Environmental Politics in Japan: Networks of Power and Protest*. New York: Cambridge University Press.

Brockett, Charles. 2005. *Political Movements and Violence in Central America*. Cambridge: Cambridge University Press.

Brooker, Megan. 2018. "Indivisible: Invigorating and Redirecting the Grassroots." In *The Resistance: The Dawn of the Anti-Trump Opposition Movement*, edited by David Meyer and Sidney Tarrow, 162–86. Oxford: Oxford University Press.

Brown, Hana, and Jennifer Jones. (2016). Immigrant rights are civil rights. *Contexts*, 15(2), 34–39.

Brown, Phil, Rachel Morello-Frosch, and Stephen Zavestosk, eds. 2012. *Contested Illnesses: Citizens, Science, and Health Social Movements*. Berkeley: University of California Press.

Broyles-Gonzalez, Yolanda. 1994. *El Teatro Campesino: Theater in the Chicano Movement*. Austin: University of Texas Press.

Buechler, Steven. 2004. "The Strange Career of Strain and Breakdown Theories of Collective Action." In *The Blackwell Companion to Social Movements*, edited by D.A. Snow, S.A. Soule, and H. Kriesi, 47–66. Oxford: Blackwell.

———. 2011. *Understanding Social Movements: Theories from the Classical Era to the Present*. New York: Routledge.

Bullard, Robert D. 2000. *Dumping in Dixie: Race, Class, and Environmental Quality*, 3rd ed. Boulder, CO: Westview Press.

———, ed. 2005. *The Quest for Environmental Justice: Human Rights and the Politics of Pollution*. San Francisco: Sierra Club.

———, and Beverly Wright. 2012. *The Wrong Complexion for Protection: How the Government Response to Disaster Endangers African American Communities*. New York: New York University Press.

Bunker, Stephen, and Paul Ciccantell. 2005. *Globalization and the Race for Resources*. Baltimore: Johns Hopkins University Press.

Burawoy, Michael. 1979. *Manufacturing Consent: Changes in the Labor Process under Monopoly Capitalism*. Chicago: University of Chicago Press.

———. 2017. "Social Movements in the Neoliberal Age." In *Southern Resistance in Critical Perspective*, edited by M. Paret, C. Runciman, and L. Sinwell, 21–35. New York: Routledge.

Burstein, P., R.L. Einwohner, and J.A. Hollander. 1995. "The Success of Political Movements: A Bargaining Perspective." In *The Politics of Social Protest*, edited by C.J. Jenkins and B. Klandermans, 275–95. Minneapolis: University of Minnesota Press.

Cable, Sherry. 2019. "Social Movements and Social Control." Pp. 121–36 in Mathieu Deflem, ed., *The Handbook of Social Control*. Oxford: Wiley-Blackwell.

Cai, Yongshun. 2010. *Collective Resistance in China: Why Popular Protests Succeed or Fail*. Stanford, CA: Stanford University Press.

Caniglia, Beth, Robert Brulle, and Andrew Szasz. 2015. "Civil Society, Social Movements, and Climate Change." In *Climate Change and Society*, edited by R. Dunlap and R. Brulle, 235–68. Oxford: Oxford University Press.

Carawan, Guy, and Candie Carawan. 2007. *Sing for Freedom: The Story of the Civil Rights Movement through Its Songs*. Montgomery, AL: NewSouth Books.

Caren, N., S. Gaby, and C. Herrold. 2017. "Economic Breakdown and Collective Action." *Social Problems* 64(1): 133–55.

———, K. Jowers, and S. Gaby. 2012. "A Social Movement Online Community: Stormfront and the White Nationalist Movement." *Research in Social Movements, Conflicts and Change* 33: 163–93.

Carty, Victoria. 2015. *Social Movements and New Technology*. Boulder, CO: Westview Press.

Castells, Manuel. 1983. *The City and the Grassroots: A Cross-Cultural Theory of Urban Social Movements*. Berkeley: University of California Press.

———. 2013. *Communication Power*, 2nd ed. Oxford: Oxford University Press.

——. 2015. *Networks of Outrage and Hope: Social Movements in the Internet Age*, 2nd ed. Cambridge: Polity Press.

Chang, Paul. 2015. *Protest Dialectics: State Repression and South Korea's Democracy Movement, 1970–1979*. Stanford, CA: Stanford University Press.

Chase-Dunn, Christopher. 2016. "Social Movements and Collective Behavior in Premodern Polities." Paper presented at the American Sociological Association Meetings, Seattle, August.

Chávez, Joaquín. 2017. *Poets and Prophets of the Resistance: Intellectuals and the Origins of El Salvador's Civil War*. Oxford: Oxford University Press.

Chen, Xi. 2011. *Social Protest and Contentious Authoritarianism in China*. Cambridge: Cambridge University Press.

Chenoweth, Erica, and Maria J. Stephan. 2011. *Why Civil Resistance Works: The Strategic Logic of Nonviolent Conflict*. New York: Columbia University Press.

Chun, J.J., G. Lipsitz, and Y. Shin. 2013. "Intersectionality as a Social Movement Strategy: Asian Immigrant Women Advocates." *Signs* 38(4): 917–40.

Clawson, Dan. 2003. *The Next Upsurge Labor and the New Social Movements*. Ithaca, NY: Cornell University Press.

Clemens, Elisabeth. 1997. *The People's Lobby: Organizational Innovation and the Rise of Interest Group Politics in the United States, 1890–1925*. Chicago: University of Chicago Press.

——, and Debra Minkoff. 2004. "Beyond the Iron Law: Rethinking the Place of Organizations in Social Movement Research." In *The Blackwell Companion to Social Movements*, edited by D. Snow, S. Soule, and H. Kriesi, 155–70. Malden, MA: Blackwell.

Cohn, Samuel. 1993. *When Strikes Make Sense And Why: Lessons from Third Republic French Coal Miners*. New York: Plenum.

——. 2012. *Employment and Development under Globalization: State and Economy in Brazil*. London: Palgrave.

Collins, Patricia Hill, 2015. "Intersectionality's Definitional Dilemmas." *Annual Review of Sociology* 41: 1–20.

——, and S. Bilge. 2016. *Intersectionality*. Malden, MA: Polity Press.

Collins, Randall. 2001. "Social Movements and the Focus of Emotional Attention." In *Passionate Politics*, edited by Jeff Goodwin, James M. Jasper, and Francesca Polletta, 27–44. Chicago: University of Chicago Press.

——. 2004. *Interaction Ritual Chains*. Princeton, NJ: Princeton University Press.

Connell, Raewyn. 2007. *Southern Theory: The Global Dynamics of Knowledge in Social Science*. Cambridge: Polity, 2007.

Cook, Maria Lorena. 1994. *Organizing Dissent: Unions, the State, and the Democratic Teachers' Movement in Mexico*. University Park: Pennsylvania State University Press.

Cordero Ulate, Allen. 2005. "Clases medias y movimientos sociales en Costa Rica." *Revista de Ciencias Sociales*, vol. III–IV, núm. 109–10, pp. 157-65.

Cordero Ulate, Allen. 2009. "Nuevas desigualdades; nuevas resistencias: de los ex-trabajadores bananeros costarricenses afectados por los agroquímicos." *Revista Centroamericana de Ciencias Sociales* 6,(2): 75–100.

Cress, Daniel M., and David A. Snow. 2000. "The Outcomes of Homeless Mobilization: The Influence of Organization, Disruption, Political Mediation, and Framing." *American Journal of Sociology* 105(4): 1063–104.

Cruz, Jon. 1999. *Culture on the Margin: The Black Spiritual and the Rise of American Cultural Interpretation.* Princeton, NJ: Princeton University Press.

Cunningham, David. 2004. *There's Something Happening Here: The New Left, the Klan, and FBI Counterintelligence.* Berkeley: University of California Press.

Dahlerus, Claudia, and Christian Davenport. 1999. "Tracking Down the Empirical Legacy of the Black Panther Party (or Notes on the Perils of Pursuing the Panthers)." *New Political Science* 21(2): 261–79.

Davenport, Christian. 2010. *State Repression and the Domestic Democratic Peace.* Cambridge: Cambridge University Press.

———, S. Soule, and D. Armstrong. 2011. "Protesting While Black? The Differential Policing of American Activism, 1960 to 1990." *American Sociological Review* 76(1): 152–78.

Davis, Mike. 2007. *Planet of Slums.* London: Verso.

Della Porta, Donatella. 2013. "Protest Cycles and Waves." In *The Wiley-Blackwell Encyclopedia of Social and Political Movements.* Oxford: Wiley-Blackwell.

———. 2014. "In-Depth Interviews." In *Methodological Practices in Social Movement Research,* edited by D. Della Porta, 228–61. Oxford: Oxford University Press.

———. 2015. *Social Movements in Times of Austerity: Bringing Capitalism Back into Protest Analysis.* London: Polity Press.

———, J. Fernández, H. Kouki, and L. Mosca. 2017. *Movement Parties against Austerity.* London: Polity Press.

Desmond, Matthew, and Adam Travis. 2018. "Political Consequences of Survival Strategies among the Urban Poor." *American Sociological Review* 83(5): 869–96.

Diani, Mario. 2015. *The Cement of Civil Society: Studying Networks in Localities.* Cambridge: Cambridge University Press.

———, and Doug McAdam, eds. 2003. *Social Movements and Networks: Relational Approaches to Collective Action.* Oxford: Oxford University Press.

Dicken, Peter. 2011. *Global Shift: Mapping the Changing Contours of the World Economy.* New York: Guilford.

DiGrazia, Joseph. 2017. "Using Internet Search Data to Produce State-Level Measures: The Case of Tea Party Mobilization." *Sociological Methods and Research* 46(4): 898–925.

DiMaggio, Paul, and Walter Powell. 1983. "The Iron Cage Revisited: Institutional Isomorphism and Collective Rationality in Organization Fields." *American Sociological Review* 48(2): 147–60.

Dixon, Marc. 2008. "Movements, Countermovements, and Policy Adoption: The Case of Right-to-Work Activism." *Social Forces* 87: 473–500.

———, and Vincent Roscigno. 2003. "Status, Networks, and Social Movement Participation: The Case of Striking Workers." *American Journal of Sociology* 108: 1292–327.

Dodson, Kyle. 2011. "The Movement Society in Comparative Perspective." *Mobilization* 16(4): 475–94.

———. 2015. "Gendered Activism: A Cross-National View on Gender Differences in Protest Activity." *Social Currents* 2: 377–92.

———. 2016a. "Economic Threat and Protest Behavior in Comparative Perspective." *Sociological Perspectives* 59(3).

———. 2016b. "TSMOs and Protest Participation." *Socius* 2: 1–14.

Doerr, Nicole, and Noa Milman. 2014. "Working with Images." In *Methodological Practices in Social Movement Research,* edited by Donatella Della Porta, 418–45. Oxford: Oxford University Press.

Drake, Paul. 1996. *Labor Movements and Dictatorships.* Baltimore: Johns Hopkins University Press.

Durkheim, Émile. 1984. *The Division of Labor in Society.* New York: Free Press.

Earl, Jennifer. 2004. "The Cultural Consequences of Social Movements." In *The Blackwell Companion to Social Movements,* edited by David A. Snow, Sarah A. Soule, and Hanspeter Kriesi, 508–30. Malden, MA: Blackwell.

———. 2011. "Political Repression: Iron Fists, Velvet Gloves, and Diffuse Control." *Annual Review of Sociology* 37: 261–84.

———, and R. Kelly Garrett. 2017. "The New Information Frontier: Toward a More Nuanced View of Social Movement Communication." *Social Movement Studies* 16(4): 479–93.

———, and Katrina Kimport. 2011. *Digitally Enabled Social Change: Activism in the Internet Age.* Cambridge, MA: MIT Press.

———, Andrew Martin, John D. McCarthy, Sarah A. Soule. 2004. "The Use of Newspaper Data in the Study of Collective Action." *Annual Review of Sociology* 30: 65–80

———, and Sarah Soule. 2010. "The Impacts of Repression: The Effect of Police Presence and Action on Subsequent Protest Rates." *Research in Social Movements, Conflicts and Change* 30: 75–113.

Eckstein, Susan Eva, and Timothy P. Wickham-Crowley. 2015. "The Persisting Relevance of Political Economy and Political Sociology in Latin American Social-Movement Studies." *Latin American Research Review* 50(4): 3–25.

Edelman, Marc. 1999. *Peasants against Globalization: Rural Social Movements in Costa Rica.* Stanford, CA: Stanford University Press.

———, Carlos Oya, and Saturnino M. Borras Jr., eds. 2016. *Global Land Grabs: History, Theory and Method.* New York: Routledge.

Edwards, Bob. 1995. "With Liberty and Environmental Justice for All: The Emergence and the Challenge of Grassroots Environmentalism in the USA." In *Ecological Resistance Movements: The Global Emergence of Radical and*

Popular Environmentalism, edited by Bron Taylor, 35–55. Albany: State University of New York Press.

———, and Melinda Kane. 2014. "Resource Mobilization and Social and Political Movements." In *Handbook of Political Citizenship and Social Movements,* edited by Hein-Anton van der Heijden, 205–32. Cheltenham: Edward Elgar.

———, and John D. McCarthy. 2004. "Resources and Social Movement Mobilization." In *The Blackwell Companion to Social Movements,* edited by D. Snow, S. Soule, and H. Kriesi, 116–52. Oxford: Blackwell.

———, John D. McCarthy, and Dane Mataic. 2018. "The Resource Context of Social Movements." In *The Wiley-Blackwell Companion to Social Movements,* edited by D. Snow, S. Soule, H. Kriesi, and H. McCammon, 79–97. Oxford: Blackwell.

Edyvane, Derek, and Enes Kulenovic. 2017. "Disruptive Disobedience." *Journal of Politics* 79(4): 1359–71.

Einwohner, Rachel L., and Thomas V. Maher. 2011. "Threat Assessments and Collective-Action Emergence: Death Camp and Ghetto Resistance during the Holocaust." *Mobilization* 16(1): 127–46.

———, and J. William Spencer. 2005. "That's How We Do Things Here: Local Culture and the Construction of Sweatshops and Anti-sweatshop Activism in Two Campus Communities." *Sociological Inquiry* 75(2): 249–72.

Emirbayer, Mustafa. 1996. "Useful Durkheim." *Sociological Theory* 14(2): 109–30.

Enríquez, Laura. 1991. *Harvesting Change: Labor and Agrarian Reform in Nicaragua, 1979–1990.* Chapel Hill: University of North Carolina Press.

Eyerman, Ron, and Andrew Jamison. 1998. *Music and Social Movements: Mobilizing Traditions in the Twentieth Century.* Cambridge: Cambridge University Press.

Fadaee, Simin, ed. 2016. *Understanding Southern Social Movements.* New York: Routledge.

Fanon, Franz. 1963. *The Wretched of the Earth.* New York: Grove Press.

Feagin, Joe, and Harlan Hahn. 1973. *Ghetto Revolts: Politics of Violence in American Cities.* New York: Collier Macmillan.

Figueroa Ibarra, Carlos. 1991. *El recurso del miedo. Ensayo sobre Estado y terror en Guatemala.* Costa Rica: EDUCA.

Fillieule, Olivier, and Danielle Tartakowsky. 2013. *Demonstrations.* Halifax: Fernwood.

Finlay, Barbara. 2007. *Before the Second Wave: Gender in the Sociological Tradition.* Upper Saddle River, NJ: Pearson.

Fisher, Dana, Dawn Dow, and Rashawn Ray. 2017. "Intersectionality Takes It to the Streets: Mobilizing across Diverse Interests for the Women's March." *Science Advances* 3(9): 1–8.

———, Kevin Stanley, David Berman, and Gina Neff. 2005. "How Do Organizations Matter? Mobilization and Support for Participants at Five Globalization Protests." *Social Problems* 52(1): 102–21.

Flores, Edward Orozco. 2018. *Jesus Saved an Ex-Con: Political Activism and Redemption after Incarceration.* New York: New York University Press.

Foran, John. 1997. "Discourses and Social Forces: The Role of Culture and Cultural Studies in Understanding Revolutions." In *Theorizing Revolutions*, edited by John Foran, 203–26. London: Routledge.

———. 2005. *Taking Power: On the Origins of Third World Revolutions*. Cambridge: Cambridge University Press.

———. 2009. "From Old to New Political Cultures of Opposition: Radical Social Change in an Era of Globalization." In *On the Edges of Development: Cultural Interventions*, edited by Kum-Kum Bhavnani, John Foran, Priya Kurian, and Debashish Munshi, 143–64. New York: Routledge.

Francisco, Ronald. 2005. "The Dictator's Dilemma." In *Repression and Mobilization*, edited by C. Davenport, H. Johnston, and C. Mueller, 58–81. Minneapolis: University of Minnesota Press.

Fu, L. 2016. "The Politics of Everyday Subsistence Strategies and Hidden Resistance among Herders in China." *China Journal* 76(1): 63–77.

Gaby, Sarah, and Neal Caren. 2012. "Occupy Online: How Cute Old Men and Malcolm X Recruited 400,000 US Users to OWS on Facebook." *Social Movement Studies* 11(3–4): 367–74.

Galeano, Eduardo. 1997. *Open Veins of Latin America: Five Centuries of the Pillage of a Continent*. New York: Monthly Review Press.

Gamson, William A. 1990 [1975]. *The Strategy of Social Protest*, 2nd ed. Belmont, CA: Wadsworth.

———. 1989. "Reflections on the Strategy of Social Protest." *Sociological Forum* 4(3): 455–67.

———, and David S. Meyer. 1996. "Framing Political Opportunity." In *Comparative Perspectives on Social Movements: Political Opportunities, Mobilizing Structures, and Cultural Framings*, edited by D. McAdam, J. D. McCarthy, and M. N. Zald, 275–90. Cambridge: Cambridge University Press.

Ganz, Marshall. 2009. *Why David Sometimes Wins: Leadership, Organization, and Strategy in the California Farm Worker Movement*. Oxford: Oxford University Press.

Gasim, Gamal. 2014. "Explaining Political Activism in Yemen." In *Taking to the Streets: The Transformation of Arab Activism*, edited by L. Khatib and E. Lust, 109–35. Baltimore: Johns Hopkins University Press.

Gereffi, Gary. 1994. "Capitalism, Development and Global Commodity Chains." In *Capitalism and Development*, edited by Leslie Sklair, 211–30. London: Routledge.

Gest, Justin. 2016. *The New Minority: White Working Class Politics in an Age of Immigration and Inequality*. Oxford: Oxford University Press.

Giugni, Marco. 2004. "Personal and Biographical Consequences." In *The Blackwell Companion to Social Movements*, edited by David A. Snow, Sarah Soule, and Hanspeter Kriesi, 489–507. Oxford: Blackwell.

Go, Julian. 2011. *Patterns of Empire: The British and American Empires, 1688 to the Present*. Cambridge: Cambridge University Press.

Goffman, Erving. 1974. *Frame Analysis: An Essay on the Organization of Experience*. Cambridge, MA: Harvard University Press.

Golash-Boza, Tanya. 2015. *Deported: Immigrant Policing, Disposable Labor, and Global Capitalism*. New York: New York University Press.

Goldstone, Jack. 1998. "Social Movements or Revolutions? On the Evolution and Outcomes of Collective Action." In *From Contention to Democracy*, edited by M. Giugni, D. McAdam, and C. Tilly, 125–45. Lanham, MD: Rowman & Littlefield.

———. 2004. "More Social Movements or Fewer? Beyond Political Opportunity Structures to Relational Fields." *Theory and Society* 33: 333–65.

———. 2014. *Revolutions*. New York: Oxford University Press.

———. 2015. "Demography and Social Movements." In *The Oxford Handbook of Social Movements*, edited by Donatella Della Porta and Mario Diani, 146–58. Oxford: Oxford University Press.

———, and Doug McAdam. 2001. "Contention in Demographic and Life-Course Context." In *Silence and Voice in the Study of Contentious Politics*, edited by Ronald R. Aminzade, Jack A. Goldstone, Doug McAdam, Elisabeth J. Perry, William H. Sewell Jr., Sidney Tarrow, and Charles Tilly, 195–221. Cambridge: Cambridge University Press.

———, and Charles Tilly. 2001. "Threat (and Opportunity): Popular Action and State Response in the Dynamic of Contentious Action." In *Silence and Voice in the Study of Contentious Politics*, edited by R. Aminzade, J. Goldstone, D. McAdam, E. Perry, W. Sewell, S. Tarrow, and C. Tilly, 179–94. Cambridge: Cambridge University Press.

González, Luis Armando, and Luis Alvarenga. 2002. "La huelga en el sector salud: consideraciones políticas." *Estudios Centroamericanos* 57(649–50): 1140–43.

Goodwin, Jeff. 2001. *No Other Way Out: States and Revolutionary Movements, 1945–1991*. Cambridge: Cambridge University Press.

———, James M. Jasper, and Francesca Polletta, eds. 2001. *Passionate Politics: Emotions and Social Movements*. Chicago: University of Chicago Press.

———, and Rene Rojas. 2015. "Revolutions and Regime Change." In *The Oxford Handbook of Social Movements*, edited by Donatella Della Porta and Mario Diani, 793–804. Oxford: Oxford University Press.

Gould, Deborah B. 2009. *Moving Politics: Emotion and ACT UP's Fight against AIDS*. Chicago: University of Chicago Press.

Gould, Jeffrey, and Aldo Lauria-Santiago. 2008. *To Rise in Darkness: Revolution, Repression, and Memory in El Salvador, 1920–1932*. Durham, NC: Duke University Press.

Gould, Roger V. 1995. *Insurgent Identities: Class, Community, and Protest in Paris from 1848 to the Commune*. Chicago: University of Chicago Press.

———. 2003. "Why Do Networks Matter? Rationalist and Structuralist Interpretations." In *Social Movement Analysis: The Network Perspective*, edited by Mario Diani and Doug McAdam, 233–57. Oxford: Oxford University Press.

———. 2005. "Historical Sociology and Collective Action." In *Remaking Modernity: Politics, History, and Sociology*, edited by J. Adams, E. S. Clemens, and A. S. Orloff, 286–99. Durham, NC: Duke University Press.

Gould-Wartofsky, Michael. 2015. *The Occupiers: The Making of the 99 Percent Movement.* Oxford: Oxford University Press.

Gramsci, Antonio. 1971. *Selections from the Prison Notebooks.* New York: International.

Guillemot, Jonathan R., and Debora J. Price. 2017. "Politicisation in Later Life: Experience and Motivations of Older People Participating in a Protest for the First Time." *Contemporary Social Science* 12(1–2): 52–67.

Gurr, Ted Robert. 1970. *Why Men Rebel.* Princeton, NJ: Princeton University Press.

———. 2015. *Political Rebellion: Causes, Outcomes and Alternatives.* London: Routledge.

Gutierrez, Gustavo. 1973. *A Theology of Liberation.* New York: Orbis Books.

Habermas, Jürgen. 1989. *The Structural Transformation of the Public Sphere.* Cambridge, MA: MIT Press.

Hadden, Jennifer. 2015. *Networks in Contention: The Divisive Politics of Climate Change.* Cambridge: Cambridge University Press.

Halebsky, Stephen. 2009. *Small Towns and Big Business: Challenging Wal-Mart Superstores.* Lanham, MD: Lexington Books.

Harvey, David. 2005. *A Brief History of Neoliberalism.* Oxford: Oxford University Press.

Harvey, Neil. 1998. *The Chiapas Rebellion: The Struggle for Land and Democracy.* Durham, NC: Duke University Press.

Heaney, Michael, and Fabio Rojas. 2015. *Party in the Streets: The Antiwar Movement and the Democratic Party after 9/11.* Cambridge: Cambridge University Press.

Hoffer, Eric. 1951. *The True Believer: Thoughts on the Nature of Mass Movements.* New York: New American Library.

Horowitz, Jonathan. 2017. "Who Is This 'We' You Speak Of? Grounding Activist Identity in Social Psychology." *Socius* 3: 1–17.

Hossfeld, Karen. 1990. "'Their Logic against Them': Contradictions in Sex, Race, and Class in Silicon Valley." In *Women Workers and Global Restructuring*, edited by K. Ward, 149–78. Ithaca, NY: Cornell University Press.

Howard, P. 2010. *The Digital Origins of Dictatorship and Democracy: Information Technology and Political Islam.* Oxford: Oxford University Press.

Hung, Ho-fung. 2011. *Protest with Chinese Characteristics: Demonstrations, Riots, and Petitions in the Mid-Qing Dynasty.* New York: Columbia University Press.

Huntington, Samuel P. 1991. *The Third Wave: Democratization in the Late Twentieth Century.* Norman: University of Oklahoma Press.

Hutter, Swen. 2014. "Protest Event Analysis and Its Offspring." In *Methodological Practices in Social Movement Research*, edited by Donatella Della Porta, 335–67. Oxford: Oxford University Press.

Hutter, S., H. Kriesi, and J. Lorenzini. 2018. "Social Movements in Interaction with Political Parties." In *The Wiley-Blackwell Companion to Social*

Movements, 2nd ed., edited by D.A. Snow, S.A. Soule, H. Kriesi, and H.J. McCammon, 322–37. Oxford: Blackwell.

Ince, Jelani, Fabio Rojas, and Clayton Davis. 2017. "The Social Media Response to Black Lives Matter: How Twitter Users Interact with Black Lives Matter through Hashtag Use." *Ethnic and Racial Studies* 40(11): 1814–30.

Inclán, María. 2008. "From the ¡Ya Basta! to the Caracoles: Zapatista Mobilization under Transitional Conditions." *American Journal of Sociology* 113(5): 1316–50.

———. 2012. "Zapatista and Counter-Zapatista Protests: A test of Movement–Countermovement Dynamics." *Journal of Peace Research* 49(3): 459–72.

———, and Paul Almeida. 2017. "Ritual Demonstrations versus Reactive Protests in Mexico City: Protest Participation across Mobilizing Contexts." *Latin American Politics and Society* 59(4): 47–74.

Ingelhart, Ronald. 1977. *The Silent Revolution Changing Values and Political Styles among Western Publics.* Princeton, NJ: Princeton University Press.

Ingram, P., L.Q. Yue, and H. Rao. 2010. "Trouble in Store: Probes, Protests, and Store Openings by Walmart, 1998–2007." *American Journal of Sociology* 116: 53–92.

Isaacman, Allen. 1993. "Peasants and Rural Social Protest in Africa." In *Confronting Historical Paradigms: Peasants, Labor, and the Capitalist World System in Africa and Latin America,* edited by Frederick Cooper, Allen F. Isaacman, Florencia C. Mallon, William Roseberry, and Steve J. Stern, 205–317. Madison: University of Wisconsin Press.

Jakobsen, Tor Georg, and Ola Listhaug. 2014. "Social Change and the Politics of Protest." In *The Civic Culture Transformed,* edited by Russell Dalton and Christian Welzel, 213–39. Cambridge: Cambridge University Press.

Jasper, James. 1997. *The Art of Moral Protest: Culture, Biography, and Creativity in Social Movements.* Chicago: University of Chicago Press.

———. 1998. "The Emotions of Protest: Affective and Reactive Emotions in and around Social Movements." *Sociological Forum* 13(3): 397–424.

———. 2018. *The Emotions of Protest.* Chicago: University of Chicago Press.

Jenkins, J. Craig. 1983. "Resource Mobilization Theory and the Study of Social Movements." *Annual Review of Sociology* 9: 527–53.

———, and Barbara Brents. 1989. "Social Protest, Hegemonic Competition, and Social Reform: A Political Struggle Interpretation of the Origins of the American Welfare State." *American Sociological Review* 54: 891–909.

———, and William Form. 2005. "Social Movements and Social Change." In *The Handbook of Political Sociology: States, Civil Societies, and Globalization,* edited by T. Janoski, R. R. Alford, A.M. Hicks, and M.A. Schwartz, 331–49. Cambridge: Cambridge University Press.

Jenkins, K. 2017. "Women Anti-mining Activists' Narratives of Everyday Resistance in the Andes: Staying Put and Carrying On in Peru and Ecuador." *Gender, Place and Culture* 24(10): 1441–59.

Jobin-Leeds, Greg, and AgitArte. 2016. *When We Fight, We Win: Twenty-First-Century Social Movements and the Activists That Are Transforming Our World.* New York: New Press.

Johnson, Erik W., and Scott Frickel. 2011. "Ecological Threat and the Founding of U.S. National Environmental Movement Organizations, 1962–1998." *Social Problems* 58(3): 305–29.

Johnston, Hank. 2005. "Talking the Walk: Speech Acts and Resistance in Authoritarian Regimes." In *Repression and Mobilization*, edited by C. Davenport, H. Johnston, and C. Mueller, 108–37. Minneapolis: University of Minnesota Press.

———. 2011. *States and Social Movements.* Cambridge: Polity Press.

———, Enrique Laraña, and Joseph Gusfield. 1994. "Identities, Grievances, and New Social Movements." In *New Social Movements: From Ideology to Identity*, edited by E. Laraña, H. Johnston, and J. Gusfield, 3–35. Philadelphia: Temple University Press.

Kadivar, Mohammad Ali. 2017. "Preelection Mobilization and Electoral Outcome in Authoritarian Regimes." *Mobilization* 22(3): 293–310.

———. 2018. "Mass Mobilization and the Durability of New Democracies." *American Sociological Review* 78(6): 1063–86.

Kalandadze, Katya, and Mitchell A. Orenstein. 2009. "Electoral Protests and Democratization: Beyond the Color Revolutions." *Comparative Political Studies* 42(11): 1403–25.

Karataşli, Savaş, Kumral Şefika and Beverly Silver. 2018. "A New Global Tide of Rising Social Protest? The Early Twenty-first Century in World Historical Perspective." Presented at the Eastern Sociological Society Annual Meeting, Mini-conference on Globalization in Uncertain Times. Baltimore, MD, February 22–25.

Katzenstein, Mary Fainsod. 1998. *Faithful and Fearless: Moving Feminist Protest inside the Church and Military.* Princeton, NJ: Princeton University Press.

Kauffmann, L.A. 2018. "The Republican Party Is About to Face the Wrath of Women." *The Guardian*, September 25.

Keck, M., and K. Sikkink. 1998. *Activists beyond Borders: Advocacy Networks in International Politics.* Ithaca, NY: Cornell University Press.

Kenney-Lazar, M., D. Suhardiman, and M.B. Dwyer. 2018. "State Spaces of Resistance: Industrial Tree Plantations and the Struggle for Land in Laos." *Antipode.* doi: 10.1111/anti.12391.

Khatib, Lina, and Ellen Lust, eds. 2014. *Taking to the Streets: The Transformation of Arab Activism.* Baltimore: Johns Hopkins University Press.

Kielbowicz, R., and C. Scherer. 1986. "The Role of the Press in the Dynamics of Social Movements." *Research in Social Movements, Conflicts and Change* 9: 71–96.

Kim, H., and P. Bearman. 1997. "The Structure and Dynamics of Movement Participation." *American Sociological Review* 62: 70–93.

King, Brayden G., Keith G. Bentele, and Sarah A. Soule. 2007. "Protest and Policymaking: Explaining Fluctuation in Congressional Attention to Rights Issues, 1960–1986." *Social Forces* 86(1): 137–63.

————, and Sarah A. Soule. 2007. "Social Movements as Extra-Institutional Entrepreneurs: The Effect of Protest on Stock Price Returns." *Administrative Science Quarterly* 52: 413–42.

King, Michael. 2017. *When Riot Cops Are Not Enough: The Policing and Repression of Occupy Oakland.* New Brunswick, NJ: Rutgers University Press.

Kitts, James. 2000. "Mobilizing in Black Boxes: Social Networks and Participation in Social Movement Organizations." *Mobilization* 5(2): 241–57.

Klandermans, Bert. 1988. "The Formation and Mobilization of Consensus." In *From Structure to Action: Comparing Social Movement Research across Cultures,* vol. 1, edited by B. Klandermans, H. Kriesi, and S. Tarrow, 173–96. Greenwich, CT: JAI Press.

————. 1997. *The Social Psychology of Protest.* Oxford: Blackwell.

————. 2012. "Between Rituals and Riots: The Dynamics of Street Demonstrations." *Mobilization* 17(3): 233–34.

————. 2018. "Promoting or Preventing Change through Political Participation: About Political Actors, Movements, and Networks." In *The Oxford Handbook of the Human Essence,* edited by M. van Zomeren and J. F. Dovidio, 207–18. Oxford: Oxford University Press.

Kolb, Felix. 2007. *Protest and Opportunities: The Political Outcomes of Social Movements.* Frankfurt: Campus Verlag.

Kolins Givan, Rebecca, Kenneth Roberts, and Sarah Soule. 2010. "Introduction: The Dimensions of Diffusion." In *The Diffusion of Social Movements,* edited by Rebecca Kolins Givan, Kenneth Roberts, and Sarah Soule, 1–15. Cambridge: Cambridge University Press.

Koo, Hagen. 2001. *Korean Workers: The Culture and Politics of Class Formation.* Ithaca, NY: Cornell University Press.

Koopmans, Ruud. 1993. "The Dynamics of Protest Waves: West Germany, 1965 to 1989." *American Sociological Review* 58(5): 637–58.

————. 1999. "The Use of Protest Event Data in Comparative Research: Cross-National Comparability, Sampling Methods, and Robustness." In *Acts of Dissent: New Developments in the Study of Protest,* edited by D. Rucht, R. Koopmans, and F. Neidhardt, 90–110. Lanham, MD: Rowman & Littlefield.

————. 2002. "Protest Event Analysis." In *Methods of Social Movement Research,* edited by Bert Klandermans and Suzanne Staggenborg, 231–59. Minneapolis: University of Minnesota Press.

————. 2004. "Protest in Time and Space: The Evolution of Waves of Contention." In *The Blackwell Companion to Social Movements,* edited by David A. Snow, Sarah A. Soule, and Hanspeter Kriesi, 19–46. Oxford: Blackwell.

————, and Susan Olzak. 2004. "Discursive Opportunities and the Evolution of Right-Wing Violence in Germany." *American Journal of Sociology* 110(1): 198–230.

Kriesi, Hanspeter, Ruud Koopmans, Jan Willem Duyvendak, and Marco Guigni. 1995. *New Social Movements in Western Europe: A Comparative Analysis.* Minneapolis: University of Minnesota Press.

Krinsky, John, and Nick Crossley. 2014. "Social Movements and Social Networks: Introduction." *Social Movement Studies* 13(1): 1–21.

Krishna, A. 2002. *Active Social Capital: Tracing the Roots of Development and Democracy.* New York: Columbia University Press.

Kurzman, Charles. 2005. *The Unthinkable Revolution in Iran.* Cambridge, MA: Harvard University Press.

———. 2011. "Cultural Jiu-Jitsu and the Iranian Greens." In *The People Reloaded: The Green Movement and the Struggle for Iran's Future,* edited by Nader Hashemi and Danny Postel, 7–17. New York: Melville House.

Lapegna, P. 2016. "Genetically Modified Soybeans, Agrochemical Exposure, and Everyday Forms of Peasant Collaboration in Argentina." *Journal of Peasant Studies* 43(2): 517–36.

Levitsky, Steven, and Kenneth Roberts. 2011. "Introduction. Latin America's 'Left Turn': A Framework for Analysis." In *The Resurgence of the Latin American Left,* edited by Steven Levitsky and Kenneth M. Roberts, 1–30. Baltimore: Johns Hopkins University Press.

Lewis, K., K. Gray, and J. Meierhenrich. 2014. "The Structure of Online Activism." *Sociological Science* 1: 1–9.

Lichbach, Mark. 1995. *The Rebel's Dilemma.* Ann Arbor: University of Michigan Press.

Lichterman, Paul. 2002. "Seeing Structure Happen: Theory-Driven Participant Observation." In *Methods of Social Movement Research,* edited by Suzanne Staggenborg and Bert Klandermans, 118–45. Minneapolis: University of Minnesota Press.

Lim, Chaeyoon. 2008. "Social Networks and Political Participation: How Do Networks Matter?" *Social Forces* 87(2): 961–82.

Loveman, Mara. 1998. "High Risk Collective Action: Defending Human Rights in Chile, Uruguay, and Argentina." *American Journal of Sociology* 104(2): 477–525.

Lu Y, Tao R. 2017. "Organizational Structure and Collective Action: Lineage Networks, Semiautonomous Civic Associations, and Collective Resistance in Rural China." *American Journal of Sociology* 122(6): 1726–74.

Lubeck, Paul M., and Thomas Reifer. 2004. "The Politics of Global Islam: US Hegemony, Globalization and Islamist Social Movements." In *Globalization, Hegemony and Power: Antisystemic Movements and the Global System,* 162–80. Boulder, CO: Paradigm.

Luce, Stephanie. 2017. "Living Wages: A US Perspective." *Employee Relations* 39(6): 863–74.

Luders, Joseph. 2016. "Feminist Mobilization and the Politics of Rights." In *The Consequences of Social Movements,* edited by Lorenzo Bosi, Marco Giugni, and Katrin Uba, 185–214. Cambridge: Cambridge University Press.

Lukes, Steven. 2005. *Power: A Radical View,* 2nd ed. New York: Palgrave.

Luna, Zakiya T. 2016. "'Truly a Women of Color Organization': Negotiating Sameness and Difference in Pursuit of Intersectionality." *Gender and Society* 30(5): 769–90.

Luna, Zakiya. 2017. "Who Speaks for Whom?(Mis) Representation and Authenticity in Social Movements." *Mobilization: An International Quarterly* 22(4): 435–50.

Mackin, R. 2015. Liberation Theology and Social Movements. In *Handbook of Social Movements Across Latin America*, edited by P. Almeida and A. Cordero Ulate, 101–16. New York: Springer.

Maher, Thomas V. 2010. "Threat, Resistance, and Mobilization: The Cases of Auschwitz, Sobibór, and Treblinka." *American Sociological Review* 75(2): 252–72.

Maney, Gregory, Kenneth T. Andrews, Rachel V. Kutz-Flamenbaum, Deana A. Rohlinger, and Jeff Goodwin. 2012. "An Introduction to Strategies for Social Change." In *Strategies for Social Change*, edited by G. Maney, R. Kutz Flamenbaum, D. Rohlinger, and J. Goodwin, 11–38. Minneapolis: University of Minnesota Press.

Markoff, John. 2015a. *Waves of Democracy: Social Movements and Political Change*, 2nd ed. Thousand Oaks, CA: Sage.

———. 2015b. "Historical Analysis and Social Movements Research." In *The Oxford Handbook of Social Movements*, edited by D. Della Porta and M. Diani. Oxford: Oxford University Press.

———, and Daniel Burridge. Forthcoming. "The Global Wave of Democratization and Its Aftermath." In *Democratization in a Globalized World*, edited by Christian W. Haerpfer, Ronald Inglehart, Chris Welzel, and Patrick Bernhagen, 2nd ed. Oxford: Oxford University Press.

———, and Verónica Montecinos. 1993. "The Ubiquitous Rise of Economists." *Journal of Public Policy* 13(1): 37–68.

Marti Puig, Salvador. 2012. "The Indignados: New Spanish Social Movements against the Crisis." In *The Occupy Handbook*, ed. Janet Byrne. New York: Little, Brown and Company.

———. 2012. *La Revolución Enredada*. Madrid: Los Libros de Catarata.

Martin, Andrew W. 2008. "The Institutional Logic of Union Organizing and the Effectiveness of Social Movement Repertoires." *American Journal of Sociology* 113: 1067–103.

Martin, Isaac William. 2013. *Rich People's Movements: Grassroots Campaigns to Untax the One Percent.* Oxford: Oxford University Press.

Marx, Karl, and Friedrich Engels. 1978 [1848]. "The Communist Manifesto." In *The Marx and Engels Reader*, edited by Robert Tucker, 469–501. New York: Norton.

Marx Ferree, Myra, 2005. "Soft Repression: Ridicule, Stigma and Silencing in Gender-Based Movements." In *Repression and Mobilization*, edited by Christian Davenport, Hank Johnston, and Carol Mueller, 138–55. Minneapolis: University of Minnesota Press.

Mason, P. 2013. *Why It's Still Kicking Off Everywhere: The New Global Revolutions.* London: Verso.

McAdam, Doug. 1999 [1982]. *Political Process and the Development of Black Insurgency, 1930–1970.* Chicago: University of Chicago Press.

———. 1986. "Recruitment to High-Risk Activism: The Case of Freedom Summer." *American Journal of Sociology* 92(1): 64–90.

———. 1988. *Freedom Summer.* New York: Oxford University Press.

———. 1996. "Political Opportunities: Conceptual Origins, Current Problems, Future Directions." In *Comparative Perspectives on Social Movements,* edited by Doug McAdam, John McCarthy, and Mayer Zald, 23–40. New York: Cambridge University Press.

———. 2003. "Beyond Structural Analysis: Toward a More Dynamic Understanding of Social Movements." In *Social Movement Analysis: The Network Perspective,* edited by Mario Diani and Doug McAdam, 281–99. Oxford: Oxford University Press.

———, Hilary Schaffer Boudet, Jennifer Davis, Ryan J. Orr, W. Richard Scott, and Raymond E. Levitt. 2010. "'Site Fights': Explaining Opposition to Pipeline Projects in the Developing World." *Sociological Forum* 25(3): 401–27.

———, John McCarthy, and Mayer Zald. 1996. "Preface." In *Comparative Perspectives on Social Movements: Political Opportunities, Mobilizing Structures, and Cultural Framings,* edited by D. McAdam, J.D. McCarthy, and M. Zald, xi–xiv. Cambridge: Cambridge University Press.

———, and Ronnelle Paulsen. 1993. "Specifying the Relationship between Social Ties and Activism." *American Journal of Sociology* 99(3): 640–67.

———, and W. Richard Scott. 2005. "Organizations and Movements." In *Social Movements and Organization Theory,* edited by G. Davis, D. McAdam, W.R. Scott, and M. Zald, 4–40. Cambridge: Cambridge University Press.

———, and Yang Su. 2002. "The War at Home: Antiwar Protests and Congressional Voting, 1965 to 1973." *American Sociological Review* 67(5): 696–721.

———, and Sidney Tarrow. 2010. "Ballots and Barricades: On the Reciprocal Relationship between Elections and Social Movements." *Perspectives on Politics* 8(2): 529–42.

———, and Sidney G. Tarrow. 2018. "The Political Context of Social Movements." In *The Wiley- Blackwell Companion to Social Movements,* edited by D. Snow, S. Soule, H. Kriesi, and H. McCammon, 19–42. Oxford: Blackwell.

———, Sidney G. Tarrow, and Charles Tilly. 2001. *Dynamics of Contention.* New York: Cambridge University Press.

McAllister, K.E. 2015. "Rubber, Rights and Resistance: The Evolution of Local Struggles against a Chinese Rubber Concession in Northern Laos." *Journal of Peasant Studies* 42(3–4): 817–37.

McCammon, Holly. 2003. "'Out of the Parlors and into the Streets': The Changing Tactical Repertoire of the U.S. Women's Suffrage Movements." *Social Forces* 81: 787–818.

———. 2012. *The U.S. Women's Jury Movement and Strategic Adaptation.* Cambridge: Cambridge University Press.

————, Karen E. Campbell, Ellen Granberg, and Christine Mowery. 2001. "How Movements Win: Gendered Opportunity Structures and the State Women's Suffrage Movements, 1866–1919." *American Sociological Review* 66(1): 49–70.

————, and Nella Van Dyke. 2010. "Applying Qualitative Comparative Analysis to Empirical Studies of Social Movement Coalition Formation." In *Strategic Alliances: Coalition Building and Social Movements*, edited by N. Van Dyke and H. McCammon, 292–315. Minneapolis: University of Minnesota Press.

McCarthy, John D. 1996. "Constraints and Opportunities in Adopting, Adapting, and Inventing." In *Comparative Perspectives on Social Movements: Political Opportunities, Mobilizing Structures, and Cultural Framings*, edited by D. McAdam, J.D. McCarthy, and M. Zald, 141–51. Cambridge: Cambridge University Press.

————, and Edward Walker. 2004. "Alternative Organizational Repertoires of Poor People's Social Movement Organizations." *Nonprofit and Voluntary Sector Quarterly* 33(3 supp.): 97S–119S.

————, and Mayer N. Zald. 1977. "Resource Mobilization and Social Movements: A Partial Theory." *American Journal of Sociology* 82(6): 1212–41.

————, and Mayer N. Zald. 2002. "The Enduring Vitality of the Resource Mobilization Theory of Social Movements." In *Handbook of Sociological Theory*, edited by Jonathan Turner, 535–65. New York: Kluwer.

Mckay, Steven. 2006. *Satanic Mills or Silicon Islands? The Politics of High-Tech Production in the Philippines*. Ithaca, NY: Cornell University Press.

McMichael, Philip. 2008. "Peasants Make Their Own History, But Not Just as They Please." *Journal of Agrarian Change* 8(2–3): 205–28.

McVeigh, R. 2009. *The Rise of the Ku Klux Klan: Right-Wing Movements and National Politics*. Minneapolis: University of Minnesota Press.

Melucci, Alberto. 1988. "Getting Involved: Identity and Mobilization in Social Movements." *International Social Movement Research* 1: 329–48.

Menjívar, Cecilia, and Néstor Rodriguez, eds. 2009. *When States Kill: Latin America, the US, and Technologies of Terror*. Austin: University of Texas Press.

Meyer, David S. 2002. "Opportunities and Identities: Bridge-Building in the Study of Social Movements." In *Social Movements: Identity, Culture, and the State*, edited by D.S. Meyer, Nancy Whittier, and Belinda Robnett, 3–21. New York: Oxford University Press.

————. 2004. "Protest and Political Opportunity." *Annual Review of Sociology* 30: 125–45.

————. 2014. *The Politics of Protest: Social Movements in America*, 2nd ed. Oxford: Oxford University Press.

————, and Suzanne Staggenborg. 1996. "Movements, Countermovements, and the Structure of Political Opportunity." *American Journal of Sociology* 101(6): 1628–60.

————, and Suzanne Staggenborg. 2012. "Thinking about Strategy." In *Strategies for Social Change*, edited by G. Maney, R. Kutz Flamenbaum, D. Rohlinger, and J. Goodwin, 3–22. Minneapolis: University of Minnesota Press.

———, and Sidney Tarrow, eds. 2018. *The Resistance: The Dawn of the Anti-Trump Opposition Movement.* Oxford: Oxford University Press.

———, and Nancy Whittier. 1994. "Social Movement Spillover." *Social Problems* 41(2): 277–98.

Michels, Robert. 1962. *Political Parties: A Sociological Study of the Oligarchical Tendencies of Modern Democracy.* New York: Free Press.

Milkman, Ruth. 2017. "A New Political Generation: Millennials and the Post-2008 Wave of Protest." *American Sociological Review* 82(1): 1–31.

Minkoff, Debra C., and John D. McCarthy. 2005. "Reinvigorating the Study of Organizational Processes in Social Movements." *Mobilization* 10(2): 289–308.

Monnat, S.M. 2016. "Deaths of Despair and Support for Trump in the 2016 Presidential Election." Research brief, Pennsylvania State University, Department of Agricultural Economics.

Mora, Maria de Jesus. 2016. "Local Mobilizations: Explaining the Outcomes of Immigrant Organizing in Four Central Valley Cities in California." Master's thesis, University of California, Merced.

———, Rodolfo Rodriguez, Alejandro Zermeño, and Paul Almeida. 2018. "Immigrant Rights and Social Movements." *Sociology Compass* 12: 1–20.

———, Alejandro Zermeño, Rodolfo Rodriguez, and Paul Almeida. 2017. "Exclusión y movimientos sociales en los Estados Unidos." In *Movimientos Sociales en América Latina: Perspectivas, Tendencias y Casos,* edited by P. Almeida and A. Cordero, 641–69. Buenos Aires: CLACSO.

Morris, Aldon. 1984. *The Origins of the Civil Rights Movement: Black Communities Organizing for Change.* New York: Free Press.

———. 1993. "Birmingham Confrontation Reconsidered: An Analysis of the Dynamics and Tactics of Mobilization." *American Sociological Review* 58.

———. 2015. *The Scholar Denied: W.E.B. Du Bois and the Birth of Modern Sociology.* Berkeley: University of California Press.

———, and Naomi Braine. 2001. "Social Movements and Oppositional Consciousness." In *Oppositional Consciousness: The Subjective Roots of Social Protest,* edited by J. Mansbridge and A. Morris, 20–37. Chicago: University of Chicago Press.

Mosca, Lorenzo. 2014. "Methodological Practices in Social Movement Online Research." In *Methodological Practices in Social Movement Research,* edited by Donatella Della Porta, 446–64. Oxford: Oxford University Press.

Moss, Dana. 2014. "Repression, Response, and Contained Escalation under 'Liberalized' Authoritarianism in Jordan." *Mobilization* 19(3): 489–514.

Munson, Zaid. 2010. *The Making of Pro-life Activists: How Social Movement Mobilization Works.* Cambridge: Cambridge University Press.

Nakano Glenn, Evelyn. 2004. *Unequal Freedom: How Race and Gender Shaped American Citizenship and Labor.* Cambridge, MA: Harvard University Press.

Nash, June, and Patricia Fernandez-Kelly, eds. 1984. *Women, Men, and the International Division of Labor.* Albany: State University of New York Press.

National Advisory Commission on Civil Disorders. 2016 [1968]. *The Kerner Report*. Princeton, NJ: Princeton University Press.

Nepstad, Sharon Erickson. 2011. *Nonviolent Revolutions: Civil Resistance in the Late Twentieth Century*. New York: Oxford University Press.

———, and Christian Smith. 1999. "Rethinking Recruitment to High-Risk/ Cost Activism: The Case of Nicaragua Exchange." *Mobilization* 4(1): 25–40.

Nicholls, Walter. 2014. *The DREAMers: How the Undocumented Youth Movement Transformed the Immigrant Rights Debate*. Stanford, CA: Stanford University Press.

Nolan-García, Kimberly A., and María Inclán. 2017. "Union Affiliation, Socialization, and Political Identities: The Case of Mexico." *Latin American Politics and Society* 59(2): 53–76.

Noonan, Rita. 1995. "Women against the State: Political Opportunities and Collective Action Frames in Chile's Transition to Democracy." *Sociological Forum* 10(1): 81–111.

Norris, Pippa, Richard W. Frank, and Ferran Martinez i Coma. 2015. "Contentious Elections: From Votes to Violence." In *Contentious Elections: From Ballots to Barricades*, edited by Pippa Norris, Richard W. Frank, and Ferran Martinez i Coma, 1–21. New York: Routledge.

Oberschall, A. 1973. *Social Conflict and Social Movements*. Englewood Cliffs, NJ: Prentice-Hall.

Odabas, Meltem, and Heidi Reynolds-Stenson. 2017. "Tweeting from Gezi Park: Social Media and Repression Backfire." *Social Currents*. https://doi .org/10.1177/2329496517734569

Okamoto, Dina G. 2003. "Toward a Theory of Panethnicity: Explaining Asian American Collective Action." *American Sociological Review* 68(6): 811–42.

———. 2014. *Redefining Race: Asian American Panethnicity and Shifting Ethnic Boundaries*. New York: Russell Sage Foundation.

Oliver, Pamela. 2015. "Rational Action." In *The Oxford Handbook of Social Movements*, edited by Donatella Della Porta and Mario Diani, 246–63. Oxford: Oxford University Press.

Olson, Mancur. 1965. *The Logic of Collective Action*. Cambridge, MA: Harvard University Press.

Olzak, Susan, Sarah A. Soule, Marion Coddou, and John Muñoz. 2016. "Friends or Foes? How Social Movement Allies Affect the Passage of Legislation in the U.S. Congress." *Mobilization* 21(2): 213–30.

Opp, Karl Dieter. 2009. *Theories of Political Protest and Social Movements*. New York: Routledge.

———, S.E. Finkel, Edward Muller, Gadi Wosfeld, Henry Dietz, and Jerrold Green. 1995. "Left-Right Ideology and Collective Political Action: A Comparative Analysis of Germany, Israel, and Peru." In *The Politics of Social Protest*, edited by C.J. Jenkins and B. Klandermans, 63–95. Minneapolis: University of Minnesota Press.

————, Christiane Gern, and Peter Voss. 1995. *Origins of a Spontaneous Revolution: East Germany 1989.* Ann Arbor: University of Michigan Press.

Orum, Anthony. 1974. "On Participation in Political Protest Movements." *Journal of Applied Behavioral Science* 10(2): 181–207.

Osa, Maryjane. 2003. *Solidarity and Contention: Networks of Polish Opposition.* Minneapolis: University of Minnesota Press.

Paige, Jeffrey. 1971. "Political Orientation and Riot Participation." *American Sociological Review* 36(5): 810–20.

Parsa, Misagh. 2016. *Democracy in Iran: Why It Failed and How It Might Succeed.* Cambridge, MA: Harvard University Press.

Passy, Florence. 2001. "Socialization, Connection, and the Structure/Agency Gap: A Specification of the Impact of Networks on Participation in Social Movements." *Mobilization* 6(2): 173–92.

Pawel, Miriam. 2010. *The Union of Their Dreams: Power, Hope, and Struggle in Cesar Chavez's Farm Worker Movement.* New York: Bloomsbury.

Pellow, David Naguib. 2017. *What Is Critical Environmental Justice?* London: Polity.

Peña, Devon. 1997. *The Terror of the Machine: Technology, Work, Gender, and Ecology on the US-Mexico Border.* Austin: University of Texas Press.

Perrow, Charles. 1979. "The Sixties Observed." In *The Dynamic of Social Movements,* edited by Mayer Zald and John McCarthy. Cambridge, MA: Winthrop.

Piketty, Thomas. 2014. *Capital in the 21st Century.* Cambridge, MA: Harvard University Press.

Pilati, Katia. 2011. "Political Context, Organizational Engagement, and Protest in African Countries." *Mobilization* 16(3): 351–68.

————. 2016. "Do Organizational Structures Matter for Protests in Nondemocratic African Countries?" In *Popular Contention, Regime, and Transition: The Arab Revolts in Comparative Global Perspective,* edited by Eitan Alimi, Avraham Sela, and Mario Sznajder, 46–72. Oxford: Oxford University Press.

Pinard, Maurice. 2011. *Motivational Dimensions in Social Movements and Contentious Collective Action.* Montreal: McGill-Queen's University Press.

Piven, Frances Fox, and Richard Cloward. 1979. *Poor People's Movements: Why They Succeed, How They Fail.* New York: Vintage.

Polanyi, Karl. 1944. *The Great Transformation.* Boston: Beacon Press.

Polletta, Francesca. 1999. "'Free Spaces' in Collective Action." *Theory and Society* 28(1): 1–38.

Portos, Martín, and Juan Masullo. 2017. "Voicing Outrage Unevenly: Democratic Dissatisfaction, Nonparticipation, and Participation Frequencyin the 15-M Campaign." *Mobilization: An International Quarterly* 22(2): 201–22.

Pulido, Laura, and Juan D. Lara. 2018. "Reimagining Justice in Environmental Justice: Radical Ecologies, Decolonial Thought, and the Black Radical Tradition." *Environment and Planning E: Nature and Space* 1(1–2): 76–98.

Putnam, Robert D. 2000. *Bowling Alone: The Collapse and Revival of American Community.* New York: Simon & Schuster.

Raeburn, Nicole. 2004. *Changing Corporate America from Inside Out: Lesbian and Gay Workplace Rights.* Minneapolis: University of Minnesota Press.

Raventos, Ciska, 2013. "'My Heart Says No': Political Experiences of the Struggle against CAFTA-DR in Costa Rica." In *Central America in the New Millennium: Living Transition and Reimagining Democracy,* edited by J. Burrell and E. Moodie, 80–95. New York: Berghahn Books.

Raventós Vorst, Ciska. 2018. *Mi Corazón dice No: El Movimiento de Oposición del TLC en Costa Rica.* San Jose: Editorial Universidad de Costa Rica.

Reese, E., C. Chase-Dunn, K. Anantram, G. Coyne, M. Kaneshiro, A. Koda, R. Kwon, and P. Saxena. 2015. "Surveys of World Social Forum Participants Show Influence of Place and Base in the Global Public Sphere." In *Handbook on World Social Forum Activism,* edited by J. Smith, S. Byrd, E. Reese, and E. Smythe, 64–84. Boulder, CO: Paradigm.

Reese, Ellen. 2011. *They say cutback, we say fight back!: Welfare Activism in an Era of Retrenchment.* New York: Russell Sage Foundation.

Robinson, Cedric. 2000. *Black Marxism: The Making of the Black Radical Tradition.* Chapel Hill: University of North Carolina Press.

Robinson, William. 2003. *Transnational Conflicts: Central America, Social Change, and Globalization.* London: Verso.

———. 2008. *Latin America and Global Capitalism: A Critical Globalization Perspective.* Baltimore: Johns Hopkins University Press.

———. 2014. *Capitalism and the Crisis of Humanity.* Cambridge: Cambridge University Press.

Rodney, Walter. 1981. *How Europe Underdeveloped Africa.* Washington, DC: Howard University Press.

Rodriguez, Rodolfo. 2017. "The War in the Valley: Farm Labor Organizing in a Hostile Anti-union Environment." Master's paper, Department of Sociology, University of California, Merced.

Rohlinger, Deana. 2015. *Abortion Politics, Mass Media, and Social Movements in America.* Cambridge: Cambridge University Press.

Rojas, Fabio. 2007. *From Black Power to Black Studies: How a Radical Social Movement Became an Academic Discipline.* Baltimore: Johns Hopkins University Press.

———. 2017. *Theory for the Working Sociologist.* New York: Columbia University Press.

Rolf, David. 2016. *The Fight for Fifteen: The Right Wage for a Working America.* New York: New Press.

Rollins, Judith. 1985. *Between Women: Domestics and Their Employers.* Philadelphia: Temple University Press.

Roscigno, Vincent, and William F. Danaher. 2004. *The Voice of Southern Labor: Radio, Music and Textile Strikes, 1929–1934.* Minneapolis: University of Minnesota Press.

Rosenthal, Rob, and Richard Flacks. 2012. *Playing for Change: Music and Musicians in the Service of Social Movements.* New York: Routledge.

Rosner, David, and Gerrald Markowitz. 2016. "Citizen Scientists and the Lessons of Flint." *Milbank Quarterly,* October 13. www.milbank.org/quarterly /articles/citizen-scientists-lessons-flint

Rossi, Federico. 2017. *The Poor's Struggle for Political Incorporation: The Piquetero Movement in Argentina*. Cambridge: Cambridge University Press.

Roth, Benita. 2004. *Separate Roads to Feminism: Black, Chicana, and White Feminist Movements in America's Second Wave*. Cambridge: Cambridge University Press.

Roy, Olivier. 2006. *Globalized Islam: The Search for a New Ummah*. New York: Columbia University Press.

Roy, William. 2010. *Reds, Whites, and Blues: Social Movements, Folk Music, and Race in the United States*. Princeton, NJ: Princeton University Press.

Rucht, D., R. Koopmans, and F. Neidhardt, eds. 1999. *Acts of Dissent: New Developments in the Study of Protest*. Lanham, MD: Rowman & Littlefield.

Rucht, Dieter, and Thomas Ohlemacher. 1992. "Protest Event Data: Collection, Uses and Perspectives." In *Studying Collective Action*, edited by R. Eyerman and M. Diani, 76–106. Newbury Park, CA: Sage.

Sandoval, Salvador. 2001. "The Crisis of the Brazilian Labor Movement and the Emergence of Alternative Forms of Working-Class Contention in the 1990s." *Revista Psicología Política* 1(1): 173–95.

Santoro, Wayne A., and Gail M. McGuire. 1997. "Social Movement Insiders: The Impact of Institutional Activists on Affirmative Action and Comparable Worth Policies." *Social Problems* 44: 503–20.

Schaeffer, Robert. 2009. *Understanding Globalization: The Social Consequences of Political, Economic, and Environmental Change*. Lanham, MD: Rowman & Littlefield.

Schlozman, Kay Lehman, Henry E. Brady, and Sidney Verba. 2018. *Unequal and Unrepresented: Political Inequality and the People's Voice in the New Gilded Age*. Princeton, NJ: Princeton University Press.

Schnabel, Landon, and Eric Sevell. 2017. "Should Mary and Jane Be Legal? Americans' Attitudes toward Marijuana and Same-Sex Marriage Legalization, 1988–2014." *Public Opinion Quarterly* 81(1): 157–72.

Schock, Kurt. 2005. *Unarmed Insurrections: People Power Movements in Nondemocracies*. Minneapolis: University of Minnesota Press.

———. 2015a. "Rightful Radical Resistance: Mass Mobilization and Land Struggles in India and Brazil." *Mobilization* 20(4): 493–515.

———. 2015b. *Civil Resistance Today*. London: Polity Press.

Schofer, Evan, and John W. Meyer. 2005. "The World-Wide Expansion of Higher Education in the Twentieth Century." *American Sociological Review* 70(6): 898–920.

Schumaker, Paul. 1975. "Policy Responsiveness to Protest-Group Demands." *Journal of Politics* 37(2): 488–521.

Schussman, Alan, and Sarah A. Soule. 2005. "Process and Protest: Accounting for Individual Protest Participation." *Social Forces* 84(2): 1083–108.

Scott, James. 1976. *The Moral Economy of the Peasant: Rebellion and Subsistence in Southeast Asia*. New Haven, CT: Yale University Press.

———. 1985. *Weapons of the Weak: Everyday Forms of Peasant Resistance*. New Haven, CT: Yale University Press.

———. 1990. *Domination and the Arts of Resistance: Hidden Transcripts.* New Haven, CT: Yale University Press.

Seidman, Gay. 1994. *Manufacturing Militance: Workers' Movements in Brazil and South Africa, 1970–1985.* Berkeley: University of California Press.

Selbin, Eric. 2010. *Revolution, Rebellion, Resistance: The Power of Story.* London: Zed Books.

Shaw, Randy. 2011. *Beyond the Fields: Cesar Chavez, the UFW, and the Struggle for Social Justice in the 21st Century.* Berkeley: University of California Press.

Shriver, Thomas E., Sherry Cable, and Dennis Kennedy. 2008. "Mining for Conflict and Staking Claims: Contested Illness at the Tar Creek Superfund Site." *Sociological Inquiry* 78: 558–79.

Sifuentez, Mario. 2016. *Of Forests and Fields: Mexican Labor in the Pacific Northwest.* New Brunswick, NJ: Rutgers University Press.

Silva, Eduardo. 2009. *Challenges to Neoliberalism in Latin America.* Cambridge: Cambridge University Press.

———. 2013. "Transnational Activism and National Movements in Latin America: Concepts, Theories, and Expectations." In *Transnational Activism and National Movements in Latin America: Bridging the Divide,* edited by E. Silva, 1–22. New York: Routledge.

Simmons, Erica. 2014. "Grievances Do Matter in Mobilization." *Theory and Society* 43: 513–46.

———. 2016. *Meaningful Mobilization: Market Reforms and the Roots of Social Protest in Latin America.* Cambridge: Cambridge University Press.

Singerman, Diane. 2004. "The Networked World of Islamist Social Movements." In *Islamic Activism: A Social Movement Theory Approach,* edited by Quintan Wiktorowicz, 143–63. Bloomington: Indiana University Press.

Skocpol, T. 1979. *States and Social Revolutions.* Cambridge: Cambridge University Press.

———, and Vanessa Williamson. 2012. *The Tea Party and the Remaking of Republican Conservatism.* Oxford: Oxford University Press.

Small, Mario L. 2009. *Unanticipated Gains: Origins of Network Inequality in Everyday Life.* New York: Oxford University Press.

Smedley, Audrey and Brian Smedley. 2012. *Race in North America: Origin and Evolution of a Worldview.* Boulder, CO: Westview Press.

Smelser, Neil. 1962. *Theory of Collective Behavior.* New York: Free Press

Smith, Christian. 1991. *The Emergence of Liberation Theology.* Chicago: University of Chicago Press.

Smith, Jackie. 2001. Globalizing Resistance: The Battle of Seattle and the Future of Social Movements. *Mobilization* 6(1): 1–21.

———. 2008. *Social Movements for Global Democracy.* Baltimore: Johns Hopkins University Press.

———. 2014. "Counter-Hegemonic Networks and the Transformation of Global Climate Politics: Rethinking Movement-State Relations." *Global Discourse* 4(2–3): 120–38.

Smith, Jackie, Başak Gemici, Melanie M. Hughes, and Samantha Plummer. 2018. "Transnational Social Movement Organizations and Counterhegemonic Struggle Today." *Journal of World Systems Research* 24(2):372–403.

———, and Dawn Wiest. 2012. *Social Movements in the World-System: The Politics of Crisis and Transformation.* New York: Russell Sage Foundation.

Snow, David. 2004. "Framing Process, Ideology, and Discursive Fields." In *The Blackwell Companion to Social Movements,* edited by D. Snow, S. Soule, and H. Kriesi, 380–412. Oxford: Blackwell.

———, and Robert Benford. 1988. "Ideology, Frame Resonance, and Participant Mobilization." *International Social Movement Research* 1: 197–217.

———, and Robert Benford. 1992. "Master Frames and Cycles of Protest." In *Frontiers in Social Movement Theory,* edited by A. D. Morris and C. M. Mueller, 133–55. New Haven, CT: Yale University Press.

———, Robert Benford, Holly J. McCammon, Lyndi Hewitt, and Scott T. Fitzgerald. 2014. "The Emergence and Development of the Framing Perspective or 25 Years since Publication of 'Frame Alignment': What Lies Ahead?" *Mobilization* 19(1): 23–46.

———, and Catherine Corrigall-Brown. 2005. "Falling on Deaf Ears: Confronting the Prospect of Non-resonant Frames." In *Rhyming Hope and History: Activism and Social Movement Scholarship,* edited by David Croteau, Charlotte Ryan, and William Hoynes, 222–38. Minneapolis: University of Minnesota Press.

———, Daniel Cress, Liam Downey, and Andrew Jones. 1998. "Disrupting the 'Quotidian': Reconceptualizing the Relationship between Breakdown and the Emergence of Collective Action." *Mobilization* 3(1): 1–22.

———, and Doug McAdam. 2000. "Identity Work Processes in the Context of Social Movements: Clarifying the Identity/Movement Nexus." In *Self, Identity, and Social Movements,* edited by Sheldon Stryker, Timothy J. Owens, and Robert W. Wright, 41–67. Minneapolis: University of Minnesota Press.

———, E. Burke Rochford, Steven Worden, and Robert Benford. 1986. "Frame Alignment Processes, Micromobilization, and Movement Participation." *American Sociological Review* 51: 464–81.

———, and Sarah Soule. 2009. *A Primer on Social Movements.* New York: Norton.

———, and Danny Trom. 2002. "Case Study and the Study of Social Movements." In *Methods of Social Movement Research,* edited by B. Klandermans and S. Staggenborg, 146–72. Minneapolis: University of Minnesota Press.

———, Rens Vliegenthart, and Pauline Ketelaars. 2018. "The Framing Perspective on Social Movements: Its Conceptual Roots and Architecture." In *The Wiley-Blackwell Companion to Social Movements,* edited by D. Snow, S. Soule, H. Kriesi, and H. McCammon, 392–410. Oxford: Blackwell.

———, Louis Zurcher, and Sheldon Ekland-Olson. 1980. "Social Networks and Social Movements: A Microstructural Approach to Differential Recruitment." *American Sociological Review* 45: 787–801.

Sobieraj, Sara. 2011. *Soundbitten: The Perils of Media-Centered Political Activism.* New York: New York University Press.

Somers, Margaret. 2008. *Genealogies of Citizenship: Markets, Statelessness, and the Right to Have Rights.* Cambridge: Cambridge University Press.

Somma, Nicolás. 2010. "How Do Voluntary Organizations Foster Protest? The Role of Organizational Involvement on Individual Protest Participation." *Sociological Quarterly* 51(3): 384–407.

———. 2012. "The Chilean Student Movement of 2011–2012: Challenging the Marketization of Education." *Interface* 4(2): 296–309.

———. 2018. "When Do Political Parties Move to the Streets? Party Protest in Chile." *Research in Social Movements, Conflicts and Change* 42: 63–85.

Sosa, Eugenio. 2012. "La contienda política tras el golpe de Estado oligárquico de la resistencia en las calles hacia la disputa político/Electoral." *Bajo el Volcán* 11(17): 21–42.

———. 2013. *Dinámica de la protesta social en Honduras.* Tegucigalpa: Editorial Guaymuras.

———. 2015. "The Movement against the Coup in Honduras." In *Handbook of Social Movements across Latin America,* edited by P. Almeida and A. Cordero, 313–26. New York: Springer.

———. 2016. *Democracia y movimientos sociales en Honduras: de la transición política a la ciudadanía indignada.* Tegucigalpa: Editorial Guaymuras.

———. 2018. "El alzamiento popular contra el fraude electoral en Honduras." *Envío* 16(54, February): 11–22.

Soule, Sarah A. 2004. "Going to the Chapel? Same-Sex Marriage Bans in the United States, 1973–2000." *Social Problems* 51(4): 453–77.

———. 2009. *Contention and Corporate Social Responsibility.* Cambridge: Cambridge University Press.

———, and Susan Olzak. 2004. "When Do Social Movements Matter? The Politics of Contingency and the Equal Rights Amendment, 1972—1982." *American Sociological Review* 69: 473–97.

Spalding, Rose. 2014. *Contesting Trade in Central America: Market Reform and Resistance.* Austin: University of Texas Press.

Spronk, Susan, and Philipp Terhorst. 2012. "Social Movement Struggles for Public Services." In *Alternatives to Privatization in the Global South,* edited by David McDonald and Greg Ruiters, 133–56. New York: Routledge.

Stanley, William. 1996. *The Protection Racket State: Elite Politics, Military Extortion, and Civil War in El Salvador.* Philadelphia: Temple University Press.

Stearns, Linda Brewster, and Paul D. Almeida. 2004. "The Formation of State Actor-Social Movement Coalitions and Favorable Policy Outcomes." *Social Problems* 51(4): 478–504.

Strang, D., and S.A. Soule. 1998. "Diffusion in Organizations and Social Movements: From Hybrid Corn to Poison Pills." *Annual Review of Sociology* 24: 265–90.

Stryker, Sheldon. 2000. "Identity Competition: Key to Differential Social Movement Participation?" In *Self, Identity, and Social Movements,* edited by Sheldon Stryker, Timothy J. Owens, and Robert W. Wright, 1–21. Minneapolis: University of Minnesota Press.

Suh, Cha, Ion Bogdan Vasi, and Paul Y. Chang. 2017. "How Social Media Matter: Repression and the Diffusion of the Occupy Wall Street Movement." *Social Science Research* 65 (2017): 282–93.

Swarts, Heidi, and Ion Bogdan Vasi. 2011. "Which U.S. Cities Adopt Living Wage Ordinances? Predictors of Adoption of a New Labor Tactic, 1994–2006." *Urban Affairs Review* 47(6): 743–74.

Szasz, Andrew. 1994. *Ecopopulism: Toxic Waste and the Movement for Environmental Justice.* Minnesota: University of Minnesota Press.

Tarrow, Sidney. 1989. *Democracy and Disorder: Protest and Politics in Italy, 1965–1975.* Oxford: Oxford University Press.

———. 2005. *The New Transnational Activism.* Cambridge: Cambridge University Press.

———. 2011. *Power in Movement: Social Movements and Contentious Politics,* 3rd ed. Cambridge: Cambridge University Press.

———. 2013. *The Language of Contention: Revolutions in Words, 1688–2012.* Cambridge: Cambridge University Press.

———. 2018. "Rhythms of Resistance: The Anti-Trumpian Moment in a Cycle of Contention." In *The Resistance: The Dawn of the Anti-Trump Opposition Movement,* edited by David Meyer and Sidney Tarrow, 187–206. Oxford: Oxford University Press.

———, and Doug McAdam. 2005. "Scale Shift in Transnational Contention." In *Transnational Activism and Global Contention,* edited by D. Della Porta and S. Tarrow, 121–47. Boulder, CO: Rowman & Littlefield.

Taylor, Dorceta. 2014. *Toxic Communities: Environmental Racism, Industrial Pollution, and Residential Mobility.* New York: New York University Press.

Taylor, Keeanga-Yamahtta. 2016. *From #BlackLivesMatter to Black Liberation.* Chicago: Haymarket Books.

Taylor, Verta. 1989. "Social Movement Continuity: The Women's Movement in Abeyance." *American Sociological Review* 54(5): 761–76.

———, Katrina Kimport, Nella van Dyke, and Ellen Ann Andersen. 2009. "Culture and Mobilization: Tactical Repertoires, Same-Sex Weddings, and the Impact on Gay Activism." *American Sociological Review* 74(6): 865–90.

———, and Nella Van Dyke. 2004. "'Get Up, Stand Up': Tactical Repertoires of Social Movements." In *The Blackwell Companion to Social Movements,* edited by David A. Snow, Sarah A. Soule, and Hanspeter Kriesi. Oxford: Blackwell.

———, and Nancy Whittier. 1992. "Collective Identity in Social Movement Communities: Lesbian Feminist Mobilization." In *Frontiers in Social Movement Theory,* edited by A. D. Morris and C. M. Mueller, 104–29. New Haven, CT: Yale University Press.

Terriquez, Veronica. 2015a. "Intersectional Mobilization, Social Movement Spillover, and Queer Youth Leadership in the Immigrant Rights Movement." *Social Problems* 62(3): 343–62.

———. 2015b. "Training Young Activists: Grassroots Organizing and Youths' Civic and Political Trajectories." *Sociological Perspectives* 58(2): 223–42.

————. 2017. "Legal Status, Civic Organizations, and Political Participation among Latino Young Adults." *Sociological Quarterly* 58(2).

————, Tizoc Brenes, and Abdiel Lopez. 2018. "Intersectionality as a Multipurpose Collective Action Frame: The Case of the Undocumented Youth Movement." *Ethnicities* 18(2): 260–76.

Tilly, Charles. 1978. *From Mobilization to Revolution.* Reading, MA: Addison-Wesley.

————. 1984. "Social Movements and National Politics." In *Statemaking and Social Movements,* edited by C. Bright and S. Harding, 297–317. Ann Arbor: University of Michigan Press.

————. 1999. "From Interactions to Outcomes in Social Movements." In *How Social Movements Matter,* edited by M. Giugni, D. McAdam, and C. Tilly, 253–70. Minneapolis: University of Minnesota Press.

————, and Lesley Wood. 2012. *Social Movements, 1768–2004.* Boulder, CO: Paradigm.

Touch, S., and A. Neef. 2015. "Resistance to Land Grabbing and Displacement in Rural Cambodia," Conference Paper no. 16, Chiang Mai University, Thailand.

Touraine, Alain. 1985. "An Introduction to the Study of Social Movements." *Social Research* 54(2): 749–87.

Trejo, Guillermo. 2012. *Popular Movements in Autocracies: Religion, Repression, and Indigenous Collective Action.* New York: Cambridge University Press.

Trejos, María Eugenia. 1988. "¿Desnacionalización el ICE?" Cuaderno de Estudio, no. 9. San José: Centro de Estudios para la Acción Social.

Uba, Katrin. 2008. "Labor Union Resistance to Economic Liberalization in India: What Can National and State Level Patterns of Protests against Privatization Tell Us?" *Asian Survey* 48(5): 860–84.

Useem, Bert. 1998. "Breakdown Theories of Collective Action." *Annual Review of Sociology* 24: 215–38.

Valdez, Zulema. 2011. *The New Entrepreneurs: How Race, Class, and Gender Shape American Enterprise.* Palo Alto, CA: Stanford University Press.

Van Dyke, Nella. 2017. "Movement Emergence and Resource Mobilization: Organizations, Leaders, and Coalition Work." In *The Oxford Handbook of US Women's Social Movement Activism,* edited by H. J. McCammon, V. Taylor, J. Reger, and R. L. Einwohner, 354–75. Oxford: Oxford University Press.

————, and Bryan Amos. 2017. "Social Movement Coalitions: Formation, Longevity, and Success." *Sociology Compass* 11(7): 1–17.

————, and Marc Dixon. 2013. "Activist Human Capital: Skills Acquisition and the Development of Commitment to Social Movement Activism." *Mobilization* 18(2): 197–212.

————, Marc Dixon, and Helen Carlon. 2007. "Manufacturing Dissent: Labor Revitalization, Union Summer, and Student Protest." *Social Forces* 88(1): 193–214.

————, Doug McAdam, and Brenda Wilhelm. 2000. "Gendered Outcomes: Gender Differences in the Biographical Consequences of Activism." *Mobilization* 5(2): 161–77.

———, and Holly McCammon. 2010. "Introduction: Social Movement Coalition Formation." In *Strategic Alliances: Coalition Building and Social Movements*, edited by N. Van Dyke and H. McCammon, xi–xxviii. Minneapolis: University of Minnesota Press.

———, and David S. Meyer. 2014. "Introduction." In *Understanding the Tea Party Movement*, edited by N. Van Dyke and D. S. Meyer, 1–14. Burlington, VT: Ashgate.

———, and Soule Sarah. 2002. "Structural Social Change an the Mobilizing Effect of Threat: Explaining Levels of Patriot and Militia Organizing in the United States." *Social Problems* 49(4): 497–520.

———, Sarah A. Soule, and Verta A. Taylor. 2004. "The Targets of Social Movements: Beyond a Focus on the State." *Research in Social Movements, Conflicts and Change* 25: 27–51.

———, and Verta A. Taylor. 2018. "The Cultural Outcomes of Social Movements." In *The Wiley-Blackwell Companion to Social Movements*, 2nd ed., edited by D. A. Snow, S. A. Soule, H. Kriesi, and H. J. McCammon, 482–98. Oxford: Blackwell.

Van Laer, J. 2010. "Activists Online and Offline: The Internet as an Information Channel for Protest Demonstrations." *Mobilization* 15(3): 347–66.

Van Stekelenburg, J., and B. Klandermans. 2017. "Individuals in Movements: A Social Psychology of Contention." In *Handbook of Social Movements across Disciplines*, edited by C. Roggeband and B. Klandermans. Handbooks of Sociology and Social Research. Cham: Springer.

Vasi, Ion Bogdan. 2011. "Brokerage, Miscibility, and the Spread of Contention." *Mobilization* 16(1): 11–24.

———, David Strang, and Arnout van de Rijt. 2014. "Tea and Sympathy: The Tea Party Movement and Republican Precommitment to Radical Conservatism in the 2011 Debt-Limit Crisis." *Mobilization* 19: 1–22.

———, and Chan S. Suh. 2016. "Online Activities, Spatial Proximity, and the Diffusion of the Occupy Wall Street Movement in the United States." *Mobilization* 21(2): 139–54.

———, Edward T. Walker, John S. Johnson, and Hui Fen Tan. 2015. "'No Fracking Way!' Documentary Film, Discursive Opportunity, and Local Opposition against Hydraulic Fracturing in the United States, 2010 to 2013." *American Sociological Review* 80(5): 934–59.

Vela Castañeda, Manolo, 2012. *Guatemala, la infinita historia de las resistencias.* Guatemala City: La Secretaría de la Paz de la Presidencia de la República de Guatemala.

Velasquez Nimatuj, Irma. 2016. "¿Hasta dónde la corrupción definió la participación de los pueblos indígenas en el 2015?" In *La Fuerza de las Plazas*, edited by R. Solís Miranda, 201–33. Guatemala City: Fundación Friedrich Ebert.

Verba, Sidney, Kay Lehman Schlozman, and Henry E. Brady. 1995. *Voice and Equality: Civic Voluntarism in American Politics.* Cambridge, MA: Harvard University Press.

Verhoeven, Imrat, and Jan Willem Duyvendak. 2017. "Understanding Governmental Activism." *Social Movement Studies* 16(5): 564–77.

Vommaro, Pablo. 2015. *Juventudes y políticas en la Argentina y en América Latina. Tendencias, conflictos y desafíos.* Grupo Editor Universitario. Buenos Aires.

Von Bülow, Marisa. 2011. *Building Transnational Networks: Civil Society and the Politics of Trade in the Americas.* Cambridge: Cambridge University Press.

———, and Germán Bidegain Ponte. 2015. "It Takes Two to Tango: Students, Political Parties, and Protest in Chile (2005–2013)." In *Handbook of Social Movements across Latin America,* edited by Paul Almeida and Allen Cordero Ulate, 179–94. New York: Springer.

Viterna, Jocelyn. 2013. *Women in War: The Micro-processes of Mobilization in El Salvador.* New York: Oxford University Press.

———, and Fallon Kathleen. 2008. "Democratization, Women's Movements, and Gender-Equitable States: A Framework for Comparison." *American Sociological Review* 73: 668–89.

Voss, Kim, and Rachel Sherman. 2000. "Breaking the iron law of oligarchy: Union revitalization in the American labor movement." *American Journal of Sociology* 106(2): 303-49.

Vreeland, James. 2007. *The International Monetary Fund: Politics of Conditional Lending.* London: Routledge.

Walgrave, Stefaan, and Dieter Rucht, eds. 2010. *The World Says No to War.* Minneapolis: University of Minnesota Press.

———, and Joris Verhulst. 2011. "Selection and Response Bias in Protest Surveys." *Mobilization* 16(2): 203–22.

———, and Ruud Wouters. 2014. "The Missing Link in the Diffusion of Protest: Asking Others." *American Journal of Sociology* 119(6): 1670–709.

Walker, Edward. 2014. *Grassroots for Hire: Public Affairs Consultants in American Democracy.* Cambridge: Cambridge University Press.

———, Andrew Martin, and John D. McCarthy. 2008. "Confronting the State, the Corporation, and the Academy: The Influence of Institutional Targets on Social Movement Repertoires." *American Journal of Sociology* 114(1): 35–76.

Walsh, Edward, Rex Warland, and Douglas Clayton Smith. 1997. *Don't Burn It Here: Grassroots Challenges to Trash Incinerators.* University Park: Penn State University Press.

Walton, John. 1998. "Urban Conflict and Social Movements in Poor Countries: Theory and Evidence of Collective Action." *International Journal of Urban and Regional Research* 22(3): 460–81.

———, and David Seddon. 1994. *Free Markets and Food Riots.* Oxford: Blackwell.

Ward, Michael. 2016. "Can We Predict Politics? Toward What End?" *Journal of Global Security Studies* 1(1): 80–91.

Weber, Max. 1978. *Economy and Society,* vol. 1. Berkeley: University of California Press.

Weyland, K. 2014. *Making Waves: Democratic Contention in Europe and Latin America since the Revolutions of 1848.* Cambridge: Cambridge University Press.

White, James W. 1995. *Ikki: Social Conflict and Political Protest in Early Modern Japan.* Ithaca, NY: Cornell University Press.

Whitman, Gordon. 2006. "Beyond Advocacy: The History and Vision of the PICO Network." *Social Policy* 37(2).

———. 2018. *Stand Up! How to Get Involved, Speak Out, and Win in a World on Fire.* Oakland, CA: Berrett-Koehler.

Whittier, Nancy. 2004. "The Consequences of Social Movements for Each Other." In *The Blackwell Companion to Social Movements,* edited by D. Snow, S. Soule, and H. Kriesi, 531–52. Oxford: Blackwell.

Wickham-Crowley, Timothy. 1992. *Guerrillas and Revolution in Latin America: A Comparative Study of Insurgents and Regimes since 1956.* Princeton, NJ: Princeton University Press.

———. 2014. "Two 'Waves' of Guerrilla-Movement Organizing in Latin America, 1956–1990." *Comparative Studies in Society and History* 56(1): 215–42.

Williams, Eric. 1944. *Capitalism and Slavery.* Chapel Hill: University of North Carolina Press.

Wilson, John. 1973. *Introduction to Social Movements.* New York: Basic Books.

Wolford, Wendy. 2010. *This Land Is Ours Now: Social Mobilization and the Meanings of Land in Brazil.* Durham, NC: Duke University Press.

Wood, Elisabeth Jean. 2003. *Insurgent Collective Action and Civil War in El Salvador.* Cambridge: Cambridge University Press.

Wood, Lesley. 2012. *Direct Action, Deliberation, and Diffusion: Collective Action after the WTO Protests in Seattle.* Cambridge: Cambridge University Press.

———. 2015. "Horizontalist Youth Camps and the Bolivarian Revolution: A Story of Blocked Diffusion." In *Handbook of World Social Forum Activism,* edited by Scott Byrd, Ellen Reese, Jackie Smith, and Elizabeth Smythe, 305–19. New York: Routledge.

Wood, Richard, and Brad Fulton. 2015. *A Shared Future: Faith-Based Organizing for Racial Equity and Ethical Democracy.* Chicago: University of Chicago Press.

Young, Ralph. 1991. "Privatisation in Africa." *Review of African Political Economy* 51: 50–62.

Zatz, Marjorie, and Nancy Rodriguez. 2015. *Dreams and Nightmares: Immigration Policy, Youth, and Families.* Berkeley: University of California Press.

Zepeda-Millán, Chris. 2017. *Latino Mass Mobilization: Immigration, Racialization, and Activism.* Cambridge: Cambridge University Press.

Zermeño, Alejandro. 2017. *Strength-based interaction rituals: The impact of sweatlodges and danza Mexica on Mexican American wellbeing* (unpublished master's thesis). University of California, Merced.

Zhao, Dingxin. 2001. *The Power of Tiananmen.* Chicago: University of Chicago Press.

Index